# MOTOR RAIL LTD

The precise identities of these two 20hp petrol locomotives is not known, but there is reason to believe that they could be MR 5072 and 5080 of 1930 supplied to M.A. Boswell, contractor, of Wolverhampton. Judging by the piling behind the last wagon they could be on a pipeline contract. The trench would have been excavated and the wagons filled by the Ruston Bucyrus excavator, itself relatively modern and having a diesel engine, judging from the radiator seen through the open doors.
*H.W. Robinson. Collection Industrial Railway Society*

# MOTOR RAIL LTD

## Alan M. Keef

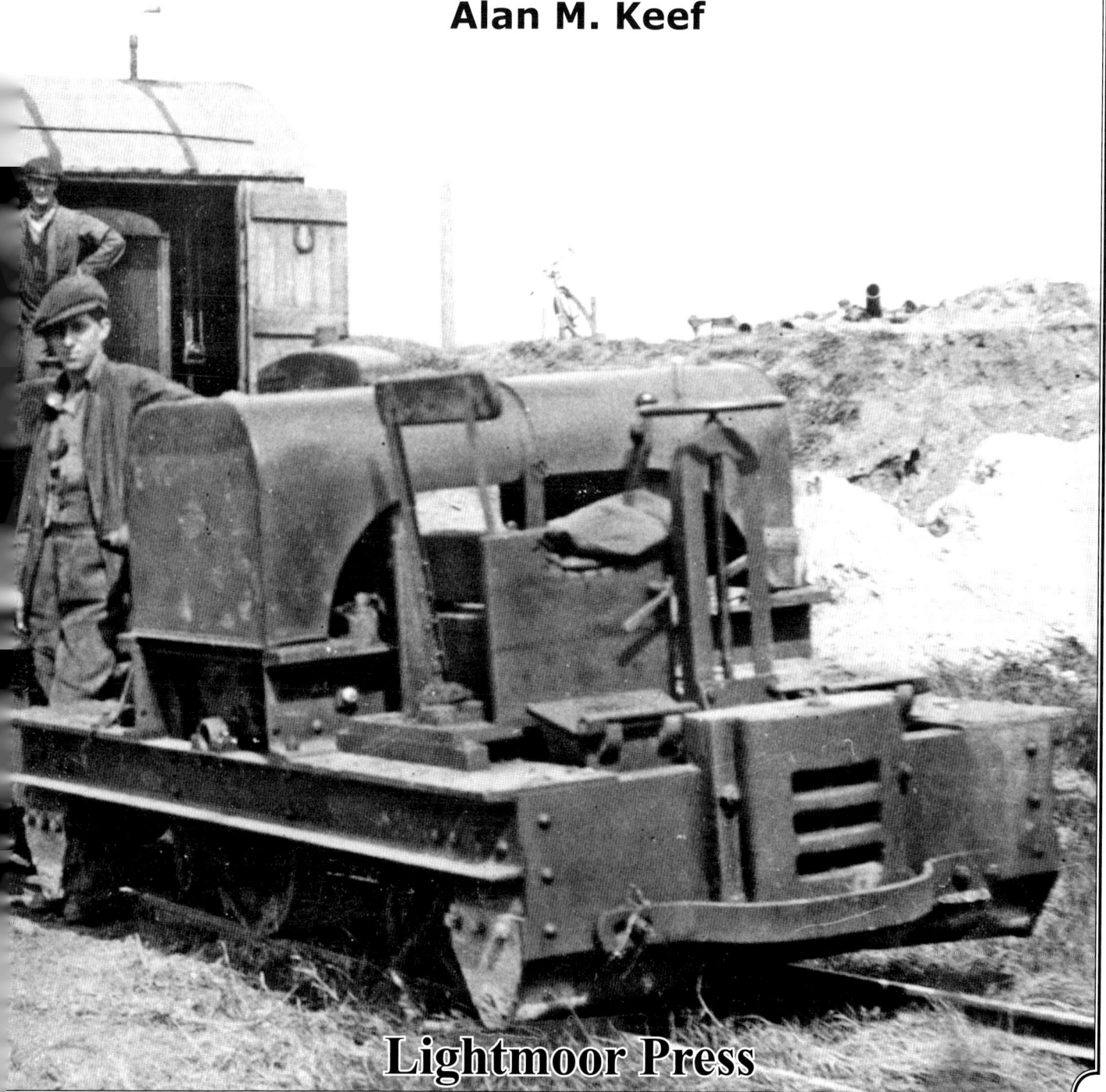

Lightmoor Press

*This book is dedicated to all those who worked for Motor Rail Ltd,*
*its predecessors and successors, over the last hundred years or so.*

# Contents

© Alan M. Keef and Lightmoor Press 2016.
Designed by Nigel Nicholson.

British Library Cataloguing-in-Publication Data. A catalogue
record for this book is available from the British Library.
ISBN 9781911038092

**LIGHTMOOR PRESS**
**Unit 144B, Lydney Trading Estate, Harbour Road, Lydney, Gloucestershire GL15 5EJ**
**www.lightmoor.co.uk**
*Lightmoor Press is an imprint of Black Dwarf Lightmoor Publications Ltd.*

Printed in Poland; www.lfbookservices.co.uk

1. This is a well-known Motor Rail picture and may have been taken for publicity purpose shortly after delivery of either MR 10272 of 1951 or MR 10409 of 1954. Both locomotives were new to the Leighton Buzzard Light Railway and this picture hung in their offices in Church Square, Leighton Buzzard. Whilst patently not new, the locomotive is in fairly pristine condition and shows off well with a normal load of twenty-four wagons of sand behind it. This is now the site of Pages Park Station on the Leighton Buzzard Railway.

# Preface

The genesis of this book is a manuscript that followed from a great deal of archive research by Frank Jux. This was done largely for his own pleasure and he then handed it to me with the comment that I could do as I liked with it! Generous indeed. Thus it is largely his book up to about Chapter 8 and I have taken it on from there with particular emphasis on the non-railway facets of the business together with the task of finding all the pictures.

Quite independently we had both visited the Simplex Works in Bedford in the 1950s. Frank had got there first in 1952 whilst researching material for the Industrial Railway Society. I got there in 1958 whilst working on a proposed article on the Leighton Buzzard Light Railway that was eventually included in *Narrow Gauge Tracks in the Sand* by Rod Dingwall. We both met Mr Tysoe who welcomed us warmly and helped with what we wanted. What is more remarkable is that I arrived at St Johns Station on my way to school every day, and within a long stone's throw of the Motor Rail offices, without realising that 'here be narrow gauge locomotives'!

The connections continued with Frank taking a ride on the Leighton Buzzard Light Railway in the days when they still operated the ex-War Department Light Railways 40hp locomotives, and as part and parcel of my first job I became involved in not only the Light Railway itself but also in the affairs of the major sand quarry companies as well. If at that time anyone had suggested that I might become a significant customer of Motor Rail Ltd and that I would eventually take over their business, the world would have laughed loud and long at such nonsense. But so it turned out to be!

Originally formed as the Motor Rail & Tramcar Co. Ltd with the prime purpose of building petrol driven tramcars for the founder's interests in East India Tramways in Karachi, it was not until the middle of the First World War that it came to build locomotives. These locomotives were a scaled down version of the proven tramcar design and were instantly successful in their own right. The concept was an inspired design, soundly engineered and simple in both operation and maintenance. Thus the story of the company

2. This is the Leighton Buzzard Light Railway that Frank and Alan knew in the late 1950s. Arnold's No. 42, MR 7710 of 1939, hammers up the 1 in 25 of Marley's Bank in a cloud of black diesel exhaust. This locomotive was originally sold to Sir Robert McAlpine Ltd as a 5 ton machine, came to the Leighton Buzzard Light Railway Co. Ltd in 1956 and was transferred to Joseph Arnold & Co. Ltd stock in 1958.

encompasses much of the history of British internal combustion driven locomotives. In its day the company was a leader, if not *the* leader, in its field, but the economics of materials handling change and today the use of rail haulage, particularly narrow gauge, for industrial purposes has shrunk to near vanishing point. This history should have been written much earlier when those who played the leading roles in the forming of the company were still alive to answer all the questions that should have been asked forty years and more ago.

Added to this is the fact that Motor Rail fundamentally only made 'widgets' and did not take a huge interest in what they made or where it was sold. With the rise of railway enthusiasm, especially for narrow gauge railways, the fact that those 'widgets' were locomotives took on a whole new significance. Most were sold through agents, almost 100% for overseas sales, and thus the paraphernalia of a marketing office is singularly lacking. To put this in perspective, their locomotive production is assiduously recorded by enthusiasts but no such record exists for the dumpers they made – let alone trailers!

Therefore my input to this history starts in the early 1970s when I became a customer of Motor Rail Ltd for the purchase of spare parts for their locomotives. Thus I saw the company from the outside looking in and, whilst I had a good rapport with the business, it was always a bit remote. A great deal of information came to Alan Keef Ltd with the purchase of the company, some of it useful, some of it less so, and this has been drawn upon for the later years of its operation.

## Locomotive Numbering

I have followed the nomenclature used by the Industrial Railway Society and others to identify locomotives. This starts with an abbreviation of the manufacturer's name followed by the works number followed by, where appropriate, the year of manufacture. For the purposes of this book we are only concerned with four names:

AK    Alan Keef Ltd, Ross-on-Wye.
K     Kitson & Co. Ltd, Leeds.
MR    Motor Rail Ltd, Bedford. This also covers Motor Rail & Tramcar Co. Ltd.
SMH   Simplex Mechanical Handling Ltd. Successor to Motor Rail Ltd as from 1972.

Thus a locomotive might be designated MR 8882 of 1944, SMH 101T018 of 1979 or AK 36 of 1990. In addition, Alan Keef Ltd add an R to the works number where a locomotive is rebuilt dramatically away from its original format, an extreme example being MR 5877 of 1935 which became AK 93R of 2012 when its method of propulsion was changed to steam.

## Spellings

The spelling of the Indian, and later Pakistani, province of Sindh is variable, sometimes including the h and sometimes not. For the purposes of this book I have used the commonest spelling, as Sindh. In 1955 the Pakistan Government decreed that it should be merged into the province of West Pakistan. The spelling of Kiamari

is interchangeable with Keamari. The former seems to be the norm in document form, and is used herein, but the latter appears on tram destination boards and the like.

I have used the contemporary spellings of street names and places although some of these tended to vary over the years. Many have been changed completely; for instance Bundar Road is now M.A. Jinnah Road.

I have used imperial units of weights and measures, for although Simplex leaflets often gave metric dimensions the manufacturing process was entirely imperial. Similarly I have used pre-decimal currency with only occasional conversions.

## Photographs

Many of the photographs come from the collections of Alan and Patrick Keef, and from those inherited from Motor Rail by Alan Keef Ltd. The latter are not well documented as to just what, when or where they were taken; they also include a very large number taken of manufacturing details which are irrelevant to this story. None of these are credited.

## Acknowledgements

Again, Frank Jux has generously provided a number of photographs, and I am particularly grateful to the collection of the late Jim Peden from the Industrial Railway Society for a wide variety of pictures both in time and subject matter. These have been credited to the individual photographers as appropriate. Also to Bob Darvill for the supply of sundry information and to Andrew Neale for providing the title page photograph. Thanks to Terry Russell for permission to reproduce the map of East India Tramways and entrusting me with his ticket collection from Karachi. Similarly to the Narrow Gauge Railway Society library and to Jim Hay and John Rowlands of the Moseley Railway Trust for their efforts on my behalf. This particularly applies to the latter for allowing me verbatim use of his plan of the works and associated text. At the eleventh hour John Bryant came up with an MR&T Co. catalogue running to 124 pages with a handwritten date on it of 1924. This has been used extensively for early photographs. Don Skevington, a former employee, shareholder, now Simplex Mechanical Handling Spares Ltd, provided much useful information on that side of the business.

I am further grateful to a number of individuals and organisations for the use of pictures provided, some of which are copyrighted, and these are credited against the individual image. Those from the Imperial War Museum and Bedfordshire Archives are credited accordingly. There are at least a few for which I have no record and if one of those is your photograph, my apologies, and please let me know for future reference.

I make no apology for the fact that many of the pictures involve areas of the author's expertise, such as the railways around Leighton Buzzard, the products of Alan Keef Ltd and those parts of the world where I have been particularly involved.

Finally, I have endeavoured to find images which have not been seen too often before and are shots of locomotives in action rather than posed works photographs, even if, as a consequence, the quality is not what one might wish. This particularly applies to Terry Russell's snaps of East India Tramways, but the photographs of the system in action are essential.

# 1

# An Indian Adventure

## 1883–c.1910

The use of mechanical traction on street tramways in Britain was authorised by an Act of Parliament passed in August 1879. As a result the 1880s saw a great expansion in the construction of tramways in Britain and the application of steam haulage to these. Not unnaturally, British entrepreneurs lost no time in promoting companies to establish tramways in foreign lands: the countries of the Empire and India, the jewel in the Imperial crown, did not escape attention.

Development of a harbour at Karachi – in what is now Pakistan – started in 1854 with the commencement of a breakwater, although work on the project was not finished until 1883. This marked the start of the importance of the town as a port and was further established by its selection as the terminus for the 5ft 6ins gauge Sindh Railway, work on which started in 1859. A jetty was built at Kiamari, some two miles from the town near the eastern breakwater, although it was considerably more via the circuitous route laid around the mangrove swamps to the Cantonment Station from which the railway was built inland to Kotri. Construction of this line was engineered by John Brunton who later became engineer to the completed railway.

By the 1880s the town had grown in importance and the Government had plans to expand the facilities of the port further to cater for the steamships of the era. The railway company did not provide a passenger service on its line to the Merewether Pier at Kiamari and traffic to the harbour had to make its own way via the causeway known as the Napier Mole that connected the town with the Kiamari wharves. It was perceived by a number of businessmen with Indian connections that there was an opening for a passenger and freight service that could connect all parts of the town with the Native Port and Kiamari. For this they applied for a concession to lay down a tramway along the route. Meanwhile John Brunton had returned to England where he gained suitable experience as engineer to Oxford Tramways. He was thus well placed to be consultant and engineer to East India Tramways Ltd. Official approval was given to the project by an Act passed by the Bombay authorities on 8th February 1883 and ratified by the Government of India on 26th March.

Armed with this concession a company was formed in England on 31st January 1884 with a prospectus being issued the following day to raise funds for the venture. The authorised capital of the company was £85,000 with the directors being as follows:

J. Percy-Leith. A director of the Eastern Bengal Railway.
W.H. James. Formerly with the Public Works Department, railway branch.
C. Steer. Formerly a High Court Judge in Calcutta.
W. Fletcher-Gordon. A director of the Bombay Gas Company.

In addition to John Brunton, J. Claxton Fidler was joint engineer to the company. The contract for the construction and equipment of the line was given to E.D. Mathews of London for a contract price of £76,500. The rolling stock that Mathews provided included six tram engines built by Kitson of Leeds in 1885 and numbered 144–149 in their tramway locomotive list. Starbuck & Co. of

3. A works photograph of one of the steam tram engines used by Karachi Tramways. Built by Kitson & Co. of Leeds in 1885 it lacks the condensing apparatus on the roof which was typical of most steam tramways. The dual controls are very prominent and, presuming that the track is standard gauge, the further side must be standing on blocks for the photographer's benefit!
*Courtesy Stephenson Locomotive Society*

| ORDER No. | BUILT FOR | GAUGE | CYLINDERS | | BOILER | | | | TUBES | | HEATING SURFACE | | | CONDENSING SURFACE | GRATE AREA | WATER CAPACITY | FUEL CAPACITY | BOILER PRESSURE | WHEELS DIAMETERS, WHEEL BASE AND WEIGHTS | DATE |
|---|---|---|---|---|---|---|---|---|---|---|---|---|---|---|---|---|---|---|---|---|
| | | | DIA. | STROKE | BARREL LENGTH | DIA. | F'BOX SHELL LENGTH | BREADTH | NO. | DIA. | TUBES | F'BOX | TOTAL | | | | | | | |
| 144-9 | KARACHI | 4'-0" | 8" | 12" | 4'5" | 2'9" | 2'9" | 3'.02" | 73 | 1 5/8" | 106 | 23 | 129 | — | 6 | 105 COLD 40 COND. | CUB: FT: 9 | 160 | 2'4½"  2'4½"  ◄— 5'-0" —► | 1885 |

| NAME OF COMPANY | MAKERS No. | | ADHESIVE | TOTAL WEIGHT | REMARKS | Co's No. | CYLs. | DIA. BOILER. FIREBOX. TUBES. TOTAL. | GRATE AREA | DATE OF TRIAL | REMARKS | WATER PER MILE | FUEL | COKE PER MILE |
|---|---|---|---|---|---|---|---|---|---|---|---|---|---|---|
| Karachi | 144-9 | | | | | | | 8×12. 2.9  23  106. 129.  6 Sep 85 | | | | | | 12.06 |

4. A section from the Kitson records relating to the Karachi locomotives that provides most of the technical information that could be needed. With 8ins x 12ins cylinders and a wheelbase of only 5ft these locomotives neither large nor powerful machines.

*Courtesy Stephenson Locomotive Society*

Birkenhead supplied the rolling stock which comprised nineteen carriages made up of two First class carriages, four composite and thirteen Third class as well as two parcels vans and twenty-three goods wagons. The rails of 70lbs/yd were supplied by Bolling & Lowe along with the other permanent way materials, apart from points and crossings which came from Ransomes & Rapier of Ipswich. Work on construction of the tramway started in Karachi on 26th August 1884 and shipment of the material was completed exactly a year later. With a rail gauge of 4ft 0ins interchange with the Sindh Railway was neither intended nor possible. As completed the line had a track length of about nine miles including sidings. The track was laid using grooved rail of a type designed by Brunton that he had already used in Oxford. From the list of equipment it will be seen that whoever had specified the requirements of the line had seen it as being as much a light railway as a passenger tramway. The line was completed in 1885 with the opening ceremony being performed by the Commissioner of Sindh on 20th April outside the Scots Kirk (St Andrew's Anglican Church). These dates are well attested but do not quite tally with Kitson records that suggest that the locomotives were tested in September 1885. Perhaps one was despatched early or the opening was with horse trams only. Either way, this was a creditable performance in construction. A further offering of shares was made in June 1885 when a glowing picture of the financial prospects of the company was painted, a dividend of 7% per annum being guaranteed for three years with earnings of 10% per annum being believed to be easily obtainable. The tramway was expected to replace bullock cart haulage between the city and the docks and monopolise traffic on the route.

As was so often the case, the enterprise that had been described did not reap its expected rewards. The problems were partly of the company's own making, and a report by the secretary in March 1886 after a visit to Karachi had much to say on the shortcomings of the line together with suggestions for its improvement. The tram engines had caused complaints from the residents of the streets that they traversed on the grounds of noise and were not economical to work. The trains were made up of First, Second and Third class carriages with the former being but sparsely filled. The vast bulk of the passengers required only Third class accommodation and it was suggested that a more frequent and therefore more profitable service could be provided using light horse drawn cars. The steam engines would be retained only for heavy work such as 'commuter' runs to the docks at Kiamari and for freight traffic. Much general haulage continued to be done by the bullock carts which had not been driven off the roads as had been hoped. The main freight traffic was in bagged grain from two large warehouses either to the main line goods depot or to the native harbour for onward shipment by dhow. This traffic was intermittent and unfortunately the distance from the tramway depot to the warehouses involved the locomotives in running light for five miles to and from their work. The recommendations of the report were adopted and by 1st January 1887 the service was operated by seven cars with twenty-nine horses, although this was increased to eleven cars and fifty-eight horses during the ensuing year. This in turn had reached eighteen cars (including one larger 'two-horse' car) and eighty-three horses by 1889. In 1890 fares had to be reduced to counter increasing competition from so-called dog-carts.

The other problem that greatly affected the company's prospects was the formation of the North Western State Railway in 1886 and the continued development of the harbour facilities at Karachi. The company was aware of the policy regarding the harbour expansion but seems to have discounted any possible adverse effects on its business; indeed it may have seen the development prospects as a point in its favour for the future. The formation of the North Western Railway may have been accompanied by a more active freight development policy and certainly led to the establishment of a depot near the native harbour at the shoreward end of the Napier Mole. So far as the harbour was concerned the Karachi Port Trust was set up on 1st April 1887 to administer the port and take over responsibility for its development. At that time the only rail-served facility was the Merewether Pier connected to the original Sindh Railway branch. Only one steamer at a time could be handled at the pier whilst two more berths were available at the newly completed Erskine Wharf. A further extension to Erskine Wharf was in hand to accommodate three more ships while facilities for smaller craft were also being expanded. This expansion of capacity naturally required an improvement of the railway layout not least because the sidings laid to connect with Merewether Pier were inconvenient to work. The North Western Railway accordingly put in hand a new line from their McLoed Road (City) railway station to Kiamari via the Napier Mole. This crossed the Chinnar Creek on its own railway bridge and paralleled the mole before crossing the road and tramway to reach the new wharves. The first train to run via this new route, loaded with railway material, reached Kiamari on 4th May 1889 and the line was fully opened later that year.

5. The hand-written caption is barely decipherable but prominently states: *'The first petrol tram in the world – Karachi, 1910. 46-seat open type. 8 miles to the gallon with petrol at 7 annas per gallon, weight unloaded 3 tons. Designed by John Abbott, Chairman, with J.R. Abbott, his father. Lucas Valveless engine and Dixon Abbott Patent Gearbox.'*

6. (*Below*) Early days in Karachi. Probably about 1914 and taken from an early MR&T Co. catalogue. The destination board on the left-hand car reads Boulton Market, the other is illegible. It is an interesting social comment that at this stage the white passengers (in topees) were happy to share the seating indiscriminately with the local population. *Courtesy John Bryant*

These various changes had a serious effect on the tramway company's freight business in particular and it lost 75% of its goods traffic. Henceforth it had to rely solely on passenger fares to survive. Thus, at the end of 1889, the steam locomotives were laid up permanently after only a very short period of use

Facilities at the port were constantly being improved to deal with an expanding trade. In May 1894 work was started on a new import yard for the Port Trust adjacent to the North Western Railway goods yard next to the Custom House, again at the shoreward end of Napier Mole. This was accompanied by the construction of a new roadway at the joint cost of the North Western Railway, the Port Trust and the Municipality – Queens Road – to the south of the railway yard from the end of the Napier Mole bridge. The new import yard encroached upon Bundar Road and the line of the tramway had to be relocated slightly to the north. Christened Mansfield Yard, it was officially opened on 20th November 1895.

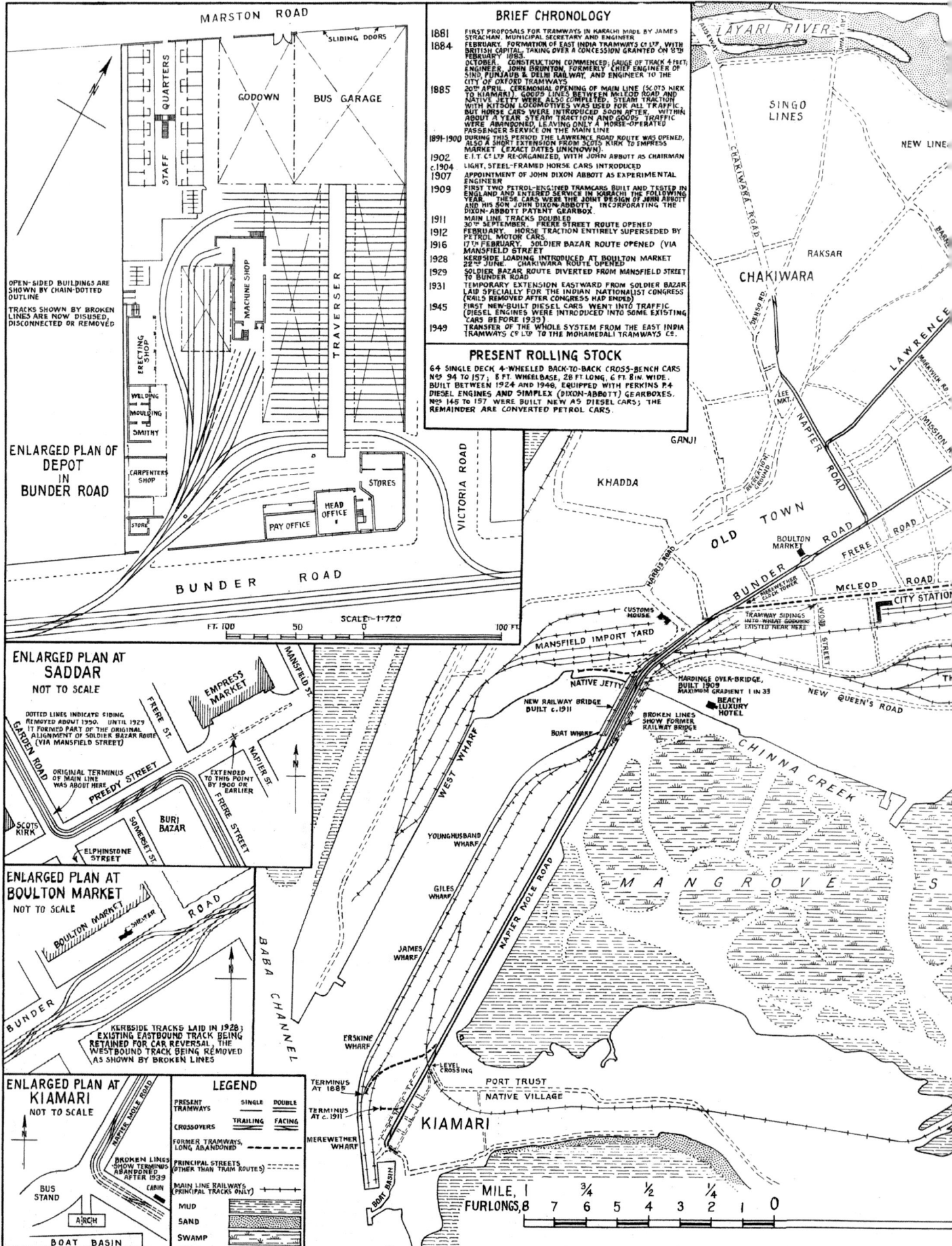
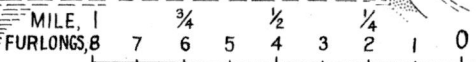

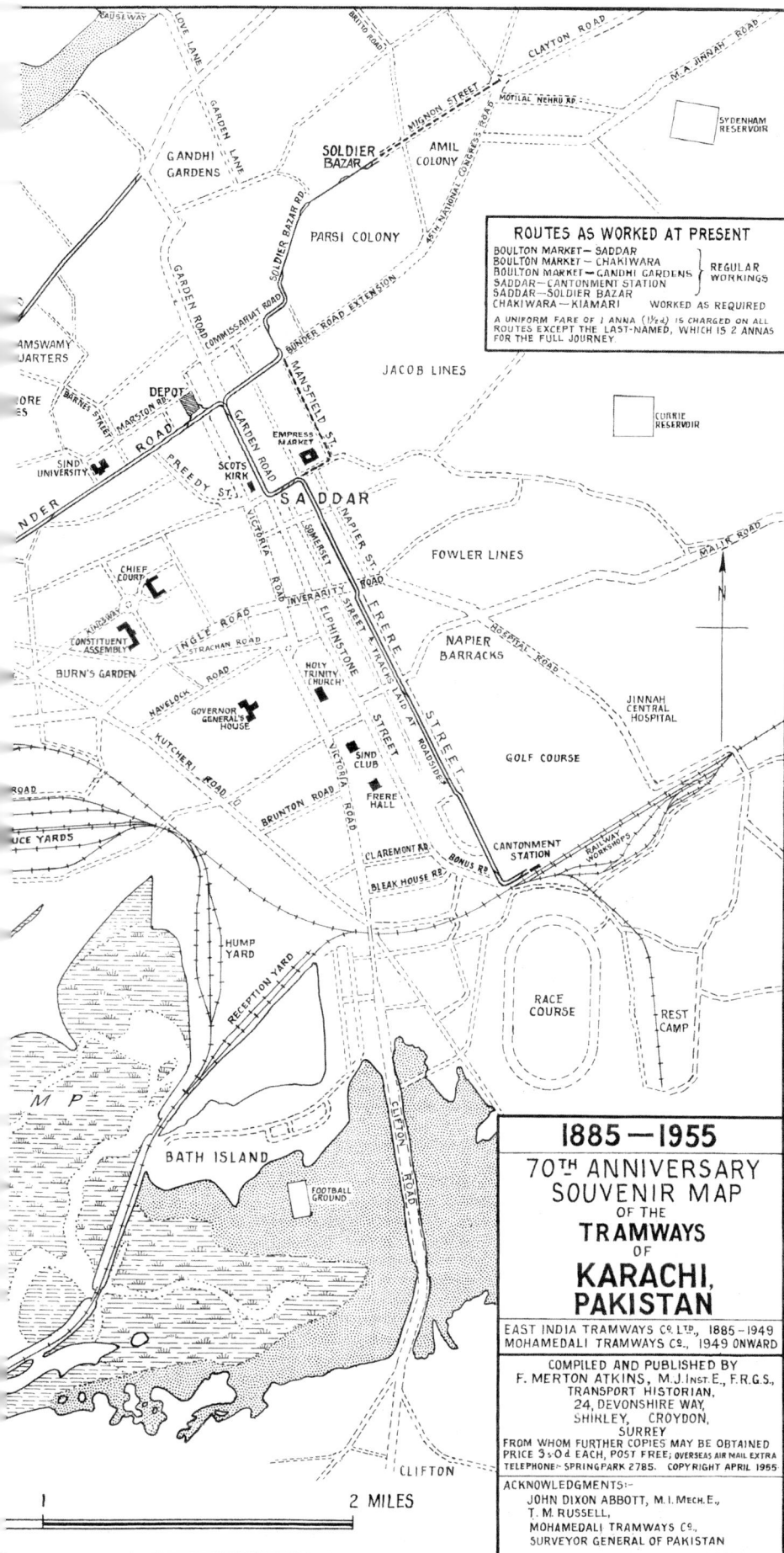

## Map labels

CAUSEWAY
LOVE LANE
GARDEN LANE
BRITO ROAD
CLAYTON ROAD
M.A. JINNAH ROAD
MIGNON STREET
MOTILAL NEHRU RD.
GANDHI GARDENS
SOLDIER BAZAR
AMIL COLONY
SYDENHAM RESERVOIR
45TH NATIONAL CONGRESS ROAD
PARSI COLONY
SOLDIER BAZAR RD.
COMMISSARIAT ROAD
GARDEN ROAD
BUNDER ROAD EXTENSION
JACOB LINES
...AMSWAMY ...UARTERS
...ORE ...ES
BARNES STREET
SIND UNIVERSITY
DEPOT
MARSTON RD.
GARDEN ROAD
PREEDY ST.
MANSFIELD ST.
EMPRESS MARKET
SCOTS KIRK
SADDAR
CURRIE RESERVOIR
VICTORIA ROAD
SOMERSET STREET
NAPIER ST.
ELPHINSTONE STREET
FRERE STREET
MALIR ROAD
FOWLER LINES
CHIEF COURT
KINGWAY
CONSTITUENT ASSEMBLY
INGLE ROAD
INVARARITY ROAD
STRACHAN ROAD
BURN'S GARDEN
HAVELOCK ROAD
HOSPITAL ROAD
NAPIER BARRACKS
HOLY TRINITY CHURCH
JINNAH CENTRAL HOSPITAL
GOVERNOR GENERAL'S HOUSE
KUTCHERI ROAD
SIND CLUB
VICTORIA ROAD
GOLF COURSE
FRERE HALL
BRUNTON ROAD
ROAD
...UCE YARDS
CLAREMONT RD.
BLEAK HOUSE RD.
BONUS RD.
CANTONMENT STATION
RAILWAY WORKSHOPS
TRACKS LAID AT ROADSIDE
HUMP YARD
RECEPTION YARD
RACE COURSE
REST CAMP
M P
BATH ISLAND
FOOTBALL GROUND
CLIFTON ROAD
CLIFTON
N

### Map legend (centre)

**ROUTES AS WORKED AT PRESENT**

BOULTON MARKET — SADDAR
BOULTON MARKET — CHAKIWARA
BOULTON MARKET — GANDHI GARDENS } REGULAR WORKINGS
SADDAR — CANTONMENT STATION
SADDAR — SOLDIER BAZAR
CHAKIWARA — KIAMARI            WORKED AS REQUIRED

A UNIFORM FARE OF 1 ANNA (1½d) IS CHARGED ON ALL ROUTES EXCEPT THE LAST-NAMED, WHICH IS 2 ANNAS FOR THE FULL JOURNEY.

### Map title block

**1885 — 1955**
70TH ANNIVERSARY
SOUVENIR MAP
OF THE
**TRAMWAYS**
OF
**KARACHI,
PAKISTAN**

EAST INDIA TRAMWAYS Cº. Lᵀᴰ., 1885-1949
MOHAMEDALI TRAMWAYS Cº., 1949 ONWARD

COMPILED AND PUBLISHED BY
F. MERTON ATKINS, M.J.Inst.E., F.R.G.S.,
TRANSPORT HISTORIAN,
24, DEVONSHIRE WAY,
SHIRLEY, CROYDON,
SURREY
FROM WHOM FURTHER COPIES MAY BE OBTAINED
PRICE 3s·0d EACH, POST FREE; OVERSEAS AIR MAIL EXTRA
TELEPHONE- SPRINGPARK 2785.    COPYRIGHT APRIL 1955

ACKNOWLEDGMENTS:-
JOHN DIXON ABBOTT, M.I.MECH.E.,
T.M. RUSSELL,
MOHAMEDALI TRAMWAYS Cº.
SURVEYOR GENERAL OF PAKISTAN

2 MILES

While these developments had been going on the tramway company had not been entirely inactive. It had submitted a claim for compensation for the disruption of its traffic caused by the building of the North Western Railway branch to the harbour, which crossed its line on the level, and in 1890 managed to extract £5,450 from the Government as a result. It had also gained authority to extend the lines in town for a further two miles and seven chains along Napier and Lawrence Roads to a terminus at the Government Gardens. Construction of this extension had already started when a prospectus was written in 1890 for the issue of £30,000 of 5% Mortgage Stock. This was to provide funds for the work and for the repayment of earlier debenture issues. According to this prospectus passenger journeys had shown a strong upward movement rising from 856,123 in 1887 to 1,550,082 in 1888, no doubt due to the introduction of horse trams in addition to those still being operated by locomotives.

Despite this the financial results of the company were poor, partly due to the capital structure set up by the promoters with 1888 being the only year in which a surplus was earned. The guarantee given in 1885 of a dividend on the £8,000 of shares then issued was not covered by profits and the burden of the interest entailed by issuing fixed interest bearing stock made it more difficult to earn a return for the ordinary shareholders. One can only assume that when the funds were needed they could not otherwise have been obtained. The initial operating period from April to December 1885 had resulted in a loss after payment of interest of £5,645 and this was followed by a deficit of £7,932 in 1886 and of £3,306 in 1887. The surplus in 1888 amounted to £1,132 but slipped into a deficit of £372 the following year. Thereafter the losses increased, fluctuating from year to year, but adding up to an accumulated deficit of £31,538 by the end of 1898. Interest on the mortgage debentures was only partly paid in 1893 and not paid at all in 1894 and 1895. The company could not continue to operate in this way without making itself vulnerable to a take-over bid. Therefore it is not surprising that in 1902 a capital reconstruction was undertaken. The old company went into

This map was prepared for the 70th anniversary of Karachi's tramway system in 1955 and shows it at its greatest extent. It is surprising how little it changed over the years with very few early closures.                    *Courtesy Terry Russell*

liquidation and a new company retaining the old name of East India Tramways Ltd was formed under new direction and with an improved capital structure. The only stock bearing a fixed rate of interest were 7,500 5% preference shares credited as having 10 shillings (50p) paid up. The ordinary shares were reduced from 75,070 that had been issued under the old company to 33,433 and there were 30,000 shares of a new deferred class. Only when dividends of 5% had been paid on the ordinary shares would the

deferred shareholders receive a dividend but they were then entitled to the balance of profits remaining. There were also several levels of potential reward with only a small burden on the profits of the company. The new Board of Directors was headed by John Abbot as Chairman, the other members being G. Dugald Buckler and H. Dixon Kimber with George Gale acting as Secretary. The offices of the new company were at 79 Lombard Street, London with the company being formally registered on 25th July 1902.

7. Khibandarrd. An early motor tram passes down Bunder Road past the Max Denso Hall on the right. The library attached to this hall was the first in the city available to the native population. This picture is consistently quoted as being from 1900, however the car appears to be an early D series and these were not available until 1911 at the earliest, which would date the picture to say 1912-14. The absence of any form of motor transport together with the ox carts tend to confirm this, but the plethora of telephone wires could make it somewhat later. Certainly the car is not horse drawn which it would have been in 1900.
*Wikipedia*

The series of photographs (Plates 8-15) was taken by Terry Russell whilst serving with the RAF in Pakistan in 1953/54, by which time the system had become Mohamedali Tramways (MTC). They are very much 'snaps', but they do show the system in the full flight of its everyday operations.

8. (*Above*) A busy scene at Saddar in EIT days and near to the Scots Kirk which was the first terminus of the tramway. Note the policeman holding back the traffic as two cars round the corner into Garden Road.

9. (*Above*) CIT Car No. 128 passes another on its way from Boulton Market to Cantonment Station. Note the children with plates selling food to travellers; a feature of travel in many countries across the world.

10. (*Below*) Bunder Road Depot hardly changed over the years of the tramway's existence. This is the traverser between the two car sheds which remained hand operated to the end. The building in the distance is the bus garage which seems to have a few occupants.

12. The approach to the depot from Bunder Road with the fuel pumps the first port of call for incoming cars. The two men are 'rail cleaners', presumably to mitigate the possibility of derailment. Did they operate only within the depot or did their duties spread further afield? If so it must have been at night as trams or surrounding traffic would have mown them down!

11. As far as passengers were concerned Boulton Market was the hub of the system and car No. 96 loads at the kerbside for a routine trip to Ghandi Gardens. This car has also been given its MTC roundel.

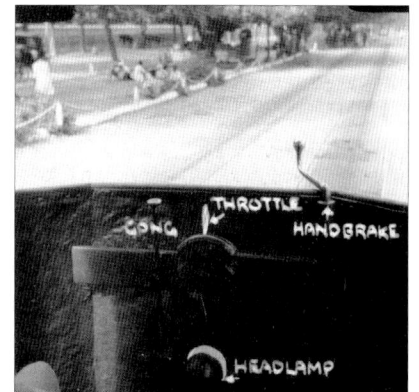

13. A view of the driver's controls. The handbrake is no doubt a standard of its era with a ratchet at floor level for which the driver kicked the pawl on or off as required. The throttle is convenient to his left hand with that other vital piece of equipment, the gong, next to it. The forward/reverse and change speed levers together with the clutch pedal would have operated across the vehicle after the style of MR 2262 (see Plate 65).

14. (*Right*) An internal view showing the cross-bench seating which appears to have a hard seat but with a cushioned backrest. Also visible are the sash window type blinds to keep out both sun and rain.

15. (*Below*) Car No. 150 is recorded as having been completely rebuilt and it would have acquired a Perkins 4.236 diesel engine in the process. It has also gained stiffening bars across the dash which would be desirable judging by the damage that some cars seem to have received in this area. It can be seen that the car has also acquired a Mohamedali Tramways roundel and Arabic inscription above the headlight. It is here pulling away from Boulton Market.

16. (*Right*) An order from East India Tramways from August 1947. Although described as tramcar side frames the detail suggests that these were in fact complete, or near complete, frames, with the reference to engine bearers and brake crossbars. Delivery is lengthy but judging by the dates from quote to order the postal service was very good indeed!

*Courtesy Bedford County Record Office*

Cable Address: "IVORIDE, LONDON."
Code: BENTLEY'S COMPLETE PHRASE.
Telephone: MANSION HOUSE 7417.

**ORDER No. 7622**

From The East India Tramways Co., Ltd.,
34, Nicholas Lane,
London, E.C.4.

22nd August, 19 47.

To Messrs Motor Rail Ltd.,
Simplex Works, Bedford.

*PLEASE SUPPLY the undermentioned goods, packed for Export :*

PLEASE
NOTE.

INVOICES required in quadruplicate : 2 copies on official form A with certificate of origin and all copies signed.

Packages must be distinctly marked with the following SHIPPING MARK :

**TRAMWAYS KARACHI.**

No. 7622 /1 & upwards.
(Marks not to be enclosed in lines or squares.)

DELIVERY DATE 2 Sets 8 months
Balance 12 months.

Marks on and descriptions of packages must correspond with particulars in invoices.

5 sets Tramcar side frames W.27457/29309/23152. Each consisting of one pair of parts 460/1A/2/3/4/5/8 rivetted together; with cleated engine channels 720/1 and two brake corssbars, as supplied to E.I.T. Order No. 6842 but including 2 brake crossbars.

@....................£79. 4s. 8d. per set.

In accordance with your quotation of the 19th August 1947 to our Consulting Engineer Mr. J. D. Abbott.

TERMS nett

DELIVERY Bundled and delivered F.O.R. Bedford £1.10.0. extra.

Please apply for shipping instructions to Messrs. M.A.T. Transport Ltd., of Ling House Dominion Street, London, E.C.2. stating marks numbers measurements and gross weights of packages and sending them copy of the invoice.

FOR AND ON BEHALF OF THE EAST INDIA TRAMWAYS CO. LTD.

Secretary.

25 AUG 1947

Phones: Office : 7100 / 7662
Proprietor : 7528
Residence : 7217

Cables: "TRAMWAYS"

# MOHAMEDALI TRAMWAYS Co.

Bunder Road

Ref. No._____ KARACHI _____

17. (*Left*) The new order. Headed notepaper from Mohamedali Tramways.
*Courtesy Terry Russell*

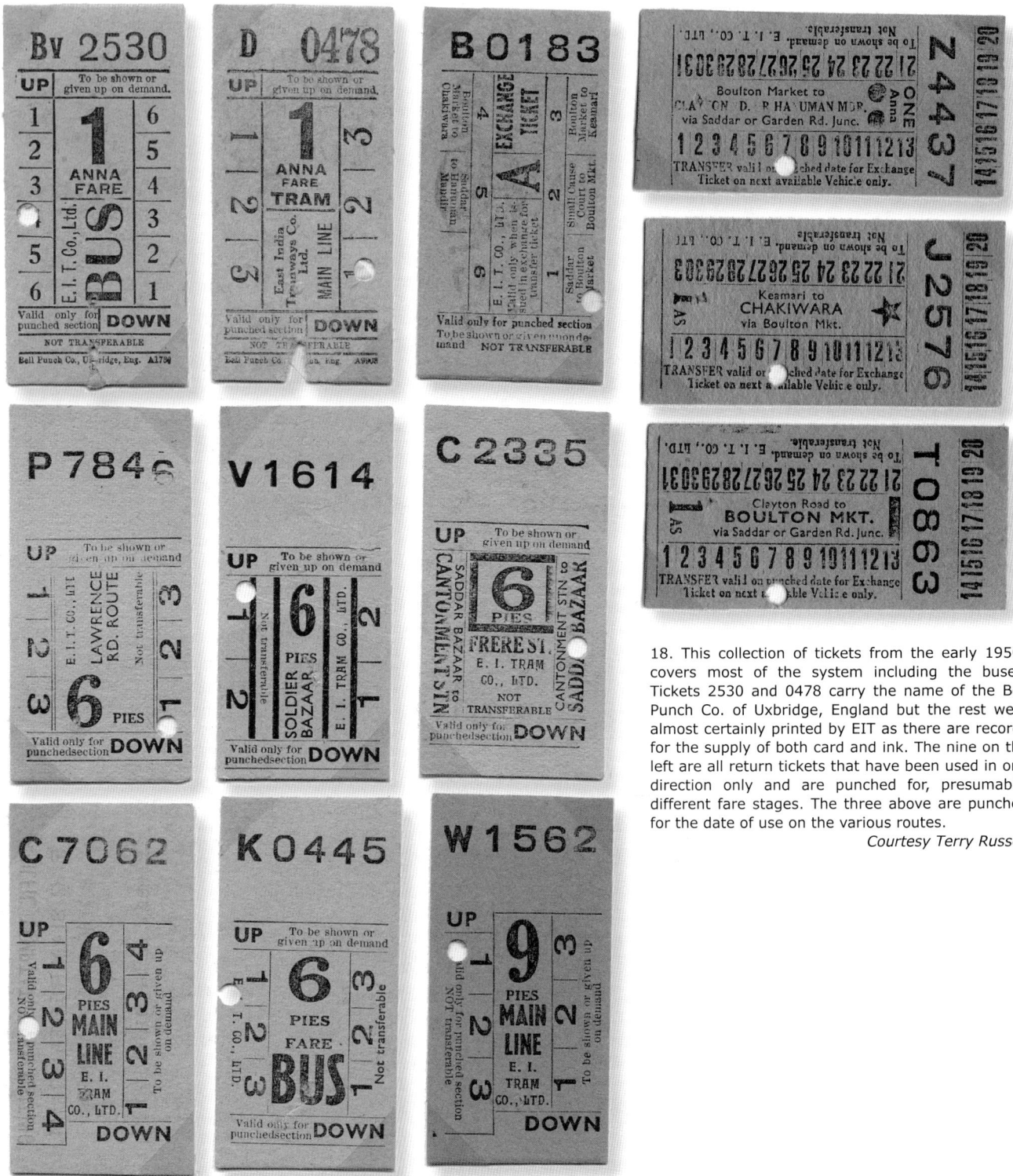

18. This collection of tickets from the early 1950s covers most of the system including the buses. Tickets 2530 and 0478 carry the name of the Bell Punch Co. of Uxbridge, England but the rest were almost certainly printed by EIT as there are records for the supply of both card and ink. The nine on the left are all return tickets that have been used in one direction only and are punched for, presumably, different fare stages. The three above are punched for the date of use on the various routes.

*Courtesy Terry Russell*

19. It is not known just when these tokens date from or how they were used. However, the collection of tram tickets above suggests that at that time, the early 1950s, most fares were either 1 Anna or 6 Pies. The tokens are likely to have been on sale at the company offices or local shops. Although the tokens are of East India tramways origin it is likely that they continued in use into Mohamedali Tramways days when inflation could have made them redundant. They may have been an effort to both speed up ticket sales and reduce losses in cash handling. The 1 Anna token on the left is blue and the 6 Pies on the right is green. There was also a 9 Pies token which was black.     *Photos courtesy Oesha and Kushi*

# 2

# East India Tramways Ltd

## 1910–1972

The new company continued to operate the tramway as before with a moderate annual surplus. However, the port continued to become busier and the Stock Exchange Yearbook for 1897 contained a note that the company was negotiating a claim for compensation for a further proposed crossing of its track. This was presumably in connection with the planned expansion by the Karachi Port Trust but work did not start on any major extensions until 1906 when further extensions to the wharves and a rearrangement of the facilities were commenced. It was decided to lay out a new import yard within the port boundaries exchanging the Mansfield Yard for the North Western Railway yards at Kiamari. Main line traffic had increased so much by this date that the two tracks that had emerged from the import yard en route for Kiamari were insufficient and provision was made to replace these with six lines. As a result an overbridge became necessary to avoid interruption of both road and tramway traffic during shunting operations. This involved the demolition of the Old Custom House and the relocation of the tramway over the new bridge.

Understandably, the tramway resisted this change which would entail them in considerable operating problems. The gradients leading onto the bridge were too great to be negotiated by the horse hauled cars unaided and a new means of locomotion would now have to be found or additional horses provided for working over the bridge. Negotiations between the East India Tramways and the Karachi Port Trust were lengthy and as an agreement could not be reached the Port Trust proposed to petition the Commissioner for Sindh asking for an Act to be passed to allow them to compulsorily acquire the length of road required. Work on the bridge was held up in the meantime although it was by then 75% complete and it was not until 1910 that compensation of £9,500 was accepted by the tramway company to cover the extra costs of working their line. The Port Trust also paid the cost of diverting the tramway tracks over the new bridge. The bridge was formally opened and christened the Hardinge Bridge by the Viceroy of India on 12th April 1911.

Whilst the negotiations for compensation had been going on the Directors had been considering their problem and decided to experiment with internal combustion engined vehicles rather than adopt electrification of their track which would have been expensive and beyond their resources. There had been some experimentation with petrol engined trams in England prior to this but these had not always been successful. Many of the early internal combustion engined railcars had been single ended necessitating turning facilities at the end of the route. This feature was a result of their evolution from omnibus design as opposed to being designed specifically for rail usage. Although there were a number of firms such as Drewry Car Co. and McEwan Pratt that produced railcars, these were only

recently established and John Abbott preferred to draw up his own design and specification with the assistance of his son John Dixon Abbott.

It is possible to trace the ideas being followed by the company, for on 16th September 1907 the publication *Motor Traction* reported as follows:

*We have received an important export enquiry for petrol motor trams for use on ordinary tramway lines, gauge 4ft. They are required to run in places where electric mains are not allowable on account of the effect on certain delicate instruments in neighbouring buildings. Trucks without bodies, but with engines, are wanted with drawings and full description.*

This undoubtedly related to Karachi but responses, if any, were not reported. However, a fortnight later the same publication included a letter headed 'Motor Tractor for Tramway Work':

*Sir, What I am – and for some years have been – looking for is one simple yet reliable motor tractor for tramways, of about 14–20 horse power, capable of replacing to advantage single horse traction abroad. It would be necessary to haul on tram rails a gross load of 3 tons – ex tractor – at a speed of about 10 miles per hour in either direction at a running cost of not more than 2d per mile. It must stop and start frequently – as is necessary in tramway service – without any intermediate speed gears. At one of the exhibitions about two years ago or more I saw a small car with a friction drive off a flat face flywheel, the principle of which was stated to be successfully used by some Vienna omnibus company, but have heard nothing of any further adoption of the system since. I should like to know if this method of gear driving has stood the test of experience and could be seen in regular work. It would be futile to send abroad what has not stood a continuous test in Europe.*

*As no steering, differential gear or passenger accommodation is needed, such a tractor ought not to be difficult or expensive to produce but somehow the few attempts in this direction have not been satisfactory.*

*JOHN ABBOTT*

Again the editor promised to forward any replies but we have no record of any response.

It seems that in the silence that followed this correspondence John Abbott chose to design his own machine to suit the specific conditions obtaining in Karachi. For the record the friction drive that John Abbott mentions was later used very successfully by D. Wickham & Co. Ltd in their small maintenance trolleys.

The statements given to the shareholders with the accounts for 1909 and 1910 provide some background but little detail of the design work carried out.

*In view of the increasing traffic and the impending introduction of heavier gradients over an important part of the tramway system than will be possible to work satisfactorily by means of horses, the Directors have deemed it advisable to make a working trial with a few motor driven cars. This will ascertain practically whether this form of traction may not be more suitable for general use and at the same time give a more speedy service than is obtainable by means of horses, which, during the hot season suffer considerably. As, however, the directors could not find any tramcars in practical operation that would in their judgement be satisfactory, they had recourse to experiments with various forms of motors modified in various particulars at the suggestion of the Chairman. In the result they succeeded in producing a motor they have every reason to hope will be eminently satisfactory and a few cars specially constructed with this form of motor are being sent out to Karachi to further test their economy and practicality in use. Should they prove successful it is the intention of the board to gradually, but as quickly as possible, adopt them to the entire exclusion of horses.*

*The extension of the line down Frere Street has now been sanctioned subject to Government approval.*

The extension was officially opened on 30th September 1911.

The subsequent report for the year ended 31st July 1910 reported on the success achieved:

*In last year's report reference was made to the trial that was being made with motor driven cars. These trials have been so far successful that the Directors have determined to gradually supersede all the horse cars by motors. Orders are consequently being given for the building and supply of motors as quickly as circumstances will permit consistent with the training of native drivers and the embodiment of such minor improvements as experience with the new form of traction indicates. It will be remembered that the introduction of a more powerful form of traction was necessitated through the building by the Karachi Port Trust of an overbridge with heavy gradients. 14,702 miles run by motor traction at a running cost of 2¾d per mile. This favourable result is largely due to the 'Dixon Abbott' patent two speed reversing gear which combined with the 'Lucas Valveless' motors provides an exceptionally simple and direct driving mechanism the maintenance and depreciation of which, it is believed, will prove to be correspondingly light.*

The gradient over the Hardinge Bridge is variously quoted as 1:30 and 1:38. Initially the experimental cars ran between the horse trams but this obviously was not satisfactory due to their difference in speed and it is readily seen that the Directors wished to change to the new method of traction as soon as possible.

20. Possibly brand new, but at the very least just out-shopped from the workshops behind it, is this very smartly turned out car, No. 130. Elaborate lining out was not a feature of East India Tramways! Cars can be seen in the car shed to the right and, more interestingly, to the left a vehicle labelled 'Break Down Car'. Judging by the position of the steps, this could just possibly be the chassis of an enclosed car from steam tramway days.

21. (*Right*) Car 139 has been similarly refurbished but so far at least without the lining. The boxed-in middle seat that covers the engine and gearbox can be seen. Possibly as a warning to increasing motor traffic a red tail light has been affixed to the right of the destination blind.

*The improved result is largely due to the better service enabled by the 'Simplex' motor trams which after three years careful development are now operating at the unusually low cost of 1.77d per mile for power, repairs and maintenance, which for cars carrying 46 passengers is probably a record for tramway or light railway traffic. Their mechanism is moreover of such a simple character that subsequent maintenance and depreciation are not likely to prove a heavy charge.*

It had been stated in the *Tramway and Light Railway Gazette* for 8th July 1909 that it was reported from India that 10hp motors were about to be used on the Karachi tramways. If this is correct then the initial trams had a smaller engine than the main batch for the standard engine adopted for the bulk of the cars was a Lucas Valveless engine of 25hp. This was a two stroke design with unusual features in that the two cylinders each drove separate crankshafts which rotated in opposite directions and were geared together with both pistons rising and falling in unison. The drive was taken through a gearbox giving two speeds in either direction, the design being the subject of a patent taken out by John Dixon Abbott in 1909 (number 18314). Both engine and gearbox were manufactured by David Brown & Sons of Huddersfield who produced them as a unit in a supporting frame made up of rolled steel joists. This unit was fitted transversely across the tram car enabling the drive to be taken from the main shaft of the gearbox to an axle by heavy roller chain, thus dispensing with the need for bevel gears or a worm drive. By the date of an article in *The Commercial Motor* on 17th August 1911, eighteen of these units had been supplied for the East India Tramway Co. Ltd by David Brown. A further twenty-four were in course of manufacture by the Motor Rail & Tramcar Co. Ltd which had been formed to take over the gearbox patent and manufacture of tramcars. The completed tramcars weighed between 3¼ and 3½ tons and seated forty-six passengers on 'toast rack' open cross-bench seating made of teak, fixed on a steel chassis, and with an overall canopy with side curtains that could be used if required. The exact number supplied to Karachi is not clear since an article in *Tramway & Railway World* on 8th August 1912 quoted a figure of trams in use as thirty. This figure was repeated in an article in another journal in May 1914 with the addition that six more were in transit to Karachi and four more were to be constructed. It is possible that the balance of the units mentioned in the 1911 article were sent out as spares or were ordered by the Motor Rail & Tramcar Co. Ltd with other customers in mind.

There is no doubt that these trams were a great success and transformed the company's prospects, converting a profit of hundreds of pounds into thousands. John Dixon Abbott was made the company's engineer and went to Karachi to oversee the changeover from horse to petrol traction and remained there for three years until this was done, with the final elimination of horse traction being achieved in February 1912. It is unfortunate that the details of the design and construction of these tramcars was not given in any of the articles published that contained information provided by the company. It was stated that two cars were sent to Karachi in 1909 after two years experimental running in this country but where this was carried out has not been traced. It would, in any case, have been difficult to achieve as the number of 4ft gauge tramways in the UK was always minimal. These two cars may have been different from the production batches as the

1911 article on the Lucas Valveless engined trams states that the first car had been in use for over 12 months rather than the 18 months that had elapsed since the end of 1909. David Brown & Sons provided the engine and gearbox unit but it is not known who supplied the tram chassis and assembled them although it is possible that final erection was done in Karachi. They were larger than the horse cars which only seated thirty passengers, and a new car shed with parallel tracks served by a traverser was provided to house them in the depot off Bundar Road.

Profits for the year to 31st July 1912 amounted to £8,540, out of which £3,495 was transferred to a suspense account from which the cost of doubling the company's tracks and introducing the new trams was to be met along with the extension along Frere Street to the North Western Railway's Cantonment Station. The following year the figure was £9,714 – a very satisfactory operating ratio of 43% of the gross takings – with £6,141 placed to suspense. Work on the extension was expected to be completed in late 1913 or early 1914 bringing the track mileage to about seventeen with a route mileage of eight and a half. The three main routes being:

| | | |
|---|---|---|
| Sadar Bazaar to Kiamari | 5 miles | Fare 2 annas (1d) |
| Max Denso Hall to Government Gardens | 2 miles | Fare 9 pies (¾d) |
| Sadar Bazaar to Cantonment Station | 1½ miles | Fare 9 pies (¾d) |

At its greatest extent the route mileage was ten and a half miles, most of which was double track.

With the report for 1913 the Directors were justified in claiming that:

*The result, obtained with fares averaging less than a penny each, amply justifies your Directors adoption of the Simplex motor trams, which, for the fourth year since introduction show an average cost for working expenses of 4.93d per car mile inclusive of 0.82d depreciation.*

The Deferred shareholders who, it will be recalled, received no dividend until the other shareholders had been paid 5% were able to benefit from their faith in the company and reserves of £20,000 were allocated to them in the form of an issue of an equivalent amount of Deferred shares.

1914 saw a further successful year with a profit of £8,862 of which £2,000 was placed to reserve and authority was received for extensions of the line to Soldiers Bazaar and along the Lawrence Road. In 1913 six char-a-banc type omnibuses with open sided cross-bench seating had been supplied by Tilling-Stevens and Thorneycroft. It was intended that these should provide feeder services to the tramway system although initially they were put into service on the routes of the proposed tramway extensions. More came later during the war years when there were problems obtaining spare parts with which to keep the tramcar fleet in operation, presumably due to War Office commitments at Bedford (see Chapter 4). As an experiment they were not deemed successful but served their purpose for a few years. The average cost of working was 5.39d per car mile although this probably took into account the higher cost for operation of the buses, since in the following year the Simplex trams ran 599,725 miles at a cost of 4.31d per car mile (with receipts of 9.52d per car mile). The road buses in the same year ran 31,708 miles at a cost of 8.97d per mile (with receipts of 9.99d per mile).

Although the company had thought that the authorised extensions might have to be postponed following the outbreak of the First World War, that from Empress Market to Soldiers Bazaar was taken in hand and opened for traffic on 18th February 1916. On the tramway there was a frequent service of the motor trams varying from every six minutes on the busiest route to every fifteen minutes on that less patronised. The war was to have a momentous impact on the future of the Motor Rail & Tramcar Co. Ltd to which company John Dixon Abbott had assigned his gearbox patent. It also seriously affected the East India Tramway Co. Ltd since Government control of engineering production resulted in the cessation of the supply of spare parts to Karachi with which to keep the trams running. This makes it all the more surprising

GOING HOME TIME—IN KARACHI

PERKINS DIESEL

KEAMARI

129

HERE IS ONE OF A FLEET OF DIESEL ENGINED TRAMS OPERATED BY THE EAST INDIA TRAMWAY CO. LTD. OF KARACHI. TRAMS AND BUSES OWNED BY THIS COMPANY ARE FITTED WITH PERKINS DIESEL ENGINES

Perkins HIGH SPEED DIESELS . . . F. PERKINS LTD., 73 LINCOLN ROAD, PETERBOROUGH. 'PHONE 4021/2 FOR VEHICLE, MARINE AND INDUSTRIAL APPLICATIONS

22. Overshadowed by the Perkins logo, an already well loaded tramcar is rapidly becoming overloaded! This a well-known Perkins advertisement in *Transport World* for 12th August 1948 shows the conductor (in white) with his Bell punch clinging on before the car takes off for Kiamari.

that they were able to obtain buses during the war years and to extend the route mileage! Although as much repair work as possible was done using the facilities in Karachi, the trams slowly began to grind to a halt. At the meeting held to report on the accounts for the year ended 31st July 1916 the death of the Chairman, John Abbott, was reported to shareholders and his son John Dixon Abbott was accordingly made a Director to fill the vacancy with H.D. Kimber taking over as Chairman. The Simplex trams ran a total of 625,391 miles in that year at a cost of 4.96d per mile but by the following Annual General Meeting the war shortages had resulted in a large proportion of the rolling stock being off the road. It was only when two-thirds of the trams were inoperable awaiting repair that the Government could be persuaded to allow replacement engines to be exported. As a consequence losses were incurred on operations during the year ending 31st July 1918.

However, receipt of the new engines and consequent return of the rolling stock to service soon remedied most of the problems, although the price of petrol remained high and running costs were never to return to the low figures of pre-war years.

The war changed the attitudes of many people and brought a great deal of change in its wake. The directors of East India Tramways Co. Ltd were not unaffected and reported with the 1919 results that they were:

> pleased to report a satisfactory increase in gross receipts consequent on their having been able to send out to Karachi new engines and spare parts for the re-equipment of worn out machinery in the cars which had to be withdrawn from service during the period of the war when it was impossible to repair them.
>
> The Directors are replacing the worn out rolling stock by a fleet of improved cars of the corridor type closely approximating to the usual type of electric car. Although these cars will not accommodate quite so many passengers as at present, it is hoped, by reason of their greater comfort their popularity will make up for their slightly less earning capacity. The first car of the new type is being despatched this month. [The report was dated 4th December 1919.]
>
> Mr H.J. Mahon, who has been connected with the company in Karachi for seventeen years and has been their Manager since 1904 is retiring at the end of the year. One of the Directors, Mr J.D. Abbott, who is also the company's Consulting Engineer, has gone to Karachi to report on the general position regarding the tramway service and as to the appointment of a successor to Mr Mahon. Mr Abbott will also supervise the inauguration of the new cars, in the same way as in 1909 he put the present fleet into proper running condition.

The Board of Directors had again changed by the death in September 1918 of G.D. Buckler, and G. Gale was made a Director with E.P. Williams taking over the position of Secretary. The company moved back into profit, a surplus of £3,767 being earned in the year to July 1919 which was increased to £13,931 the following year, aided by an increase in the value of the rupee and increased fares.

Ten of the new trams had been received by the end of 1920 giving a total of forty-one trams in service. The new vehicles were built by the Motor Rail & Tramcar Co. Ltd at Bedford, the first being supplied complete, but the rest as chassis only with the bodies to be constructed in Karachi. They had 40hp Dorman 4JO petrol engines, together with the standard Dixon Abbot 2-speed gearbox and seats for thirty-eight passengers. The body was 26ft 6ins long and 6ft 9ins wide with the passenger accommodation enclosed but with a completely open driving platform at each end. The wheelbase was 7ft 6ins, the weight about 8 tons and they were designed for a maximum speed of 15mph. The company still had six omnibuses but there was less need for these and they were withdrawn from service in the ensuing year with two being retained for service as required. A reflection of the changes resulting from the world war was that average running costs were now 14.04d per mile, with receipts at 14.6d and the profit resulted from the high number of miles run (643,659) rather than a high operating ratio. A further result was the incidence of a short strike by workers in February 1920, mirroring the wave of labour unrest around the world at that time. A Mr Charles Howat was appointed General Manager in Karachi, but due to ill health was forced to relinquish the post which was taken over in June 1921 by W.B. Hossack. J.D. Abbott remained in Karachi over this period during which a new car shed was built, two blocks of workmen's dwellings rebuilt and improvements made to the workshops. He was expected to return to England in time to attend the 1921 Annual General Meeting of the company due to be held on 24th November, having arranged for a further ten of the new type of car to be built; these being put into service the following year.

The double track section between Sadar Bazaar and the Hardinge Bridge was relaid during 1925/26 and in 1927 work commenced on doubling some of the busiest lines in Napier Road and Lawrence Road. The company was also asked by the Karachi Municipality to extend their routes westward across the old river bed with the new route to Chakiwara being opened on 28th October 1928. These and other improvements enabled the company to remain profitable with over ten million passenger journeys a year by 1929. In 1929 the line in Mansfield Street was closed and in 1931 a temporary half mile extension was installed from Soldiers Bazaar to the site of the 45th National Congress meeting. This was lifted after the event.

The company then began to feel the effect of the depression in trade and increased competition. Traffic, however, showed a steady increase due to the policy of charging as low a fare as possible in order to make competition unprofitable. Unfortunately this resulted in a reduction in the level of profits from £16,003 in 1931 to £10,310 in 1932. The company had resumed running a bus service at this point in time but now it was at least meeting its operating costs. In August 1932 it was agreed to offer to repay ordinary shareholders at par and this was accepted. The Preference shareholders then became the sole owners of the company. This repayment of capital no doubt partly accounted for the reduction in profit in 1932/33, but fares had again been reduced, with a satisfactory increase in passengers, almost fourteen million journeys being made that year. Traffic enjoyed a further surge in 1933/34 to over 17,800,000 and profits were once more on a rising trend, £12,989 being earned in 1933/34 and £14,016 in 1934/35. The bus routes failed to match this progress and remained only a marginal operation; although

the company was to remain a bus operator even though this soon involved them in losses.

During this period new trams were built or rebuilt at Karachi to a new design, no new chassis being sent from England. This was the DG class, introduced in 1927 and carrying running numbers 109-118 with later batches carrying the numbers up to 128. These used the Dorman 4JUS engine. In 1934 the Karachi municipal engineer suggested that the bodies be modified to give better protection from the weather to front and rear passengers, with the result being class DG/1 with an overall roof and front panels. These were numbered 129-138. A further modification drawn up in 1944 produced the DG/2 class with diesel engines and running numbers up to 158.

The drift towards war was reflected in the accounts for the year to 31st July 1939 with labour unrest (blamed on communist agitation) leading to a 5½ day strike and profit reduced to £7,907. George Gale died in 1942, when E.P. Williams, the Company Secretary, became a director. With the repayment of the ordinary shares in 1932 there were only a limited number of people holding shares and the published company reports become perfunctory as a result, few comments being included on the day-to-day operations. There was no evident change in the fleet of trams or buses due to the war but with increasing usage the profits rose, reaching a peak of £20,247 in 1944, before receding to £11,805 in 1948 and a loss for the period up to February 1949. The first diesel trams were introduced in 1945 and in due course the Perkins Engine Co. made considerable publicity out of this unusual use for their engines.

In August 1947 the granting of political independence to India, and its partition, resulted in Karachi becoming the main port of the new state of Pakistan. British owned business faced an uncertain future as the new rulers of the country made it clear that they wished to see industry and commerce in the hands of Pakistani nationals. The Directors therefore decided to sell the business to local interests as soon as possible and invited offers for the undertaking. Several bids were received and in March 1949 it was agreed to sell the business to Salahuddin Batlay for 27 lacs of rupees (£202,500). For some reason, however, this deal was not concluded and on 27th June 1949 the purchaser was amended to Mohamedali & Sons with the sale price remaining the same. This was a very substantial sum of money for the time, representing around £6.5m in today's terms, and the buyers must have had very considerable faith in both the tramway and the future of their fledgling country.

The assets were handed over as from 1st March 1949 although legal difficulties did not allow the formal transfer until 21st September 1950. The Chairman, H.D. Kimber died on 4th September 1950 with J.D. Abbott taking over the post for the short period until 15th November 1950 when it was formally decided to place the company into liquidation.

Although the trams had been rebuilt with diesel engines, commencing in 1945, the programme was not completed until 1952. By 1971 the remaining trams had all been rebuilt to a standard design using Perkins 65hp engines as replacements. There is a good deal of correspondence with Bedford in 1959/62 about Mohamedali Tramways starting a programme of replacing five trams per year into the foreseeable future. To this end they set about getting the necessary permissions to import components from England and quotations were provided for this. These were based on uplifting previous figures as Motor Rail appeared to have lost the appropriate drawings! In fairness East India Tramways was something of a personal fiefdom of J.D. Abbott and he may have been the only one who knew what drawings were involved. Although he had retired by then he was obviously still well regarded in Karachi as Mohamedali speak of how pleased he would have been with this development. It is not obvious as to whether anything came of this.

There are in private collections plastic (or more likely, Bakelite) tokens for use on East India Tramways. Just when these were in circulation or how they were used remains a mystery but the intention was no doubt to speed up ticket sales and help to control cash handling. They exist in denominations of 1 Anna and 6 pies with a black one of 9 pies being on record as well. There are suggestions that there were other values and in a multitude of colours, possibly for different routes.

The records also show just how much business Motor Rail lost with the sale of EIT – to whom they supplied not only the obvious spare parts for engines, gearboxes and brake blocks (300 at a time)

but a great many more esoteric things ranging from printers ink and card for tickets (literally by the ton) to an Aveling Barford road roller in 1952.

In its later days at least, the organisation was vast. In 1953 there was a major strike in Karachi, probably extending beyond just the tramway company, but no less than 700 of the company's staff were taken into custody, leaving only about 80 to run the system.

However, as happened elsewhere, the tram routes were gradually being replaced by buses and the last tram ran on 30th April 1975, considerably later than the often assumed date of closure as being in the mid 1960s. There are also strong suggestions from various sources that the tramway closed because of the activities of the local 'transport mafia'. If there is any truth in this, one can only presume that it comprised strong-arm tactics against the tramway owners and/or its staff on behalf of the bus operators within the city. Or was this the precursor to the major run of car bomb attacks in the city and elsewhere some ten years later that could have been orchestrated from the same source?

23. One of the Ministry of Munitions 16-seat railcars on test on the Bedford to Hitchin branch of the Midland Railway. On this occasion it was also being demonstrated to the railway press and has here stopped at Shefford Station, 10 miles into the trip, for closer inspection. Speeds up to 40mph were registered.
*MR&T Co. catalogue.*
*Courtesy John Bryant*

24. This is the prototype 38C tramcar for Karachi designed in 1919. There was a perceived need for increased comfort and this enclosed corridor car was MR&T Co.'s answer. The 40hp Dorman 4JO petrol engine and gearbox had very largely disappeared under the floor leaving the petrol tank under the central seat. Driving controls were standard Karachi practice except that both axles were now driven. Electric lighting is now provided and the car has a service speed of up to 25mph. However, loading and unloading were slow and although some twenty were built (nineteen supplied chassis only) they eventually reverted to the normal toast rack pattern.
*MR&T Co. catalogue.*
*Courtesy John Bryant*

# 3

# The Motor Rail & Tram Car Co. Ltd

## 1912–1927

Following the success of the Karachi tramcars, John Abbott decided that there was a future for a firm to manufacture and sell similar cars to other tramways and he arranged for the formation of a company having these objectives. Thus was the Motor Rail & Tram Car Co. Ltd registered on 20th March 1911. The registered office was at 79 Lombard Street, London, which it shared with the East India Tramways Co. Ltd, this being the office of their solicitors. The shares were held by himself (1,000 shares) and George Gale, secretary to the tramway company who held 100 shares. A further 1,000 shares were issued to his son, J.D. Abbott, in exchange for the gearbox patents that had been registered in a number of countries. It was thus a distinct offshoot of East India Tramways although having no financial connection with it. Advertisements were placed in some of the leading British tramway and engineering periodicals, including the *Indian and Eastern Engineer*, several of which had already carried reports of the success of Karachi trams. The company took over responsibility for the supply of tramcars to Karachi but did not have any manufacturing capacity itself, buying the engine and gearbox units from David Brown and Sons as before. An extant register of drawings records as its first three entries:

- Chassis for closed car 4ft 0ins gauge 8ft 0ins wheelbase x 25ft 10ins overall                                3.4.1911
- Arrangement for closed car 4ft 0ins gauge 8ft 0ins wheelbase x 21ft 0ins body                                16.5.1911
- Chassis for open or closed car 4ft 0ins gauge 8ft 0ins wheelbase, x 25ft 10ins                                15.5.1911

Due to the unusual gauge these can only have been for East India Tramways. Unfortunately the record also states that these drawings were missing or destroyed in 1957. It is unusual, and most annoying, that Motor Rail only rarely put dates on their drawings but it seems that they did so at this early stage. It was not until an order was received in May 1912 from John Birch & Co. for one car and a trailer for Siam that J.D. Abbott was elected as a director and appointed Works Manager as from 6th May 1912 at a salary of £100 per annum. However, this order was cancelled a month or two later and no action appears to have been taken to acquire a works. In spite of this a drawing for the ubiquitous 2-speed gearbox appears in the register for February 1912, followed in June by *'Chassis for closed car 4' 8½" gauge x 7' 0" wheelbase 20' 0" body & 28' 0" overall, Coventry Simplex motor entirely below floor'*, which vehicle would have been a good many years ahead of its time.

To emphasise the close ties between the two companies it was then decided to try and promote sales by contacting tramway companies in India and asking Brunton (Engineer to East India Tramways Ltd) to undertake the canvassing. Unfortunately he was in ill health and that company's General Manager, Mahon, was asked to undertake the work during his furlough. This action was prompted by negotiations for the sale of trams for use in Baroda, an order for ten trams being received at the end of 1912 at a price of £539 per chassis. The Baroda Tramway Co. Ltd had been formed by local interests in Bombay in 1908 and opened the first three miles of its planned seven miles of route in the same year, using horse traction with rails and rolling stock being bought from the Bombay Electricity Supply and Tramways Co. Ltd which was then electrifying its lines. Baroda is situated in the Gujarat province of India very roughly half way between Bombay and Karachi (at that time, of course, all one country – India) so it is more than likely that the authorities knew all about what was going on in Karachi. It is nowhere stated just what the rail gauge of this tramway was but as the records of the car sizes are exactly the same as Karachi one can reasonably assume 4ft again.

Alongside all this the company became aware that there were proposals to build a tramway in Aden. Aden had been occupied by the East India Company in 1839 and was used by Britain primarily as a coaling station on the strategic sea route to India. Aden itself was very small, only 75 square miles, but treaties with local chiefs established a protectorate over a further 42,000 square miles. This took it up to the boundary with lands falling within the Turkish Empire, thus becoming politically sensitive. In 1905 a local firm, Cowasjee Dinshaw Bros, obtained a concession from the Sultan of Lahaj for the construction of a railway to connect his territory to the port of Aden. This was opposed by the Indian authorities, for political reasons, who feared that it might be connected to the Hedjaz Railway that was then in the planning stage.

However, the Sultan and Aden businessmen were in favour of a railway or tramway scheme and between 1909 and 1911 proposals were submitted by a range of interested firms and individuals that included E.R. Calthorp, Orenstein & Koppel and Decauville. On the 2nd May 1912, East India Tramways wrote from Karachi that J.D. Abbott would be calling at Aden at about the end of May on behalf of the Motor Rail & Tramcar Co. regarding the feasibility of introducing Simplex motor trams similar to those in Karachi. He seems to have convinced the authorities that these would be more practical than using steam locomotives to haul trains. This was followed up by a letter from England in March 1913 to the Railway Board at Simla in India under whose aegis this project presumably came. In this he offered:

*'As sole manufacturers of these trams and similar tractors we submit the following designs:*
*Drg X15   Tramcar similar to Karachi to take 46 passengers on 4' 0" gauge.*
*Drg X12   Alternative design with driving pair of wheels at one end and four wheel bogie at the other.*

*Drg X48   Petrol locomotive with both axles driven by worm gearing.'*

In June of 1913 Motor Rail & Tramcar Co. said that they would consider the construction and operation of the tramway at their own risk. However, terms could not be agreed upon and the project was overtaken by the First World War during which a metre gauge railway was built by the army utilising rolling stock from India. This line continued after the war for public use but did not pay and was closed in 1929. The significance of this project is that it was the first suggestion that MR&T should build locomotives in addition to tramcars. In this case it was proposed that the locomotives should be for freight traffic. No detailed design has come to light but it seems that a machine with 7ft wheelbase and a 4-cylinder petrol or paraffin engine was envisaged, including the possibility of using two engines in each unit. The suggestion to drive the axles with worm gearing is slightly surprising as the Karachi tramcars always used roller chains and Motor Rail were wedded to this form of final drive until the end. The following year, however, they started using shaft

drive in their railcars and they were no doubt looking for a customer for whom to build a prototype.

This made manufacturing facilities essential, with the town of Lewes, in what is now East Sussex, being selected as a suitable location. This was perhaps an unlikely base for their activities, the explanation for which may have had something to do with the fact that at the time John Abbott lived in nearby Eastbourne. An arrangement was made with John Every, the proprietor of the long established Phoenix Ironworks at Lewes, by which the tramcars were built at his works. The ironworks was established around 1832 after the demise of the Wealden iron industry and produced a wide range of structural and other ironwork. These ranged from manhole covers to iron pavilions and piers, with the firm also having a sizeable machine shop. It is not clear whether Every acted as a sub-contractor under J.D. Abbott's supervision or if the company rented part of the premises and employed its own staff. Since there is no mention of the purchase of plant and machinery in the company's minute books the former option seems the most likely. In May 1913 a significant event was the allocation of further shares in the

THE MOTOR RAIL & TRAM CAR CO. LTD.

Cars in Service on the

East India Tramway Co.'s

System.

SIMPLEX WORKS, BEDFORD, ENGLAND.

73

25. From that catalogue again, two pictures of EIT 38C tramcars posed for the camera but, as was the convention at the time, with the background faded out. The top one tells us that: '*Your quickest way to the sea is to TRAVEL BY TRAM to Keamari, Build wealth by safeguarding health. 5 to 10 minutes service from Saddar. Last car leaves Keamari at 9.45 pm.*' The left-hand advertisement advise that '*For weak eyes and spectacleware you should consult Patel & Sons*' whilst the inner one warns '*Safety First … Motorists drive slowly past cars*', but the second line is unreadable. The lower car is perhaps painted in a dark green, lined out and has an elaborate EIT logo on the side.        *MR&T Co. catalogue. Courtesy John Bryant*

26. Car No. 94 was the first of the SC type and reverted to cross-bench seating. These were never supplied complete from Bedford but in various stages of disassembly for final completion in Karachi. The power unit was a Dorman 4JUS petrol/paraffin engine later upgraded through Meadows and Perkins diesel engines. The windows and door openings were fitted with pull-down blinds.

*MR&T Co. catalogue.*
*Courtesy John Bryant*

27. (*Right*) This advertisement in the *Railway Gazette* for November 1929 encapsulates the Motor Rail & Tramcar Co.'s production of rail vehicles, other than locomotives, in its entirety up to that date. Clockwise from top left:

a) This metre gauge car was one of three supplied to South Indian Railways in 1915, before the works was taken over building rail tractors for the Ministry of Munitions. One of these was requisitioned at Aden on its way to India and was replaced in 1925 by a slightly longer and more powerful vehicle. The engine was fitted above the frame driving through the usual Dixon Abbott 3-speed gearbox but with shaft drive to a worm box on the bogie axle – altogether well ahead of its time.

b) The pair of 750mm gauge cars supplied in 1927 to the Onda–Castellón railway in Spain in 1927 were very superior vehicles and MR&T Co. were rightly proud of them. Fitted with 105hp Aster engines they would have had a good turn of speed for the twenty or so passengers that each carried. As with the South India cars the engine was on the chassis with shaft drive to a worm box on the axle and the coupling rods to the other bogie axle. Even if the background is faded out this is taken outside the works at Bedford.

c) Effectively MR&T Co.'s last effort in the way of railcar production was this standard gauge tower wagon supplied to the Mexican Railway Co. in January 1929. As so often, the body was built upon arrival which means that this picture of the completed vehicle must have been supplied by them. The tower was operated by compressed air and the controls arranged for driving at each end. Once again the engine is fitted longitudinally with a worm box on one axle only.

d) The three 3ft 6ins gauge cars for the Western Australian Government Railways supplied in 1921 were nearer to being railcars than tramcars. Fitted with electric lighting and vacuum brakes they were used over a selection of lightly laid branch lines where an occasional passenger service was required. The bodies were built at the company's Midland Junction workshops and could seat thirty to forty people and tow a 20-seat trailer if needed. They are reputed to have operated until around 1950 with one converted to a works trailer surviving until 1965.

e) This 9 seat lightweight railcar for the Darjeeling Himalaya Railway was intended to provide a premium express service for important passengers but the need to fit in with steam trains rather nullified the concept. With facilities to turn locomotives at each end it has only a single driving position. It was luxuriously fitted out with cushioned seats for all passengers including the driver.

f) Six of these 'lorry' type vehicles were supplied to the Buenos Aires Great Southern Railway in 1927. Of 5ft 6ins gauge they were fitted with 65hp White & Poppe engines driving through a 3-speed gearbox to a worm box on the rear axle. The body was of 10 tons capacity and the driver sat sideways allowing running in either direction, but in practice they were usually turned if at all possible.

company, 200 more being applied for by J.D. Abbott and 1,000 by Thomas Dixon Abbott, his brother, who was to play a major part in the activities of the company in the future.

Work on the ten cars for Baroda was quickly put in hand, three being well on their way to completion by April 1913 with all being completed and despatched by 14th September 1913. The engine and gearbox assemblies continued to be supplied by David Brown & Sons. Not a great deal is known about these vehicles but, not least because of the speed of manufacture, one can assume that they were very similar, if not identical, to the cars being supplied to Karachi The company was unfortunate with its first major order in that after paying for the first six of the cars shipped, the Baroda Tramway Co. ran out of funds and the remaining four cars had to be put into store in India awaiting payment. This was still not forthcoming by April 1914 and, since to sue them would probably result in the liquidation of the tramway company, an offer to take over the management of the undertaking was provided instead. The result of this approach is not recorded but the tramway company appointed new managing agents and funds seem to have been found as a result, since it was reported at the company's annual general meeting in December 1914 that the last four trams had by then arrived in Baroda.

During 1914 three further orders were received, the first resulting from the Lombardy Road Railways Co. Ltd, a London company operating a standard gauge tramway from Milan to Giossano. This company had been founded in 1881 and owned a fleet of fifteen Henschel steam tramway locomotives. They also still had the last of five Fox Walker locomotives and with other local tramways being electrified had decided to improve their service by the acquisition of two Simplex motor tramcars. John Abbott went to Milan to finalise the details of the order, the drawings for which were approved in July, subject to any regulations to be laid down for their use by the Italian authorities. These were to be supplied as chassis only with the bodies to be built in Milan. One of the cars was shipped early in 1915 and the other was ready by June of that year but was held back at the request of the customer, presumably due to the war conditions then prevailing in Europe. Shipping space was found at the end of the year and both cars were completed and ready for service in Italy during 1916. However, the tramway company had other problems due to the war, chiefly lack of fuel for both their steam locomotives and petrol vehicles, and the railcars could not be put into service. The end of the war also saw the end of the operation which was taken over by the Edison company for the conversion of its lines to electric traction. The fate of the Simplex cars has not been traced but it seems entirely possible that they were never used.

28. This is the chassis for the Darjeeling car and its light weight is readily visible by the way that the frame members, themselves of folded steel sheet, are cut away to remove unnecessary weight. Thus the tare weight was reduced to a mere 3½ tons. The driver would have sat at the right hand front corner with all the controls readily to hand.
*MR&T Co. catalogue. Courtesy John Bryant*

29. Designated 28C, the cars for Siam were, if anything, a development of the 38C cars for Karachi. Nine chassis were produced in 1922/23 together with six trailers over the same period. Shown on the test track at Elstow Road this neatly shows the position of engine and fuel tanks. These are believed to have been for use on the street tramways of Bangkok prior to electrification. Compare the 'buffer' with those on the 20hp locomotive on the front cover.

The second order in 1914 resulted from a tender submitted to the South Indian Railway for the supply of three metre gauge rail coaches to carry seventy passengers each. The Motor Rail & Tram Car's price was £1,435 each and this was the successful tender. These railcars are described in an article in the *Engineer* for 16th April 1915 that included a photograph of a completed coach at the Lewes Works. Power was provided by a 45hp 4-cylinder Dorman petrol engine driving through the usual 3-speed gearbox supplied by David Brown. Because the coach was mounted on two 4-wheel bogies the traditional Simplex layout could not be used and the engine was mounted lengthwise at one end of the chassis with the drive being via the gearbox and couplings to worm gearing on one axle of the front bogie. A series of rods and levers gave the driver control from each end. The bodywork, 40ft long, was supplied by Brush and designed to be dismantled for shipment. Altogether these were a very sophisticated and advanced design for their time. The total vehicle weight was 12 tons and the railcars were intended for use on the Pamban viaduct line of the South Indian Railway, at the extreme south-eastern point of the country. A further railcar was supplied in 1925 but this was fitted with a White & Poppe engine of 65hp, engines of this size having been used as replacements for the originals. Reputedly one of these cars was diverted to the Aden Railway during the First World War whilst it was in transit to India and this latter car was in fact a replacement for the one thus lost. At least one of these cars was rebuilt with a diesel engine in 1935 using parts supplied by Motor Rail.

The final order of the year was for another Indian railway, the Bhavnagar State Railway, and again obtained by tender with the order being placed by the railway's consulting engineers. This was an order for a single vehicle of metre gauge vehicle and to seat fifty passengers. It seems to have been similar to the Baroda cars (and hence those at Karachi) with a wheelbase of 8ft and an overall length of 25ft 10ins. The prices quoted for its supply had been £700 if fitted with an open body or £840 if enclosed. It was completed and awaiting shipment by September 1915, and despite the exigencies

of war it does seem to have been despatched. This unit was fitted with a Dorman engine and may have been the start of the long association between the two companies. It has been suggested that the supply of engines to Motor Rail & Tramcar Co. Ltd helped to put the firm of W.H. Dorman Ltd from Stafford on its feet. This in turn accounted for the extended credit allowed to Motor Rail which only came to an end when Dorman were taken over by the English Electric Co.

Although this is the total of the cars built at Lewes, other enquiries were dealt with. The company considered offering two cars to the London County Council on a trial basis for use on their Liverpool Road section of tramway where horse trams were to be withdrawn. It also had negotiations with the Edinburgh City Tramways but seems to have been in some doubt about offering any trial vehicle in view of the gradients ruling on parts of the city tramway system. The most promising prospect was for the supply of trams to Australia. An offer was made to the Banfield Tramway Co. to supply trams and accept payment in 10% Cumulative Preference shares of that company with the price of the cars being £1,300 each and open platform wagons to go with them at £580 each. In the event three chassis only, of 3ft 6ins gauge, were supplied to the Western Australian Government Railways in 1921 with the bodies to be made in their Midland Junction workshops and fitted upon arrival. These trams were used indiscriminately across a series of lightly laid branch lines where an occasional passenger service was required. Due to the sparsity of the population they were even available for hire in the manner in which one would nowadays hire a road coach!

Whilst the company's business changed dramatically with the success of its 20hp and 40hp tractors for use on the Western Front it is proposed to complete the story of railcar production here, even if this is not chronologically correct.

The contracts for military locomotives (covered in the next chapter) were not cancelled until December 1918 and this was counterbalanced by the placing of an order for twenty-five 20hp

30. This tiny vehicle, to seat only six passengers, fitted with just a 20hp engine and 2-speed gearbox was for the Chinese Engineering & Mining Co. for use on their 50 mile private branch line. Built in 1920 it is recorded that spares were supplied at least as late as 1937.
*MR&T Co. catalogue. Courtesy John Bryant*

31. MR&T advertised these inspection railcars but only two were built in 1920 for the Cameroons. Effectively they were a 20hp tractor in a different frame with a different body and were thus probably too expensive. *MR&T Co. catalogue. Courtesy John Bryant*

inspection cars by the Ministry of Munitions. Of these, twenty were built to 5ft gauge for shipment to Murmansk in Russia to which place the British had despatched an expeditionary force to aid the 'White' Russians on their fight against the Bolsheviks. The remainder were built to standard gauge and these were tested and demonstrated on the Midland Railway line from Bedford to Hitchin. This was done on a Sunday and was attended by representatives from trade periodicals including *The Engineer* and *Railway Gazette*.

If the aforementioned drawing register is to be believed they also envisaged that the internal combustion engined passenger vehicle had a significant future and there are many proposed arrangement drawings of which the following are a random selection:

- Simplex Double Bogie semi-enclosed tram car 1 metre gauge.
- 40hp loco and closed corridor railcar, 60 passenger, 914mm gauge.
- Road finishing machine with 20hp Simplex unit. *(What on earth was this?)*
- 40hp double deck tramcar, 16 inside, 24 outside, 4ft 8½ins gauge.
- 105/165hp corridor rail coach, 4ft 8½ins rail gauge – seating 40 Third and 16 First class passengers. *(Possibly the vehicle in Plate 32.)*
- 3ft 6ins gauge pump trolley, double geared. *(Also a single geared and 2ft gauge version.)*

There are no dates with these but the early 1920s seems likely and again the drawings are recorded as having been 'scrapped' in 1941.

After the batch of inspection cars for the Ministry of Munitions, orders tended to be for individual units and in 1920 a 9-seat light railcar was built for the 2ft gauge Darjeeling Himalaya Railway. With the renowned gradients of that railway this was indeed light at only 3½ tons tare weight. This vehicle was intended to provide a fast service at a premium fare for those who wanted to avoid the toiling steam trains and it was fitted out accordingly with leather upholstered seats for all passengers. However, in practice it had to fit in amongst those trains and thus very little time could be saved on normal schedules.

In 1921 a 6-seat enclosed railcar was supplied to Chinese Engineering & Mining Co., a London based company, for use on a 50 mile private branch line. Spare parts are recorded as having been supplied as late as 1937. In this period a variety of inspection and maintenance vehicles were supplied and although Motor Rail (and Alan Keef Ltd) dallied with this market over many years it was one that had been cornered by D. Wickham & Co. Ltd of Ware and later by continental firms, such as Geismar, so the pickings were thin indeed.

In 1922 an order was received from the Siamese State Railways for three metre-gauge tramcar chassis which was a follow up on an original quotation from 1911. These were to have bodies fitted locally and appear to have been similar in design to the East India Tramway cars type 38C. They were fitted with Dorman 4-cylinder petrol engines and must have been satisfactory as the following year an order was placed for six identical units with six trailer chassis to match. It is not known just where these were intended to be used but it is believed that they were for operation on Bangkok tramways prior to electrification.

In a more specialised line a number of larger vehicles were built that included a 'lorry' type railtruck for the Buenos Aires Great Central Railway, three 10 ton standard gauge self-propelled hopper wagons for the Associated Portland Cement Co., between 1927 and 1934, and the chassis for a motorised tower wagon for the Mexican Railway Co. in 1929.

Certainly the pair of 750mm gauge cars to Spain for the line with the lengthy title of Cia del Tranvía a Vapor de Onda al Grao de Castellón de la Plana, supplied in 1927, were something of a swansong in this market. The company was justifiably proud of these vehicles that were built after the style of the South India Railway cars. They were fitted with a longitudinal 105hp Aster petrol engine mounted in its own engine room with shaft drive to the bogie beneath it which in turn was fitted with outside connecting rods to couple the axles. Engine cooling was from a radiator under the floor. The saloon was fitted with tramcar type reversible seats and had accommodation for twenty passengers. They were designed to pull two or three centre-door trailers that were built locally. They must have served their purpose well as they are recorded as having been converted into ordinary coaches as late as 1955.

The future was with locomotives, however, and whether there was a conscious decision to abandon the railcar market or it 'just happened' is not known.

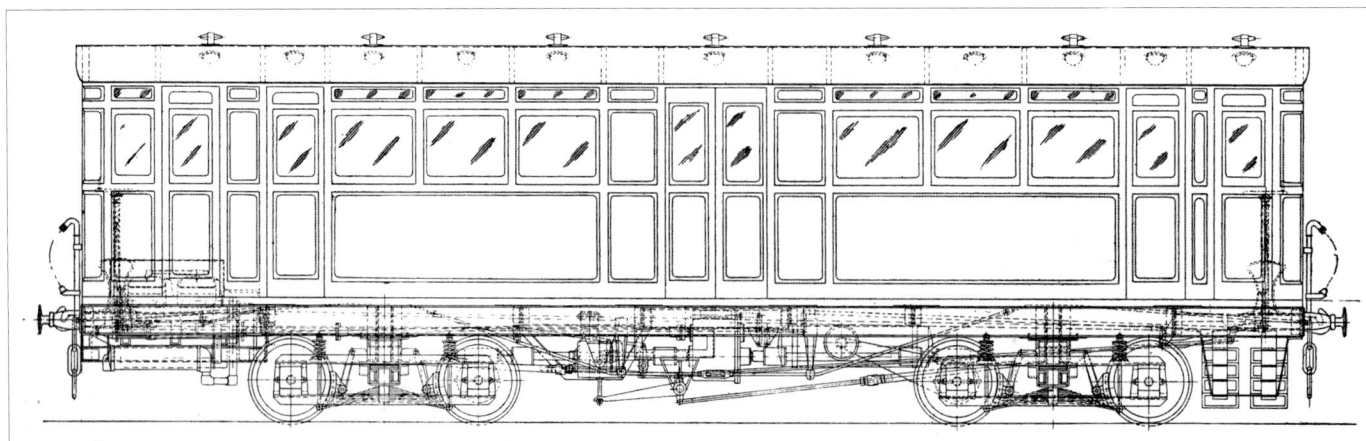

32. Was this the forerunner of the modern DMU? Or did it anticipate Forbes on the County Donegal Railways by many years? This comes from their 1924 catalogue and is quoted as having a 140hp engine giving speeds up to 45mph. From what can be seen, the engine was to be mounted at one end driving to (presumably) a 3-speed gearbox in the middle of the vehicle with shaft drive to one bogie, all of which was common technology to the company at that time.

*MR&T Co. catalogue. Courtesy John Bryant*

# 4

# The First World War and its Aftermath

## 1918-1925

The three members of the Abbott family in the company were all engineers and there seems to have been an early intention to build petrol locomotives as well as trams if the opportunity arose.

These plans would eventually come to fruition as a result of the First World War into which Britain was drawn in August 1914. This seems to have had an immediate effect at Lewes as many of the workmen volunteered for military service and it soon became difficult to obtain labour and materials. The Germans had anticipated the need for light railways in any coming war, as, to a certain extent, had the French (see also Appendix I). T.D. Abbott had seen evidence of this and contacted the War Office in 1914 seeking an order for petrol locomotives – perhaps based on the outline design of 1912 – but was informed by Lord Kitchener that a need for light railways was not envisaged. Nevertheless, provisional

33. There are several pictures of King George V being shown the front whilst being propelled by a 20hp tractor. This one from the Motor Rail records is an enlargement from a larger picture when the King was visiting a Forestry Corps working in Hesdin Forest in August 1917. The bonhomie of the accompanying general and perhaps the King himself, can be compared with the worried looks of the locomotive crew, no doubt fearful of tipping their monarch head first into the Flanders mud!

drawings were completed soon after the outbreak of war. By 1916 the armies had fought themselves to a standstill and the front lines had become more or less stationary. Some better form of transport in the forward areas behind the front line became vital and finally the need for this form of transport was perceived.

The range of the guns was between 3,000 and 6,000 yards so that main line railheads – which represented the most efficient means of transportation – could not be located nearer than this to the front line and, in practice, were kept some ten miles or more away. Transport between railhead and the front line was generally by horse or petrol-driven lorries along with much manhandling upon reaching a destination. A few London buses, and a larger number of Paris buses, were used to move troops but most had to march. Initially the French continued to maintain the roads, but the number of vehicles using what were unmetalled secondary roads led to the necessity for the British to maintain the roads within their own sector. Much of the roadstone had to be brought from distant quarries in France, Belgium and even the Channel Islands, although colliery waste tips and even sand dunes were also utilised. The quantities became enormous, especially during the severe winter conditions of 1915/16, and soon revealed the difficulties of keeping any sort of road transport on the move.

There had been some use of tramways around the trenches to move supplies and ammunition to the trenches, but these were either man or horse powered and used very light rails. They were envisaged for bridging the final gap from the nearest point on the front line to which horse drawn transport could venture.

The War Office then decided to experiment with petrol rail tractors (as they were then called) and invited tenders for the supply of 'trench tractors' of 60cm gauge to a specification drawn up by their consulting engineers, Rendell, Palmer & Tritton. This required the tractors to have an axle load of not more than one ton per axle and an ability to haul a 15 ton load at 5mph. Their design for a tractor was submitted and further discussions led the Motor Rail & Tram Car Co. to believe that their proposals would lead to an order in due course.

The company had already decided to look for an alternative site for a works due to the difficulties being experienced at Lewes and had visited several towns, including Bedford, in the latter part of 1915. In January of 1916 an arrangement was made with the Bedford Engineering Co. for the manufacture of any orders received at the latter's works in Bedford. This firm had been founded about 1890 and, although general engineers, they specialised in the manufacture of steam cranes. They had also built a few railway locomotives with vertical boilers that included many crane parts and thus had considerable relevant experience. Although in agricultural surroundings, Bedford had a broadly based engineering industry that included the agricultural engineers J. & F. Howard

34. (*Left*) This line up of two open 40hp tractors and a string of 20hp tractors is often quoted as being at an unknown location in France. In fact it is at Bedford Engineering before the move to Elstow Road. The building does not quite tally with other shots in that location but the crane does appear; also note the stack of six 20hp frames on the extreme left.
*Courtesy Industrial Railway Society*

35. (*Below*) This is believed to be the first batch of 20hp tractors to have been built at the newly acquired works in Elstow Road, Bedford. Certainly they are of later origin as the handbrake column on the earlier designs was a much wider affair. Note the hand Klaxon horn and the hook carrying a vertical coupling link beside the buffer. The pegs poking through the floor operate the front and rear sanding gear.
*W.J.K. Davies/NGRS Library Collection*

36. An early Motor Rail & Tramcar Co. Ltd works plate from MR 1029 of 1918. Having been built for the Ministry of Munitions in September of that year it may never have reached France. It is later recorded as having been with Abdon Clee Stone Quarry, Ditton Priors, near Bridgnorth, Shropshire.

who also manufactured light railway material Grafton & Co. who made steam cranes, Saunderson & Gifkin[1] who as motor engineers were also early makers of agricultural tractors, wind pumps and a very few locomotives, Adams Manufacturing Co. who made both cars and 'Igranic' electrical components, and finally W.H. Allen & Co. Ltd who were to become world renowned for their stationary and marine diesel engines. It thus had a much larger pool of skilled labour than did Lewes as well as being in a reasonably central position for the supply of material.

The company still relied on David Brown & Sons for its gearboxes and thus acted as designer and main contractor only, with all the processes of manufacture being handled by sub-contractors under their supervision. W.H. Dorman Ltd now supplied the engines because David Brown had abandoned the manufacture of Valveless cars and engines by this time. The exact nature of their agreement with Bedford Engineering Co. is not known but when that firm's manager was called away for war duties, the two Abbott brothers are understood to have taken over control with the production of locomotives then being the main output. The frame was made in-house while most of the components were bought in. After assembly the locomotives were tested on a circular track laid out at the rear of the works although examples were also sent to

the Royal Engineers at Longmoor for their evaluation. J.D. Abbott was the company's Engineer and his brother, T.D. Abbott, the Assistant Engineer, the latter being released from military service in February 1916 for the purpose. Both brothers were named in the patent application submitted in 1918 that set out the details and layout of the Simplex locomotive designs for the War Office, so it may be assumed that both may have had a hand in the detailed work involved. When it finally came, the first order from the War Office was for only three tractors. Although the details are not clear, the minutes of a directors' meeting in March 1916 merely state that progress was being made with the three tractors on order and that a tender for a further four tractors had been submitted. The 20hp tractor appears in the drawing register from this date to be followed by a 40hp version in early 1917. The prospect of future work seems to have been good, however, since it was decided to rent an office in Bedford, although it was intended that the accounting would continue to be undertaken in the London office, no doubt under the supervision of George Gale who was an accountant.

A further issue of shares was made in June 1916 when it was reported that an office had been opened at 33 Houghton Road, Bedford and a typist engaged. John Abbott, who, was founder of the company and its Chairman, died on 23rd August 1916 and control passed to his sons. John took over as Chairman whilst

1.  My late mother in law was in some way related to the Saundersons.

37. A 40hp protected tractor, MR 503 of 1917, 'somewhere in France' but possibly further back from the front as the trees have branches with leaves upon them. The old engineers adage that 'If in doubt, try a larger hammer' may apply here; it even looks as though someone has tried to drive something that was too tall out of the shed!

*Courtesy Industrial Railway Society*

38. (*Above*) Photographs of the armoured version of the 40hp tractor seem to be a little bit rare so this one of MR 463 of 1917 is useful. Apart from a glimpse of the inside, with the water pump and magneto prominent, it shows the heavily armoured roof with mere slits for the driver to see through. These had a shutter on the inside so that they could be closed off. Thus, although not protected from artillery fire the driver stood a reasonable chance with something less destructive.

*Courtesy Industrial Railway Society*

39. A close up of the armoured 40hp tractor in 'shut up' condition. A good many of these locos and their protected sisters in their latter days show large cut outs in the armour plating intended to cool both engine and driver. These were covered with a plate raised off the bodywork to allow a steady flow of air. From the fading out of the picture this would appear to be a works photo in the yard at Elstow Road.

*W.J.K. Davies/NGRS Library Collection*

Thomas took his place as a director having been appointed to that office on 18th July 1916.

T.D. Abbott went to Audruicq in France in April 1916 to test the first Simplex tractor to be delivered. Unfortunately the radiator had been damaged in transit and the clutch shaft brake was out of adjustment. Once these matters had been rectified he instructed six servicemen in the use of the tractor and it was put on the test track. This was 300yds in length, roughly pear shaped in layout and included gradients of 1 in 25. The locomotive was tested with loads slightly in excess of specification and performed entirely satisfactorily. It was then loaded away for use elsewhere. This exercise lasted slightly over two weeks.

The War Office was the sole customer and following these tests provided a steady flow of orders. During 1916 these were all for the 20hp locomotives which, having been designed for trench tramway use, were without cabs and weighed a little over two tons. At the beginning of 1917 the War Office decided that light railways should be actively developed. Thus a heavier 40hp design for use on longer hauls was designed and this was produced in three forms. The iconic heavy-plate curved ends acted as ballast to bring the weight up to 5½ tons (with further cast iron floor plates added it could reach 6 tons) and at its simplest had a protective cover for the driver who sat over the engine. The protected variety had a more substantial roof and side doors so that the driver was protected from straying rifle fire and ricocheting bullets. The armoured version was totally enclosed in heavy steel plate with the driver having only a narrow slit through which to see, and even this could be closed off. Orders for, primarily, the protected and armoured types were received in increasing quantities during 1917 and 1918, with day, night and Sunday shifts being worked to increase the flow of locomotives

40. A line up of protected and armoured 40hp tractors at an unknown location in France. By the way the trees are blasted it must have once been nearer to the front line than it is now. This is also an unusual situation in that the track is much more substantial than usual, appearing to be of a heavier rail section and dogspiked to wooden sleepers. Note also the Baldwin steam locomotives alongside what looks like a coaling stage in the left background.
*W.J.K. Davies/NGRS Library Collection*

41. 'The First Train Over Vimy Ridge' in April 1917. These were Canadian troops, and the Canadians were great users of their railways with a well-deserved reputation for their light railway railhead following very closely behind their advancing troops. By the style of the brake column of the leading locomotive this is a fairly early product, possibly from Bedford Engineering rather than the Elstow Road works. Along with a number of other images reproduced here, this picture hung on the wall of the office at Bedford and does the same for Alan Keef Ltd.

42. Wounded soldiers being loaded by members of the Royal Army Medical Corps at Freuchy in April 1917. Many a soldier owed his life to this apparently rough-and-ready transport by light railway. This is an interesting 'opened up' shot of a 20hp tractor. Note the high backless seat arranged by the driver. That would not only have given him a better view over his train but allowed him a quick exit if necessary!

from the works. The salary of the two engineers was more than doubled and the company was able to declare substantial dividends.

Under the impetus of these Government orders the directors decided that the company should buy its own works and on 17th January 1918 it acquired premises in Elstow Road, Bedford. These had last been occupied by the Bedford & County Laundry Co. Ltd and the price paid was £3,250. A sum of £1,000 was allocated for the purchase of machinery and a Mr L.H. Morfee was engaged as assistant engineer. The office was moved to the new works a few days later and the premises then became known as the Simplex Works. Further land was bought at the back of the works in July 1918 and on the frontage the following month. The choice of 'Simplex' for the trade name of the firm's railcars and other products would seem to be a significant decision, but the origin and reason for its selection is not known. Certainly it was in use by other firms at about the same date with a Dutch firm advertising 'Simplex' railcars and petrol engines being produced under the 'Coventry-Simplex' name. It was also used by a variety of other manufacturers for products ranging from grain silos to electrical components. Perhaps because the term was in common use, the name was not registered as a trade-mark at the time, an omission that was to cause problems later.

Although the war was still in progress a full description of the two classes of Simplex locomotive was given in the *Engineer* in its issue of 9th August 1918 and this included some interesting comments.

J. Dixon Abbott was reported as saying that he had converted horse drawn trams into self propelled vehicles in India, and that he had already drafted out designs for a locomotive when tenders were called for by the War Office. The design no doubt followed the successful layout adopted for the trams and these provided the basis for the War Office tractor design. Although the original specification called for an axle load of only one ton this was slightly exceeded in the production models. The *Engineer* quoted a weight in working order of 2¼ tons for the 20hp model and 6 tons 6 cwt for the 40hp locomotives. Despite acquisition of a new works, production continued at the Bedford Engineering Co.'s premises in order to cope with the very large orders received. In all, 724 of the 20hp tractors and 334 of the 40hp version were built to the order of the War Office with the design causing a revolution in the light railway market. It is interesting to note that J.D. Abbott foresaw gravel pits and brickworks as potential customers and these were to take many locomotives in the future. The largest single British market would prove to be the civil engineering industry that was to flourish in the upsurge of construction that followed the First World War and prior to the Second.

As the light railway system in France was wound down once the Allies gained the upper hand and the front moved forward again, many of the locomotives completed in 1918 were never sent overseas. These, together with a large quantity of track and other

43. In this obviously posed view on the Italian Front it is recorded that '*Italian men and female workers are being conveyed to their work on a British light railway.*' The 20hp tractor looks to be in 'as new' condition.                    © *IWM*

44. Railway construction with the Salonika Expeditionary Force. A trestle bridge on the Stavros line with a 40hp protected tractor on what may be an inspection trip, judging from what appear to be the same personnel in another picture of the same train recorded as such.                    © *IWM*

light railway material, were advertised for sale. The military had a very large depot at Purfleet in Essex where much of this equipment was concentrated; it certainly included various types of steam locomotive, mostly Baldwin, and a large number of Simplexes. It is not known for sure whether this included new locomotives that had not seen service in France but it seems very likely.

The First World War led to the more widespread use of light railway equipment, partly as a result of surplus equipment being made available cheaply and in large quantities, but also due to the changed economic circumstances following the war. It is perhaps significant that few of the narrow gauge steam locomotives of the War Department Light Railways (WDLR) saw use in the United Kingdom, possibly because they were too large for most British operations. In contrast, the Simplex designs filled a gap in the market by being able to run on relatively light and poorly laid track at a competitive cost. They had the further advantages of instant availability, both to buy and in use, and that there must have been a generation of men available who were familiar with them. This inspired design was the foundation of the company's business and the basic concept remained in production for the better part of eighty years.

At the date of the Armistice in November 1918 the company was working on contracts with the Ministry of Munitions to produce thirty-two 20hp and thirty-six 40hp tractors per month.

45. (*Above*) This may only be a demonstration and may not even be in France (the troops look too well dressed!), but it is marvellous what can be loaded onto a couple of light railway wagons! The caption states '*6" Mk VII Gun supported on two Class E narrow gauge rail wagons (note blocked springs) with 40hp Simplex protected locomotive.*'                      © IWM

46. (*Below*) More mundane and more typical; '*British troops taking up rails on a light railway near High Wood, October 1916*', which was fairly early on in the use of light railways by the British.                      © IWM

This represents in excess of two locomotives per day and is, by any standards, an astonishing achievement. The company also received £7,000 from the Ministry of Munitions in compensation for the cancellation of orders already in hand. Thus it emerged from the war in excellent financial shape and with an outstanding reputation.

Immediately after the Armistice it had been decided to build a 20hp inspection car and a 40hp standard gauge locomotive, these evidently completing the range of products for which demand was envisaged and which could utilise many standard components from the WDLR designs. Steps were also taken to appoint overseas selling agents with the first agreements drawn up in January 1919 for Australia and Brazil. There was also a change in the management

with a Mr Alexander Harris Brown acquiring shares in the company and being appointed a director. He took over administration while T.D. Abbott took full control of the engineering and production aspects of the business. These two directors were appointed joint managers of the company in June 1919 whilst John Dixon Abbott tendered his resignation as General Manager and Engineer on 1st May 1919. There appears to have been a disagreement between the two brothers since the Minute Book records the view that his colleagues could do better without his supervision. It seems probable that John's other commitments, including his consultancy practice and ongoing involvement with East India Tramways, proved incompatible with being General Manager of the Motor Rail

47. It is more than likely that this is the prototype standard gauge shunter being tried out in the sidings of their neighbours in Bedford, J.& F. Howard. Motor Rail never had their own sidings whereas Howard's did and the loco was trialled there. They were makers of agricultural machinery which is being loaded into Midland Railway wagons. The man with the shunter's pole does not quite look the part!
*MR&T Co. catalogue. Courtesy John Bryant*

48. (*Below*) MR 2014 *Dalmunzie* of 2ft 6ins gauge was supplied in 1920 together with these two coaches for a private railway at what became the Dalmunzie House Hotel in the Highlands of Scotland. It ran some two miles to a shooting lodge on the grouse moors. The train is shown on the zig-zag used to gain height on the valley side. This had a fearsome gradient of perhaps 1:20. With sharp eyes, or a magnifying glass, the onward track can be discerned at roughly carriage roof level. There was a second locomotive, *Glenlochsie*, MR 2086 of 1921, and a couple of flat wagons for the transport of deer carcasses. The entire railway was sold off in a family feud and, although the rolling stock survives, attempts to recreate the railway have so far come to nothing.

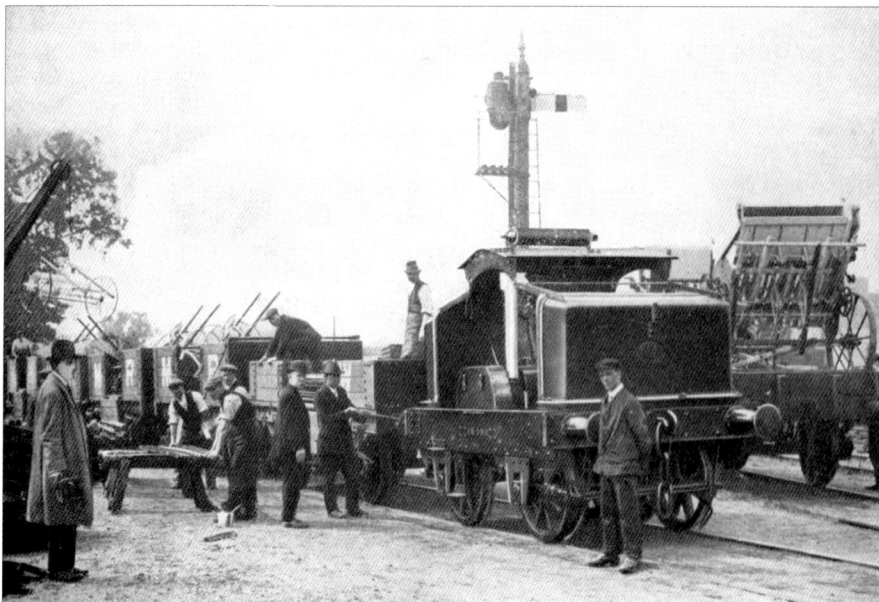

& Tram Car Co. Ltd and its operations in Bedford. Nevertheless he retained his substantial investment in the company and was appointed its consulting engineer. In September 1919 he and his brother transferred their rights to patent 127399 that had been granted to them jointly for the design of the types of locomotives built for the War Office, with the company paying them a total of £3,000 as the purchase price.

Orders flowed in during 1919 to add to the batch of railcars being built for the Government, and at the beginning of July 1919 orders in hand amounted to £20,490. The output included 20hp narrow gauge locomotives and also a satisfactory number of the new 40hp standard gauge design with fifteen being produced during the year. The company also supplied track and rolling stock in the early years at Bedford and a number of wagons were built in 1919 for Cafferata's at Newark who also purchased one of the 20hp locomotives. In August of 1919 it was decided to add a 10hp railcar to the range (although none seem to have been built), whilst in September Miss Taylor who had headed the clerical staff since the move to Bedford left their employment. There was a continued effort on the export market through the appointment of agents for further territories covering France, Holland and the Dutch East Indies, Mauritius, Spain, Portugal and Brazil – the last three being with Jones Burton & Co., that for Brazil replacing a previous agent

for this country. Not all of these were to prove successful, not least in the case of France where there already was a large number of locomotives in the Government stockpiles of surplus equipment, and these in time would add another dimension to the sales picture.

The Ministry of Munitions was the Government department charged with the disposal of surplus material and naturally it took some considerable time to sort out and catalogue the enormous volume of equipment and agree with the War Department how much was to be retained. (Appendix II gives a measure of just much material was on hand at the end of 1918.) Thus it was not until June 1919 that sales of railway material began to be made. Although some locomotives were at depots in England and some still remained in the manufacturer's works, the great majority of the Simplex locomotives were overseas in Europe and the Middle East, with a few in East Africa. In October 1919 the Ministry of Munitions advertised for sale a substantial quantity of this equipment: offering new 20hp Simplex locomotives at £400, with secondhand ones at £300 each. For the 40hp locos they asked £650 and £550 respectively. Ninety-three 20hp and thirty-three 40hp Simplexes were in store at the Royal Engineers depot at Purfleet, Essex, a number were in the repair shops at Richborough, near Ramsgate, Kent (also operated by the Royal Engineers) and further small batches were at other Government establishments. Naturally the Motor Rail & Tramcar Co. Ltd was apprehensive regarding the release of these locomotives onto the market and its effect on sales of new production. When the locomotives at Purfleet were advertised in 1920 they made a visit to inspect them and the spare petrol engines available at the same time. They decided to bid for them if the price to be paid was not too high. Since the company had insufficient cash available to purchase a large number of these locomotives, it was agreed in May 1920 that if T.D. Abbott bought any from his personal funds then the company would take them over as and when it was able to do so at the market value or below.

The very large output during the war had been achieved by using mass production methods, and locomotives continued to be built in batches. In August 1920 it was agreed to put in hand a new batch of ten 8 ton shunting locomotives while in October a batch of eight 2½ ton locomotives (as built for the War Office) and ten awnings

49, 50, 51. The two pictures dated 25.5.22 are from a 1928 publication entitled *Modern Roadmaking*, although, unfortunately, no indication is given of location. The light Jubilee track is quite well laid and the Ruston steam navvy is, along with everyone else, posed for the camera. The flat wagon on the centre track is probably carrying a tank of water to keep the beast supplied. The advert appeared within the same volume.

*Courtesy Frank Jux*

was authorised. Railcars were now only built to special order and all locomotives were to standard designs, although the range was due to be extended. There were of course variations in rail gauge and weight.

Output in the first three months of 1920 was almost £21,000 and over £36,000 in the following quarter, quite an appreciable turnover for the period. In April it was decided to increase the share capital to £50,000. Orders showed a satisfactory increase and it was decided to extend the blacksmith's shop. At the same time it was fortunate that the adjoining building of the Grosvenor Works (shown on an old plan as being occupied by the Slogger Automatic Feeder Co.) became available for purchase and this was bought at a price of £12,750. A railway track had been laid running between the two buildings after the Motor Rail & Tram Car Co. had taken over the laundry building. This was presumably used for testing locomotives and no doubt became the multi-gauge track visible in so many photographs.

The machinery of the former owners of the Grosvenor Works was auctioned in October 1920 with some being bought by its new owners who made alterations to the buildings after taking full possession on 2nd November. This addition to the works came into

use early in 1921, but a depression in trade generally was being felt and that was reflected in a slackening of orders. George Gale, who had held shares since the inception of the company, decided to work full time for it as Office Manager and to move from London to Bedford. At the same time it was agreed to pay £150 per annum to the company's solicitors, Kimber, Williams & Co., for allowing the use of their offices and staff at 79 Lombard Street for the Registered Office. Some customers had financial stringencies and £200 in debentures issued by British Glass Industries Ltd had to be taken in part payment for their 8 ton locomotive. Matters were worse with National Welsh Slate Quarries Ltd who failed to pay the balance on their account before going into liquidation in 1922. Although the company itself was short of ready cash this did not stop it developing its premises further and plans were drawn up to add further buildings between the two existing ones so that more components could be made in-house and larger locomotives produced. The range envisaged was up to 100hp and 20 tons in weight.

The construction and civil engineering industry, by its nature, has a need for the temporary supply of plant, and enquiries were received from time to time for the hire of locomotives to customers. It was decided that the company should not enter this field but that a partnership should be set up by the individual shareholders

for this purpose. This was to be known as Petrol Loco Hirers and its business and financial arrangements are covered in Chapter 13.

In October 1921 it was agreed to take on staff apprentices, perhaps a sign of confidence in the future, although the level of activity had halved since the previous year as world trade adjusted to post war circumstances. The fall in commodity prices and the value of sterling in relation to the US dollar had an effect in many industries. Government subsidies for housing were suspended in late 1920 although efforts were made to provide employment elsewhere. The road programme, when it was implemented, created a considerable outlet for light railway equipment in the years between the wars. India was also affected by wild fluctuations in the value of the rupee and Parry, Murray & Co., having been offered a position as Motor Rail agent for India early in 1922, decided not to accept as they stated that the country was overstocked with locomotives at that date.

In 1919 the British Government had sold much of their existing light railways to the French Government who had in turn set up the Ministère des Régions Libérées to take on the task of restoring the devastation caused by the war. In the area covered by this ministry's operations, mostly around Arras, the entire WDLR system had been sold to the French Government. Where appropriate it was used for both passenger and freight purposes, and some lines were taken

52. This substantial railway with its embankment, fencing and telephone wires is at Belford Hall, Northumberland and was part of an extensive forestry railway. The trainload of logs seems to be somewhat precariously balanced between a rake of small wagons and does not appear to be roped on in any way. The locomotive is MR 1074 and was despatched from the works on the day after the Armistice. It was an early sale from the storage depot at Purfleet and must have been worked hard as many spares were supplied in early 1920.

*MR&T Co. catalogue.*
*Courtesy John Bryant*

53. MR 1064 was delivered in August 1918 so may not have seen active service. Regrettably the photographer left no details of his pictures but this is believed to be on a direct labour contract for the LM&S Railway somewhere in the Stoke-on-Trent area. A date of the late 1920s seems likely as it was after the Grouping and there was a spares enquiry for this loco in 1928 from the LM&S. Certainly the men on site appear intrigued by someone wanting to photograph them and their locomotive!

*H.W. Robinson.*
*Collection Industrial Railway Society*

over by the sugar beet factories and incorporated into their existing systems. Of the remainder the authorities disposed of equipment however and wherever they could. Thus the unsold stockpiles of WDLR locomotives overhung the market and in March 1922 T.D. Abbott and A.H. Brown went to France to inspect the ninety-nine 20hp tractors advertised for sale by the French Government and lying at Arras and Barlin.

Sixty-six of these were bought at a cost of 341,067 francs (which at the then rate of exchange amounted to £7,083) under a joint venture with the London dealer William Jones with each party contributing half the cost. William Jones had been established as

a machinery dealer since the 1880s but this arrangement seems to have initiated the firm's entry into the light railway market on an appreciable scale. They went on to become import agents for Orenstein & Koppel locomotives and to manufacture wagons and trackwork in their own right. From 1922 they were based in Banning Wharf, Greenwich, moving to Westmoor Street, Charlton in 1937. The agreement with Motor Rail & Tram Car Co. provided that each party would repair and sell half of the tractors and the resulting profits would be pooled with each firm taking half of the overall total. A further twenty-seven 40hp tractors were bought in France by William Jones later in the year for the joint account. This pooling

54. Leighton Buzzard Light Railway No. 2, MR 1383 of 1918, was a 40hp protected tractor and completed in December of that year. It is seen crossing the topmost of the five level crossings in Billington Road about 1958. As part of a rationalisation of the operating of the LBLR it was scrapped a year later. The picture of a 20/28 in Plate 93 is more or less below and immediately behind the last wagon of the train.

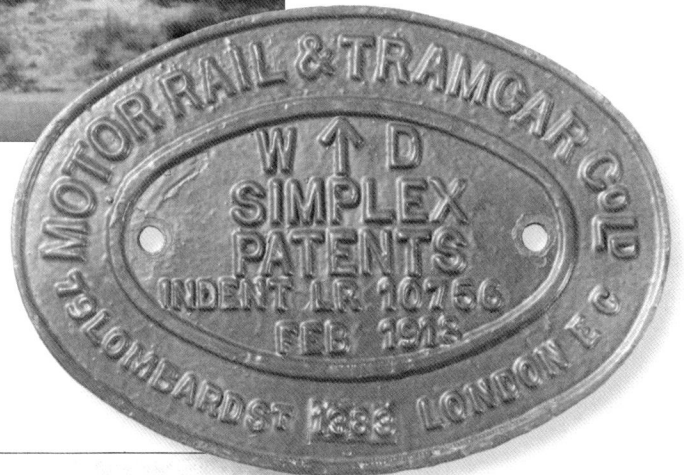

55. (Right) The works plate off Leighton Buzzard Light Railway No. 2, MR 1383. This is recorded as being despatched to the Ministry of Munitions, France on 17.12.18. The indent number would refer to the date of order. It was of the protected type and became War Department Light Railways No. 3108. It came to Leighton Buzzard in 1919.

1 cu. yd DOUBLE SIDED TIPPING WAGON

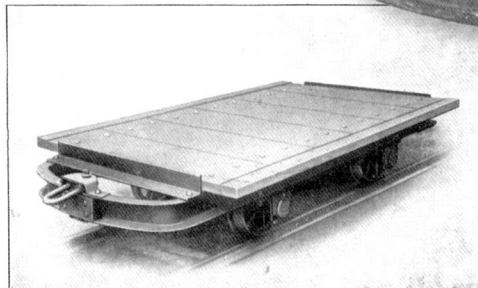

PLATFORM WAGON.

PLATFORM WAGON.

1½ cu. yd. HEAVY DOUBLE SIDED TIPPING WAGON.

56. (Left) The catalogue from which many of the early illustrations herein come included a section on wagons that Motor Rail could offer. Whilst it is possible that they manufactured some of the larger ones themselves they were at that time co-operating very much with William Jones in buying back wartime tractors. It is therefore likely that these and their like on other pages were of the latter's make.

*MR&T Co. catalogue.*
*Courtesy John Bryant*

57. Although taken in 1962 this picture could probably have been taken at any time in the previous forty years. MR 314 of 1917 looks remarkably spruce as it shunts wagons under the delivery hopper of a bucket excavator at the Chilton Brickworks of J. Browne (Bridgwater) Ltd. As can be seen these excavators worked on the principle of scraping a few inches of clay off the sloping face of the pit. The angle of the boom could be altered until eventually the whole machine and its track had to be moved sideways for another cut to be taken. *Courtesy S.A. Leleux*

58. (*Left*) Standard gauge locomotives, at least in this period, carried a makers plate that included a pair of rampant lions. This one is MR 2098 of 1922. See Chapter 14, *Rachel.*

59. Even if looking a bit careworn, MR 1944 of 1919 was still available to shunt tank wagons at Synthite Ltd's works at Mold in 1982. No mean achievement by any standards.
*A.J. Booth.*
*Collection Industrial Railway Society*

arrangement was in force until the summer of 1924 when it was terminated by mutual agreement, but whether all these locomotives had been sold on by then is unknown. It seems a bit unlikely.

It was only natural that other firms would decide to enter the market and it was a cause of considerable chagrin to the Motor Rail & Tram Car Co. that some of these were advertising reconditioned Simplex locomotives. The main culprit was Honeywill Bros, an established trading company that bought and sold a variety of commodities and saw the sale of army surplus stores including light railway equipment as simply another potential opportunity for profit. Many of the available locomotives required major repairs,

and emerged having been rebuilt to greater or lesser extent, and in the process used many of the available ex-military spare parts. Despite the fact that Motor Rail did this themselves, it was this latter aspect that particularly concerned MR&T Co.

How much of the resulting locomotive was new? And was it legitimate to advertise them as Simplex locomotives? The question was to become a persistent problem as they saw much potential business being diverted to this competitor. At least when they did it themselves the locomotive was rebuilt to their own standards, usually acquired a new works number in the process, and was thus considered to be new.

60. MR 1904 was built in 1920 as a 4 ton 20hp locomotive for Maenofferen Slate Quarry at Blaenau Ffestiniog, North Wales. Here it is seen in 1954 chain hauling wagons of waste rock on the adjoining track to the slate tips. It seems to have acquired a homemade cab and lost its bonnet covers and buffers over the years.

*V.J. Bradley.*
*Collection Industrial Railway Society*

61. In an effort to meet the competition on price the post First World War straight framed 20hp locomotive was available fitted with a Ford engine. Taken from a contemporary sales leaflet this one looks very new wherever it is working. It could have been on trial, sold, or on hire from Petrol Loco Hirers.
*Motor Rail sales leaflet.*
*Courtesy John Bryant*

In due time Honeywill Bros Ltd was to enter into the manufacture of locomotives through its subsidiary, Kent Construction Co. Ltd. There is no doubt that early Kent Construction Co. products used MR&T Co. components and these included standard gauge shunters adapted from 40hp Simplex tractors. This was patently not a case of locomotives merely being repaired. In addition, narrow gauge locomotives such as that for the Rye & Camber Tramway, were built with new frames that differed in shape from the WDLR locomotives, perhaps to avoid any conflict with the patent taken out by the Abbotts. After inspecting a locomotive shown by Honeywill Bros Ltd at the British Empire Exhibition at Wembley in 1924, MR&T Co. consulted with Marks & Clark, the patent agents, about what they saw as an attempted infringement of their patents. The result was a cautionary letter to that company and this may have had some effect on future policy since Kent Construction then produced their own designs for 10hp and 20hp locomotives in 1925 which did not have the transverse engine layout of the Simplex design.

Nevertheless it did not prevent their successors, F.C. Hibberd & Co. Ltd (whose locomotives were built under the trade name of 'Planet'), from registering the trade name of Planet-Simplex in June 1928. In this they seem to have been more astute than the Motor Rail & Tram Car Co. who failed to take similar steps. It was not until 1929 that they decided to register Simplex as a trade name in respect of internal combustion engined locomotives and rail vehicles and they then had to agree not to challenge the Planet-Simplex name that was already registered. The Registrar of Trade Marks declined to accept the Simplex name in respect of rail vehicles other than locomotives, presumably since this had already been registered and the company was forced to design a special format of the name that could be registered as a design.

From about 1925 they also had to face a great deal of competition from locomotives imported from the continent and from other manufacturers entering the market. The most successful of these imports were the 'Montania' locomotives built by Orenstein & Koppel in Germany and marketed by their erstwhile partner, William Jones Ltd, who gained a substantial number of customers in the Home Counties, especially when diesel engines came to be fitted. There were also a number of other makes imported, albeit in smaller numbers such as Austro-Daimler, Ducroo & Brauns,

62. Again this photograph was taken in 1954 but not much may have changed since this standard gauge shunter, MR 3793, was built in 1927 for Hoare Bros Ltd, Pitts Cleave Granite Quarry, Nr Tavistock. Originally fitted with a Dorman 4JO petrol engine, it was later rebuilt by Motor Rail at an unknown date with a Dorman 4DWD diesel engine.
*Courtesy Frank Jux*

63. (*Below*) The interest here is not so much the quotation itself but to whom it is being sent. The price was obviously accepted and MR 4514 was despatched to Cuffley Station almost exactly three months later.         *Courtesy Chris West*

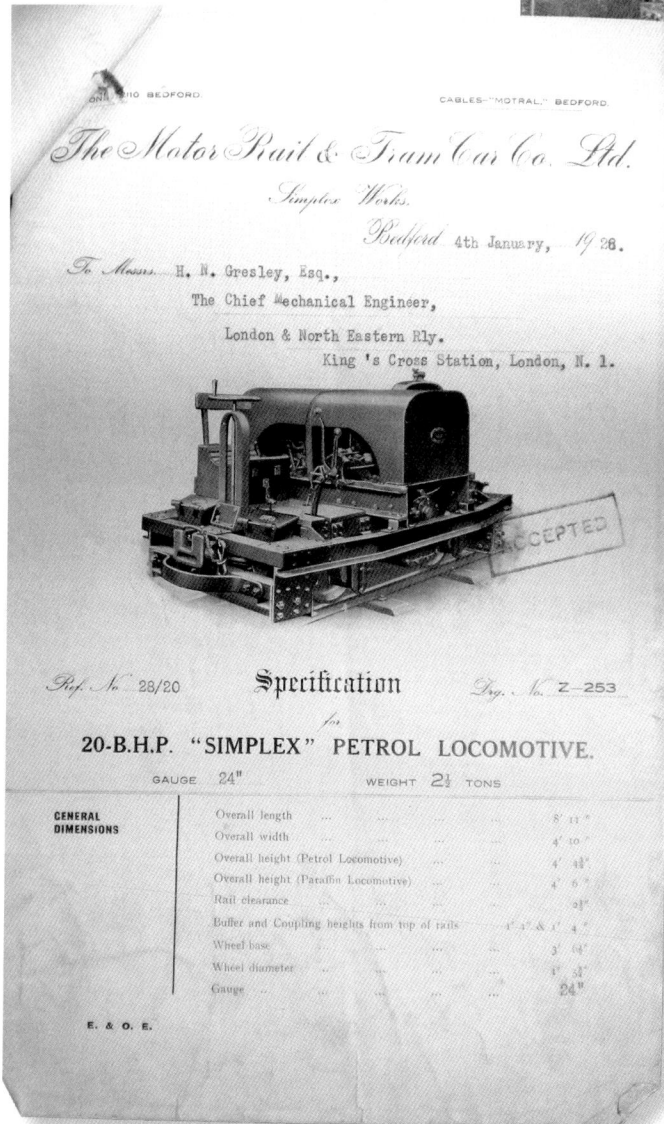

The Motor Rail & Tram Car Co. Ltd.
Simplex Works.
Bedford 4th January, 1926.

To Messrs H. N. Gresley, Esq.,
The Chief Mechanical Engineer,
London & North Eastern Rly.
King's Cross Station, London, N.1.

*Ref No. 28/20*      **Specification**      *Dwg. No. Z-253*
*for*
**20-B.H.P. "SIMPLEX" PETROL LOCOMOTIVE.**

GAUGE 24"                WEIGHT 2½ TONS

| GENERAL DIMENSIONS | Overall length | | | 8' 11" |
| | Overall width | | | 4' 10" |
| | Overall height (Petrol Locomotive) | | | 4' 4½" |
| | Overall height (Paraffin Locomotive) | | | 4' 6" |
| | Rail clearance | | | 9½" |
| | Buffer and Coupling heights from top of rails | 1' 4" & 1' 4" |
| | Wheel base | | | 3' 6" |
| | Wheel diameter | | | 1' 3" |
| | Gauge | | | 24" |

E. & O. E.

Arn Jung and Les Ateliers de Bondy, Mormuda etc. These were mostly of low power, some of as little as 6hp, and thus below the normal MR&T range. Prior to the First World War, Deutz had sold a few locomotives in this country of a type that was then copied by Ruston Proctor, but none sold in any quantity after the war. British competition in the 1920s was perhaps not so intense since it did not share the price advantage of foreign firms. This came about by the realignment of currencies following the devastation of war and, in particular, Britain reverting to the Gold Standard with the pound set at an over-valued rate. However, Kent Construction and its successors remained throughout the decade as an active competitor, as, to a lesser extent, did their near neighbour in Bedford, J. & F. Howard Ltd. There was strong competition from firms such as Muir Hill and Robert Hudson that produced designs utilising the relatively cheap Ford industrial engine used in agricultural tractors. In the former case this included the entire engine/gearbox/back axle drive train. In practical terms this was not entirely successful until a proper gearbox was fitted allowing all gearbox speeds in both directions of travel – however, they had the advantage of being very cheap. This led Motor Rail to produce a variant of their Simplex design with a Ford engine and other models with lower horse-power engines than the standard 20hp Dorman engine in order to give a wider range that could match the competition. In fact Motor Rail offered a surprisingly wide range of engines at this time, including – as well as Ford – White & Poppe, Aster (100hp), Thorneycroft (50hp), Austin light twelve, Lister and, into the diesel era, Lister again, Fowler, Ruston and McLaren. The majority of locomotives produced were narrow gauge models for use on light track and all had petrol engines. The 40hp standard gauge shunter was a successful design aimed primarily at small users with only a few wagons to move. Larger petrol locomotives did not sell well due to their capital and running costs. However, a 16 ton 65/85hp design of shunter in standard gauge was produced in 1923 with a more substantial frame and cab suitable for heavier work for the Nitrate Railway of Chile. The two other prototypes in the same batch took a number of years to sell and the design was not repeated.

The company had been extremely profitable during the war years and, as a consequence, suffered heavy taxation in 1923 when the Government levied a charge on the 'excess profits' earned as a result. This provided a temporary setback and George Gale's salary was reduced along with that of the consulting engineer, J.D. Abbott, in a reorganisation made to effect economies. The accounting work that had formerly been performed at the company's registered office in London was transferred to Bedford as part of this. The company was basically profitable, however, and in 1925 invested in additional machinery to enable it to produce its own gearboxes at a projected rate of eighty a year together with an increased volume of spare parts. In the following year it was decided to extend the buildings again to give increased accommodation for the construction of railcars.

# 5

# The Diesel Era

## 1926–1945

During the 1920s the development of diesel engine powered locomotives and railcars gathered pace especially on the Continent of Europe and in the United States of America. British-made diesel engines did not become readily available until late in the decade and the first thought given by the Motor Rail & Tram Car Co. to their use was in 1928 when the McLaren-Benz 30hp engine was considered for use in the 6 ton design. At the same time it was decided to design a 105/165hp petrol locomotive subject to it being convertible to use a McLaren-Benz diesel engine of 60hp running at 800 rpm. This was later modified to envisage a design that could use a M.A.N. 100hp diesel engine and it was also decided to consider the use of a diesel engine in the standard gauge 8 ton models. Although this is the record, its accuracy has to be queried. Logic suggests that a 60hp, even a 100hp, engine could not satisfactorily replace one of 165hp, diesel or not, without detriment to the machine's performance. General designs were drawn up for a 70hp 14 ton shunter and a 100hp 20 ton shunter, both of which had an engine layout and chassis somewhat similar to the standard gauge locomotives of Motor Rail's near neighbours, J. & F. Howard Ltd. Neither was built. The proposal for the use of a McLaren 30hp engine went ahead in somewhat modified form in that an 18hp Helios engine was offered by McLaren who supposedly had the UK agency for this German engine, although in fact the Helios company had gone into liquidation and the available engines were effectively bankrupt stock! A 2½ ton locomotive was built to take this engine but it was found to be unsuitable because the combined fuel pump/injector system could not be controlled properly and the engine had

a habit of 'running away'. Similar problems were experienced with this engine when Kerr, Stuart & Co. Ltd fitted a 6-cylinder version in a prototype diesel lorry. In due course the engine was replaced with one from McLaren-Benz (as was that of the Kerr, Stuart lorry) which was more reliable, and a number of similar locomotives were built using this 30hp power unit.

The flow of orders and profit in the year to March 1928 was satisfactory but output fluctuated widely from year to year in response to the activities of the company's customers, many of which were connected with road construction and civil engineering in general. Output was recorded as being worth £54,365 in 1926/27, £81,659 in 1927/28 and £60,143 in 1928/29, illustrating the ups and downs of the industry. In the summers of 1927 and 1928 there was a works outing arranged when the factory was closed for the purpose and the normal Saturday morning shift was not worked. This was a paid holiday but it does not seem that annual holidays with pay were yet allowed. It was not until 1929 that it was decided to give half a week's wages to employees with six months or more service, and this was followed in 1930 by the establishment of a contributory holiday pay fund.

In 1929 it was also decided to have a stand at the Roads Exhibition and Public Works Congress due to be held at the Agricultural Hall, London in November. It will be recalled that the directors visited the British Empire Exhibition at Wembley in 1924 in order examine the exhibit on the Honeywill Bros stand. They did not themselves have a stand there and it does not appear to have been until 1929 that they felt it necessary to appear at such exhibitions. Even so,

64. Usually credited with being in the 1930s, this is more likely to be shortly after the railway opened in 1919. It shows either MR 468 or 478 of 1918 at Stanbridge Road on the Leighton Buzzard Light Railway. The train is probably stationary waiting for the flagman to return to the cab after crossing the main road. By comparison with later years the amount of ballast around the track is remarkable. *Collection S.A. Leleux*

65. Three of these 65hp standard gauge locomotives were built in 1923 and whilst the first one went to Chile the other two remained in stock until 1926 and 1929. This may well be 2262, for which see *Helen* in Chapter 14. Despite the apparent position of the driver these machines are left hand drive with duplicated controls. Apart from this the mechanical arrangements are entirely typical Simplex.

they were to become regular stand-holders at successive Public Works Exhibitions in order to 'show the flag' and meet their regular customers – although few sales may have been gained as a direct result, as is normally the case with this type of exhibition. Indeed trade seems to have settled into a routine although the occasional machine tool was purchased and adjoining plots of land acquired as they became available. Thus the property adjacent to the works owned by Mr Gower that had been used as an engineering works for many years was bought in 1930. This would appear to be one of the Gower family who ran a boiler maker's business a short distance away from Motor Rail that existed at least into the 1960s.

The year 1930 saw a number of significant moves. It was decided to merge the business of Petrol Locomotive Hirers into the main company and this was done as from 30th June with a purchase price of £12,400 being paid to the owning partners. At around this time it seems to have been decided administratively to modify the system of works numbering, allocating a number series to locomotive classes rather than having a continuous run irrespective of type. It was also decided to start an auxiliary business for road haulage, as a diversification, under the name of Britannic Transport. A Leyland lorry and trailer were purchased to inaugurate this, followed by two Saurer lorries. The results were disappointing, however, showing a loss on operations, and after little more than six months in business it was closed at the year end and the lorries sold. Since it was advantageous to be able to deliver locomotives to British customers it was decided to buy a Ford six-wheeler for the company's own use.

At the end of 1930 it was evident that diesel engines had become a more practical proposition and since their main engine supplier,

W.H. Dorman & Co. Ltd, was now making a new diesel model, a definite decision was made to produce new prototype designs. It was decided to build a standard gauge locomotive with a 60hp Dorman engine at an approximate cost of £900 and a 2ft gauge 6-wheeled locomotive to incorporate a 60hp McLaren Benz engine at a cost of about £1,300. There is a drawing of a 60hp standard gauge locomotive that would have been very similar to the 8 ton 40hp design but this seems to have been abandoned in favour of a more modern 12 ton machine. This had the same transverse layout but with a proper cab at the rear in place of the traditional seat on top of the engine, but with the driver still sitting in a sideways position. The company built two of these locomotives and one was regularly hired to the organisers of the British Industries Fair at Castle Bromwich for the purpose of shunting the sidings and acting as a working exhibit. A third locomotive had an engine rated at 65/85hp and all three were rebuilt to a revised 20 ton design with the later one being for sale.

The very interesting 6-wheeled narrow gauge design had a more conventional layout of the engine and gearbox in line with the frame, and this may have partly accounted for the increased cost. According to an article in the *Railway Gazette*, a Dorman engine was fitted rather than the McLaren-Benz originally envisaged. Although an attractive and workmanlike design, no customer is recorded and it is rumoured to have been eventually broken up at Bedford. It was intended for customers that had longer hauls and required a more powerful locomotive able to run on lighter tracks. It had a 4-speed gearbox and worm drive to the centre axle. Interestingly, a copy of a drawing of this locomotive was seen by

66. (*Above*) This is probably MR 5601 of 1930, a 20hp locomotive fitted with a Dorman 2RB diesel engine, 3ft gauge and working at the Arlesey works of London Brick Co. Photographed in 1955, note the wooden end tipping wagons with extended axles at one end to catch in an end tippler. *Courtesy Frank Jux*

67. (*Right*) Not the popular idea of what a Great Western locomotive should look like! MR 3731 of 1925 was despatched to the GWR locomotive depot at Bridgwater but by 1934 had migrated back to Swindon. At 40hp and 8 tons weight it was no doubt more than capable of shunting the odd locomotive.
*Collection Industrial Railway Society*

an enthusiast among the archives of the Forges et Fonderies de Maurice in Mauritius in the 1960s and it may have been intended for the sugar estates of that country. The lack of success with this design may have soured MR&T Co.'s attitude to 'something new', compounded by the intense competition on price between the locomotive manufacturers of the day.

Although designs for railcars were drawn up and quotations submitted to a number of Spanish railways following the Onda–Castellón line contract, sales of railcars had effectively ceased. Consequently, in early 1931 the name of the company was changed to Motor Rail Ltd thus acknowledging the fact that it was intended not to compete in the that market. Although a reasonable number of tramcars and other rail vehicles had been built these had largely been for East India Tramways, or various random orders. The company had no standard designs in quantity production with

which to compete with the likes of the Drewry Car Co. Ltd and D. Wickham & Co. Ltd who sold inspection cars and trolleys in considerable numbers. The new name was officially registered on 16th April 1931 at the beginning of an inauspicious year made worse by the onset of the years of world depression. Turnover in 1931/32 was a third less than the year before, although admittedly that had been at the relatively high level of £79,669. The first few years of the decade saw great changes and many old established engineering firms and locomotive manufacturers who had suffered severely during the General Strike of 1926 and subsequent miners' strikes went out of business. These included Motor Rail's neighbours in Bedford, J. & F. Howard and the Bedford Engineering Co. The former had recently entered the internal combustion engined locomotive and light railway market and the proprietor of the latter reluctantly sold the works after forty-two years of trading. Both closed in 1932 whilst Crossley Bros who had built locomotives in the former Saunderson tractor works had closed their works shortly beforehand. Motor Rail did not take the opportunity of acquiring Howard's goodwill, such as it was, and their locomotive spares and designs were taken by their competitors, F.C. Hibberd & Co. Ltd. This may or may not have been a missed opportunity but, at the time, conserving cash was probably more important than any new venture.

Britain went off the gold standard in 1931 and this may have encouraged Empire trade. Prospects in Britain remained poor although the civil engineering industry was relatively healthy due to expenditure on roads, housing and other infrastructure projects designed to relieve unemployment. More British designed engines were also being produced by such firms as R.A. Lister, Ailsa Craig and Gardner, in addition to Dorman and McLaren. A number of firms decided to enter the market for contractor's machinery in order to utilise spare capacity. John Fowler in Leeds already produced locomotives but did not greatly affect Motor Rail's sales even if they did for a few years produce a 10hp locomotives with a transverse engine. Ransomes & Rapier also built a number of 10hp and 20hp locomotives that directly competed with Motor Rail. The most significant new entrant into the market, however, and who were to prove to be Motor Rail's main rival after the Second World War, was Ruston & Hornsby Ltd of Lincoln, successors to Ruston Proctor & Co. Ltd whose efforts with narrow gauge locomotives have already been noted. Now they had new designs that initially used Lister engines and these were in volume production from 1932. The JP series of engines came from R.A. Lister & Co. Ltd of Dursley, Gloucestershire, with the 'JP' standing for a Joint Project with Ruston & Hornsby Ltd that in practice never happened. Very soon, however, Ruston & Hornsby were manufacturing their own engines

in Lincoln and this put them in a strongly competitive position. Eventually Ruston Hornsby production would far exceed that of Motor Rail, and indeed for a very short period in the early 1960s, on the basis of sheer numbers of locomotives of all types produced, Ruston Hornsby were the world's largest locomotive builder.

R.A. Lister themselves were also competitors in the market place with a very lightweight locomotive of 1–1½ tons that used the JAP petrol engine unit from the Lister Auto-Truck and later the range of Lister air cooled diesel engines. These were popular locomotives for certain operations, such as temporary very light track on peat bogs, and Motor Rail did not seriously attempt to compete with them until the introduction of the 12hp model in the 1960s – and then not very effectively. Perhaps ironically, these latter locos were usually fitted with Lister engines!

To meet the competition Motor Rail broadened its range and was prepared to use a variety of engines both to suit the customer and to provide the power range required. The basic design remained the same, however, with the transverse layout providing simplicity and the cost saving necessary to maintain a competitive edge. Some very cheap locomotives were on the market including, notably, the aforementioned Muir Hill with a 24hp Fordson engine offered at £230. In July 1931 it was decided to produce a Simplex with a similar engine to sell at £235 and at the same time the price of a standard Simplex locomotive with a Dorman engine was to be reduced to £275. The use of a Lister engine was also considered. Four engines were ordered from Ford in January 1932 but whether all were delivered is uncertain. Only one prototype locomotive was built (MR 7001) and this was sent to Fords in May 1932 but later returned. Several firms fitted similar engines at this date and Ford may well have been having a sales drive to encourage this. The utilisation of agricultural tractor units was in vogue in a number

68. MR 5702 was built as a 12 ton locomotive with a Dorman 4RBL diesel engine rated at 50/80hp in late 1932. It was despatched to the British Industries Fair at Castle Bromwich in January 1933. It is recorded that Motor Rail exhibited a standard gauge locomotive at the fair in 1933 and 1935 so possibly this is it. The weight was later increased to 20 tons, the engine uprated to 65/85hp and as MR 5751 it was sold to Cornforth Limestone Co. in 1937 (see also Chapter 14). It was recorded as being with Wagon Repairs, Gloucester, in 1967, having by then received a Dorman 5LB engine of 120hp. Another one taken from the office wall.

of countries around the world – providing a cheap but less durable locomotive. It is a concept that has been tried by many firms, often not locomotive builders, over the years with greater or, more usually, lesser success.

With the onset of the recession in 1933 efforts were made to find other work to occupy the workshops. This was to become an obsession with Motor Rail, and later Simplex Mechanical Handling, management right up to the moment of deciding to close the business. The possibility of building larger locomotives and further railcars was mooted as was also the conversion of Bedford or Ford lorries to run on rails, but all without any practical results. One diversification achieved was the signing of an agreement with the Sure-Arc Electrode Co. Ltd in July 1933 to manufacture an AC/DC welding set to be exhibited at that year's British Industries Fair (see Chapter 13).

In October some income was gained by the letting of the 'large garage' (presumably formerly used by the haulage venture) to Shell-Mex and, encouraged by this, the company resolved to erect a further four garages to rent out. By July 1934 the four garages had been built and all had been let by the end of the year. On the strength of this a further eight garages were considered. Further development of the site was planned by the erection of a specially built bus garage at the end of the main works building, to be occupied by the Union Jack (Luton) Omnibus Co. Ltd. This was not an age when property development earned large returns but the rents received must have done their bit to tide the company through the bad years. In May 1935 a meeting was held with Mr Dwyer, a director of F.C. Hibberd & Co. Ltd but unfortunately no details of the matters discussed were recorded and Hibberd's continued to build Simplex type locomotives, thus remaining a thorn in Motor Rail's side.

In February 1936 another major step was taken with the decision to design and produce a dumper. This was a logical step in view of the company's connections with the construction industry where

69. (*Above*) MR 4802 of 1934 was originally a petrol engined locomotive but by 1959 had almost certainly been converted to diesel. Originally built for Petrol Loco Hirers it had a somewhat chequered career and is here seen at Gatwick Brick Co. Ltd. One can only guess at what is going on but one scenario is that the locomotive has pushed a train of loaded clay wagons past the empties in the loop and the driver is now chain shunting these back onto the main line. Once they are clear of the points he will couple up correctly and be on his way. He is standing to drive which requires a certain amount of skill to operate the clutch. Added to that, the nearer wheels of the middle wagon appear to be off the rails but he probably hopes that pulling them back through the turnout will correct that! *Courtesy Frank Jux*

70. (*Right*) MR 3980 of 1936 at Derbyshire Stone Quarries, Middleton, near Buxton. This photograph was taken in 1964 and the record states that spare parts had been supplied for this locomotive during the previous year.

*Collection Industrial Railway Society*

the movement of spoil was turning away from rail based equipment towards the usc of rubber tyred vehicles, and was well timed in view of the rearmament program that was soon to commence.

Muir Hill were pioneers of dumper manufacture in this country and in May 1940 wrote to Motor Rail claiming that one of their patents had been infringed. No mention of any further action is recorded in the directors' minutes and the matter must have been settled satisfactorily as Motor Rail continued to build dumpers in some numbers. Whereas the Muir Hill design was based on Ford tractor power units, Motor Rail used the Dorman engine and a slightly modified version of their locomotive gear box in their models. The first was tested between May and August 1937 and performance as well as the estimate for potential sales must have been very encouraging to justify the manufacture of an initial batch of twenty-five. The first units were put into the hire fleet so that customers could try them out without a commitment to buy.

With the economy recovering the price of materials rose and these extra costs had to be fed into the prices being charged. By

this date also, employment had picked up and in 1938 a shortage of craftsmen even led to suggestions that a night shift should be worked, although that seems to beg the question as to where the additional staff would have come from. Since competitive prices were often the order of the day it was decided to utilise Ailsa Craig engines and in January 1938 ten single-cylinder engines (at £65 each) and fifteen 2-cylinder engines (at £115) were ordered as well as a 4-cylinder engine from Ford. Motor Rail had been important customers of W.H. Dorman Ltd almost from the inception of both companies and had had engines built to their own specification. To prevent competitors using the same modified 2DWD engine design an arrangement for the exclusive use of that particular engine was made with Dorman. Under this agreement Motor Rail agreed to order at least sixty engines per year for the five-year term of the agreement at a cost of £135 each and to contribute £175 towards the cost of patterns and jigs. Preparations were thus being made for an anticipated increase in output with both new and secondhand lathes and other machinery being purchased. New offices were

71. From the fact that this locomotive has hardly had time to get dirty this would seem to be an official photograph taken upon the arrival of RS61 at ICI Cowdale Works, near Buxton, Derbyshire. It features the ubiquitous 7 ton 32/42, in this case MR 7801 of 1937, but is unusual in being fitted with full Westinghouse air brakes. There was perhaps something special about this locomotive as Alan Keef Ltd still have a large framed photograph of it that once graced the walls of Motor Rail's offices.
*P.J. Hindley (an official with ICI).*
*Collection Industrial Railway Society*

72. (*Below*) This early 20/28, MR 7077 of 1937, was originally sold to a plant hire contractor but is here seen in 1956 when with Helwith Bridge Roadstone & Granite Co. Ltd at Horton in Ribblesdale, North Yorkshire. It looks in fairly run-down condition and, interestingly, the section of track in front of it seems to be missing! Note the Settle & Carlisle line in the background.
*B. Roberts.*
*Collection Industrial Railway Society*

73. Typically the 20/28 locomotive had these plates fitted to each of the fold-over engine covers. Motor Rail always called them this whilst most of the rest of the world called them bonnet covers!

74. (*Above*) A 3 cu. yd capacity rear control dumper, 8389 of 1947, fitted with a Dorman 2DWD engine and modified locomotive gearbox. The fuel tank is prominent and is direct from the 20/28 locomotive. From the style of the chimneys, the load and the mammoth stack of bricks in the background this has to be at one of the brickworks around Bedford or possibly Peterborough. This is a publicity picture with the machine likely to be one from the company's hire fleet and, judging from the steam roller in the background, may have been on internal road making duties.

*Courtesy Moseley Railway Trust*

75. (*Left*) An unknown 6 ton 40hp locomotive propelling a train on a very spindly jetty believed to be at Junin in Chile. Neither the date or the load are recorded, but are probably 1930s and bagged nitrate. If it is at Junin the gauge would be 2ft 6ins.

also built, being first occupied in January 1938. War was seen as inevitable and by September general war precautions were being planned. By the following June these plans were extended to include air raid shelters together with other improvements including the heating of the workshops and the provision of washing facilities.

By the time war was declared in September 1939 Motor Rail had supplied a number of locomotives to contractors building ordnance factories. These orders were followed during the war years by batches of locomotives delivered to the War Office and Admiralty. Although these totalled something over three hundred – considerably less than during the First World War – if the diesel locomotives supplied by other manufacturers are added (including Simplex type locomotives from F.C. Hibberd & Co.) then the totals are almost the same. This is despite the fact that there were no tactical light railways. These numbers reflected the widespread use of light railway track and small diesel locomotives in both civil engineering works and local depot haulage. Details of just where all these locomotives were intended to be used is not recorded although it is known that many were used in storage depots around the world. However, it is a fact that a fair quantity were still in their packing cases at the war's end.

The first Government orders had been received for twenty-two of the standard 20/28hp locomotives and at the same time for the manufacture of 760 sets of gun carriage parts for two-pounder quick firing guns. In expectation of more locomotive orders, W.H. Dorman were requested to supply sixty engines so that the 2½ ton 20/28 model could be built in batches of fifty. The large garage, which had been vacated by Eastern National (successors to the Union Jack Co.) in early 1937, was adapted as an auxiliary store with a new crane being ordered for the purpose. Dumpers were also in demand and a further batch of twenty-five was put into production in March 1940 with a further sixty engines ordered in May.

It says something for the confidence in the war's outcome that in December 1939 Motor Rail were approached by A. Gloster (see Chapter 7) and W.G. Bagnall Ltd of Stafford to form a group to appropriate the worldwide business of Orenstein & Koppel who were now no longer able to provide the service they once had. Despite some hard persuasion, Motor Rail declined to get involved on the basis that the German firm would come back into the business with a vengeance after the war, and then all concerned would have great difficulty retaining whatever business they had managed to acquire, thus the not inconsiderable effort would be for nothing. Even this

76. Just when Motor Rail started this very effective way of indicating the haulage capacity of their locomotives is not recorded, but this comes from a sales leaflet of 1954. The locomotive is a 20/28, obviously of 3½ tons weight, but the location is unknown.

77. (*Below*) The ever faithful 20/28 providing vital services during the Second World War at an army depot (from the overalls, possibly REME) '*somewhere in England.'* Another picture taken from the office wall.

ignores the practical difficulties of exporting locomotives whilst hostilities lasted. They were almost certainly right. In similar vein, and with an eye to the future, they joined the Internal Combustion Export Group of the Locomotive Manufacturers Association in May 1940.

Most, but not all, of the locomotive production went to the military with the remainder being allowed to go to firms in the defence effort. A few were even sent to sisal estates in East Africa and one can only assume that sisal was considered a strategic material to the war effort. Another hundred locomotives were ordered by the War Office in February 1941 whilst at the same time the works continued to perform armament work including tank traversing gear for the Power Mounting Co. By July 1942 the supply of engines for the manufacture of locomotives and dumpers had become a problem, with only eight engines per month being

allocated by the Government controller. This meant that two-thirds of the output was munitions work, predominantly tank parts although the works were allocated a variety of other engineering work by the Government during the war period. By 1943 the availability of engines had improved and in 1944 it was possible to agree a production level of twelve units per month in order to meet War Office targets. Although the war ended in May 1945, locomotives were still being built for the military. Much of Europe was in ruins and Britain had suffered heavily in air raids. Shortages and rationing of all materials continued even into the 1950s, and with a desperate need to rebuild the country's finances priority was given to exports.

A sad event on 15th January 1942 was the death of George Gale, the oldest surviving director, who had been with the company since its inception. In 1945, with the war drawing to a close, A.H. Brown decided to resign from his position of Joint Managing Director with T.D. Abbott and a replacement was appointed as assistant to the Managing Director. This did not last, however, and in August 1945 a new post of Sales and Development Manager was created.

Many firms had given consideration to post war plans and Motor Rail was no exception. They felt they could look forward to a high level of pent-up demand for their products. Consideration was given to the construction of mining locomotives following the publication of plans for a nationalised coal mining industry. But the company did not proceed further in this direction and only a very few surface locomotives were ever built for what became the National Coal Board.

# 6

# South African Problems

## 1945–1965

At risk of putting the proverbial cart before the horse and for the sake of clarity it is better to deal with problems in South Africa as a whole before moving on to events in Bedford. These difficulties were to overshadow the operations of Motor Rail Ltd during the whole of the period from the end of the Second World War until the company became part of a larger organisation in 1965 and in the end were to become irretrievable. Appendix IV could usefully be read in conjunction with this chapter.

South Africa has a wide range of mineral resources. It is best known for its diamond and gold mines, and these two have been of vital importance in shaping its history. Since the turn of the twentieth century the gold mining industry has been of world importance and in the process utilised large quantities of railway equipment. Electric locomotives, both trolley and battery powered, had been used on the surface from as early as 1894 and underground since 1900. Petrol-engined locomotives had been tried before the First World War but it was not until the diesel engine came along that non-electric locomotives became a practical proposition. The mines are not gaseous and therefore do not require engines to be flameproofed (as in most coal mines) but exhaust conditioners were fitted as a

78, 79. These two pictures give a flavour of surface sugar operations in South Africa. The loco shed is at Delville Estates, Mposa, with a 3½ ton 20/28 (MR 20540 of 1954) passing with empty wagons and a good show of exhaust. Outside the shed is a 9 ton (MR 14020 of 1956) with possibly another lurking inside the doorway. With the train of loaded sugar cane is another 9 ton (MR 14043 of 1959) at Zululand Sugar Planters looking in very spruce, perhaps new, condition. All three were exported through A. Gloster with the latter one also passing through Lenning's hands. *Courtesy Frank Jux*

80. Whilst the precise identity of this locomotive is not known, this is what all the fuss was about in South Africa. This is a short frame 20/28 which was an intermediate design to the later 40S and 40SD. It has the Dorman 2DWD engine and is fitted with lights and an exhaust conditioner on the far side of the radiator. The engine remains hand start (very easy with the 2DWD) probably in the interests of simplicity and cost. The frame extension for the buffer head would not have been required if ballast weights were fitted as was mostly the case.

81. (*Left*) The other side of the argument. From the Motor Rail files comes this works picture of an M & R 40hp locomotive. The frame, buffers, wheels, running gear, even the driver's seat, are pure Simplex. An intermediate bracket carries the axlebox adjustment at just the frame length in the previous picture. The radiator is a fabricated version of the Dixon Abbot design and the whole layout could have emanated from Bedford.

82. (*Right*) One of very few pictures available of Simplex locomotives underground in South Africa. This is a 32/42 of 5 tons weight and looking to be in near new condition; possibly hence its being photographed. It is at Modder East Mine and appears to be of 2ft 6ins gauge. *Courtesy John Middleton*

83. (*Below*) Loraine Gold Mines, Allanridge, Orange Free State. Although this picture purports to show three 3½ ton 24ins gauge Simplexes on the 60 Level (6,000ft depth) in 1983, it is likely that these are M&R/Lenning lookalikes. The gearboxes may well be genuine Motor Rail but everything else is different. This mine had some 250 locos in its system of which 87 were Simplex. It also built 76 to its own 5 ton design! *Courtesy John Middleton*

84. (*Below Right*) 2ft 6ins gauge, 3½ ton MR 9595 of 1951. Much rebuilt by President Steyn Gold Mining Co. Ltd, Welkom, this 20/28 has a different engine and a large cooling tank in lieu of a radiator. At 2ft 6ins gauge the axleboxes on this type could be vulnerable, so the protective bars are a local addition. *Courtesy John Middleton*

matter of course to take out particulates and poisonous gases. Shortly before the outbreak of the Second World War new mining areas had been proven and although the war delayed prospecting and development, further work was being directed towards the exploration of areas in the Orange Free State. Large new goldfields were proven there and soon after the war an unprecedented mining boom ensued. Although electric mining locomotives continued to be supplied to the traditional mining areas around Johannesburg the adoption of the relatively cheap and flexible alternative of the diesel locomotive was especially prevalent in the mines opened after 1950.

Prior to this time the world market for light railway equipment had been dominated by the German firm of Orenstein & Koppel (O & K) and South Africa was no exception. Mr A. Gloster had been their British representative and after the war he started to sell Simplex locomotives into South Africa through Orenstein & Koppel's past representative in that country, E.C. Lenning (Pty) Ltd (hereinafter to be referred to simply as Lenning). Before the war this company had handled the O & K 'Montania' diesel locomotives, as were marketed by William Jones in the UK. Gloster's business went on to be incorporated as Railway, Mine & Plantation Equipment Ltd (hereinafter RMP) and these two firms were to have a dominating influence on the future of Motor Rail Ltd and between them created the company's largest overseas market. The numbers are staggering: in round figures some 880 locomotives were sold to South Africa, of which Gloster ordered no less than 200 in one batch! For the record, second on the list was East Africa where around 550 were sold mostly through Wigglesworth with equal third going to India and the Far East at 250 each.

Through the agency of Lenning, Motor Rail became one of the most important suppliers of diesel locomotives to the mines, especially those under the control of the Anglo American Corporation. In September 1948 they wrote with great enthusiasm to Motor Rail praising the Simplex radiator as the best they had known and that the locomotives themselves were very good for maintenance access. Lenning had by then ordered over seventy locomotives, many of which were used underground on a three shift continuous basis and only came to the surface once a week for maintenance purposes. There is no doubt that the simple engine and transmission arrangement of the classic Simplex design made accessibility for maintenance good and that this was appreciated in the often restricted confines of underground galleries.

At the end of 1951 the founder of Lennings died and his widow, Dagmar Lenning, wished to sell the controlling interest in the company. At this stage Motor Rail were being well served by Lennings and even if they had wanted to take that company over it was probably not possible. At the time there were exchange control regulations in force and Government permission would have been required. This would have been unlikely to be forthcoming as the purchase would have added nothing to export sales, indeed possibly the reverse.

The question of Simplex locomotives being manufactured under licence had cropped up from various directions at this time, initially from Australia. The company took the line that even in South Africa it would not be economically viable in view of the fact that the engines would have to be imported anyway. Thus the cost could not compete when the facility at Bedford was designed for large-scale production for a world market. This was possibly true, but they again misjudged the intentions of the South African Government which was to encourage local production even if the costs were higher and Motor Rail was ultimately to lose this important market as a consequence. Having said all that, both parties must have been satisfied with their position because, in 1953, they signed a ten-year contract under which Lenning were appointed sole agents for the sale of Motor Rail products in South Africa.

There may well have been a number of other considerations that applied when this agreement was drawn up. With E.C. Lenning himself having died, a long-term agreement may have been an advantage to his company if its sale was being contemplated. Motor Rail would also have wished to maintain what was a successful connection. In fact they were not averse to Lenning handling locomotives from other manufacturers if they were outside the Simplex power range. Thus, at a later stage when RMP were making arrangements to sell Baguley locomotives in South Africa, they encouraged Lenning to consider selling those models that were of larger horsepower, but without result.

T.D. Abbott made a visit to South and East Africa in July 1953, thereby emphasising the importance of these areas to the company. Subsequently applications were made to register Simplex as a trade name in both the United Kingdom and South Africa but this was not acceptable to the Registrar of Trade Marks as the name was being used by other companies for other products. Instead it was decided to apply for registration of Motor Rail as a trade name. A couple of years later the trade name of Simplex was successfully registered there as a trade mark for locomotives and internal combustion engined trucks.

The question of manufacturing locomotives under licence in South Africa was discussed following the Managing Director's

visit but the previous decision prevailed. Instead they decided to set up their own subsidiary company in South Africa and Motor Rail Simplex (Pty) Ltd (MRS) was registered on 8th June 1954. This gave the possibility of manufacturing locomotives in South Africa for sale, either by the new subsidiary, through Lenning (who now had a long term sales agreement) or through a company jointly owned by the two companies. Bedford's proposal was to set up a joint company for the manufacture and sale of Simplex locomotives but this idea was not acceptable to the new owners of Lenning who would not relinquish their exclusive control of sales. Accordingly T.D. Abbott made a further visit to South Africa to try to come to some agreement whereby Motor Rail could retain some control over any joint company. Subsequent events suggest that he was not successful.

On the technical side of matters, Motor Rail's locomotives were predominantly of low horse power and the company had not changed its designs, except in details, for many years. Those larger machines that had been built had resulted largely from customer demand. Other firms were now experimenting with different transmissions and following pressure from Lenning it was decided to design a hydraulically operated gearbox that could be used in the 20/28hp locomotive. A great deal of expense was incurred in this direction and it eventually produced the 'Simtran' transmission.

This system worked on the basis of a Vulcan Sinclair fluid coupling attached to the engine driving into a constant mesh gear box which fitted exactly where the traditional Simplex box was mounted on the engine bearers. This gearbox had internal oil operated clutches that engaged either gear and reverse. It was thus of single lever operation and in some cases had only a single gear in each direction. In addition to the pressure from Lenning it was

85. (*Above Left*) Used as a yard shunter by Buffelsfontein Gold Mining Co. Ltd, Stilfontein, this is either MR 21091 or MR 21108 of 1956/7. Of 4 tons weight it has been re-gauged to 2ft gauge but still retains its original 2DWD engine. This design ultimately became the 40S and later still the 40SD when fitted with a Deutz engine.
*Courtesy John Middleton*

86. (*Above*) It is hard to believe that this locomotive emanated from Bedford at all but it is 9 ton MR 9070 of 1954 and was originally built at 2ft 6ins gauge for the President Brand gold mine. Here it has been somewhat drastically modified to 3ft 6ins gauge for shunting main line wagons at the Sentral West Ko-op Beperk, Ventersdorp Silos. Photographed in September 1990.        *Courtesy John Middleton*

87. (*Left*) On the other hand this 9 ton locomotive, MR 9025 of 1952 must have lived a charmed life to look as smart as this forty-one years after it left Bedford! It is here seen at the rail served distribution depot of Cato Bulk Facilities (Pty) Ltd, Cato Ridge, Kwa Zulu, Natal.                                *Courtesy John Middleton*

possibly also done in response to the gearboxes being fitted to the Ruston & Hornsby LB series locomotives. These were superb in their operation, indeed still are, until serious overhaul becomes necessary. The Simtran gearbox came in both single and two speed versions and was generally fitted in locomotives larger than the 20/28. It proved to be notoriously unreliable and thus could not be considered a successful venture.

Pressure for local manufacture was being actively exerted by the South African Director of Imports and arrangements were made for the appointment of N.F. Still as General Manager of the South African subsidiary. Negotiations were started with Lenning on the terms for the supply of locally made parts with agreement being reached in 1957. This did not preclude the possibility of other firms being set up to manufacture locomotives in South Africa and this had been realised and discussed. The large mining groups dominated the market and it is perhaps not surprising that one of these, Anglo Transvaal, should have contacted Motor Rail with a proposal that their Kimberley Engineering Works Ltd should build Simplex locomotives under licence. This idea seems to have been rejected and it is difficult to see how it could have been squared with, not only their agreement with Lenning, but also with their own operations in the country. The company thus remained committed to its connection with Lenning despite a proposal from that quarter to cancel the ongoing agreement and replace it with one of only four years duration.

At this distance in time, and with the wonderful benefit of hindsight, it does seem remarkable that Motor Rail did not appreciate the scale of the market in which they were involved and react accordingly. It is also very apparent that the company was not served as well as it might have been by Lenning, who seem to have always put their own interests in front of those of Motor Rail. By the same token, Lenning were possibly equally exasperated by the ponderous attitude in Bedford and, in particular, the slow deliveries of spare parts that resulted from it. In practice herein lies the snag with the simplicity of the Simplex locomotive – it is not a very complicated machine, and to 'reverse engineer' its component parts is not at all difficult for someone minded so to do. Thus to have seriously set about making spare parts, if not complete locomotives, in the country might have saved a great deal

of aggravation and created a useful profit even if it was not as high as that at home.

Following a visit by T.D. Abbott towards the end of 1958 he reported that sales of spare parts were being affected by the production of parts by 'pirate' firms encouraged by the high profit margins added by Motor Rail's distributors, i.e. Lenning. Although they agreed to reduce their mark-up to 55% on top of the imported prices and to 45% on 'pirated' components it served to illustrate the difference of interest between Motor Rail and Lenning. Certainly at a later stage, and there is no reason to think that it was different in 1958, Motor Rail's margin was 65% over their manufacturing costs leaving every opportunity for others to make a substantial profit by selling below Motor Rail/Lenning resale prices. A great deal of Motor Rail's profit came from the sale of spare parts and they naturally did not want any loss of this market. On the other hand, Lenning wished to charge as much as possible and their profit margins seem to have become excessive. However, and in fairness, it may well be that due to the size of the country and the monopolistic internal transport arrangements in South Africa they had to maintain stocks of spare parts in several different locations in order to provide an adequate service to their customers.

The divergence of interest seems to have mirrored changes in South Africa itself. In the immediate post war years worldwide shortages of both materials and finished products were accepted as the norm and long delays on imported equipment regarded in the same light. As a supplier of a machine for which there appeared to exist an insatiable demand, Lenning prospered along with their principals. Being strong on salesmanship and in direct contact with their customers they naturally wished to supply as much as possible to meet that need. They also diversified into the production of light railway material, notably wagons and turnouts. From an early stage in their relationship they urged the Abbots to extend their product range to include battery locomotives and to fit flame-proofing to the engines together with fluid coupling transmissions in order to meet the competition head on. Eventually Motor Rail did develop new designs as a result of the urging from both the mines and Lenning, but not until the company was under new ownership.

Fundamentally, Motor Rail were conservative in their outlook and not expansionist minded like Lenning. Aside from that, as

88. Loch Athlone, Orange Free State. This pleasure line of 18ins gauge used a Simplex from the De Beers stock believed to be MR 9305 of 1948. Little more is known of this line. *Courtesy John Middleton*

they were already working to capacity they could see no point in investing heavily in new products and new machinery. Their finances were always a bit delicate and very possibly they were in no position to do so. They were a family controlled firm and any major expansion would have been very likely to have meant loss of control. Having survived the hard days of the 1930s it is understandable that they may have been more cautious than Lenning, who were in the heady period of a mining boom. As regards their locomotives, they did not wish to sell anything that was not thoroughly sound and proven and believed that they could only ensure this if they developed their own designs of transmissions – otherwise they feared that their goodwill would suffer if bought-in components failed to be satisfactory in practice. This had happened to others, and indeed did happen to Motor Rail when they used Ruston hydraulic motors in U series locomotives for Canada (see Chapter 10). A further consideration was that they reckoned to make a profit on all that they manufactured so that, ipso facto, the more they could make in house the more profit they could accrue. The 'bomb proof' radiators fitted to their standard locomotives were a good case in point, where to the very end they refused to fit a standard automotive radiator. Where flame-proofing was concerned they would have expected to meet the standards of the so-called 'Buxton certificate' (because the certification was done in Buxton) which would have allowed their products to work in British coal mines. Whether South Africa required these same high standards would have been immaterial to their thinking. To Lenning, with a large and expanding market, this attitude must have been infuriating.

Among other firms 'pirating' spare parts for imported machinery was M & R Engineering (Pty) Ltd and this company is understood to have manufactured spares for Simplex locomotives. They then decided to design and produce their own range of locomotives, at least one of which showed a remarkable resemblance to a 3½ ton Simplex. Sometime before 1959 Lenning officially took over M & R, which firm continued to market their locomotives in competition with Motor Rail who believed this to be in breach of their agency agreement with Lenning. Accordingly they gave notice to terminate that agreement in May 1959. At the Rand Show held in Johannesburg at Easter that year a 3½ ton M & R locomotive was shown on the Perkins stand. Although manufactured by M & R it was admitted that the brake gear, wheels, axles and axleboxes followed Simplex practice (and may even have been such), as did the layout. The engine, however, was from Perkins, driving an epicyclic gearbox through a Brockhouse torque convertor and layshaft to the wheels. This may have been something of a ploy to divert attention from what was going on as sales literature from 1960 shows the locomotive with a Dorman 2LB engine. Concurrent leaflets for other types of M & R locomotives, but not this one, are wholly in Lenning name.

A further factor influencing Motor Rail's position was that they had received a number of complaints from customers about the price of spare parts and the standard of service that went with them. They believed that Lenning were not employing sufficient qualified engineers to provide the first class service that was being expected. It was an unfortunate situation, particularly since Lenning owed a substantial sum of money to Motor Rail that in turn became frozen in the dispute and subsequent litigation. The divisions became even wider when Motor Rail realised that Lenning were removing all Motor Rail identification from stock locomotives, having them repainted and then sold carrying their own plates! On the other hand, when relations were good between the two companies the situation was compounded by some locomotives leaving Bedford carrying Lenning plates.

Motor Rail then decided to operate through its subsidiary – Motor Rail Simplex (Pty) Ltd – which had been given an independent existence and locomotives were sent to them to be held as stock against future sales. A number of locomotives were sold in this way but there is no doubt that this company was at a great disadvantage in attempting to compete with Lenning in any of their various guises, not least because that company sold a wide variety of other products as well. The problems the company faced at home (see Chapter 8) were encapsulated in the problems in South Africa and exacerbated by Motor Rail not grasping the opportunities that it had been offered. By comparison, Hunslet Engine Co. Ltd of Leeds had joined forces with a local firm to create Hunslet Taylor (Pty) Ltd with a factory in South Africa. They were to reap the benefit of the trading conditions by providing the broad output that Lenning envisaged. Motor Rail's products were becoming somewhat dated as competitors adopted newer types of transmission. Even Ruston & Hornsby, a much larger company with the added advantage of making their own engines were forced to adopt new designs and by 1967 had decided to opt out of locomotive building altogether. Lenning had taken on the sales agencies for Orenstein & Koppel (who within a decade would give up their own railway business) and MAK, both from Germany, whose products did not compete with the Simplex range. They had also obtained the Dorman agency with the help of Motor Rail. Having acquired M & R they were also keen to extend their manufacturing activities to include locomotives. For the purposes of distribution they had offices in Johannesburg and Durban and operated through local agencies throughout South Africa and neighbouring countries.

In August 1960 an offer was made through the agents of an unidentified principal who wished to acquire an interest in Motor Rail. This does not appear to have been followed up although it is possible to hazard a connection with Lenning. In October of the same year a proposal to make Motor Rail dumpers under licence in South Africa was mooted with the licensee being Joy Sullivan (Africa) Pty Ltd, but like most such proposals nothing further seems to have happened even though it was reported six months later that the agreement was going ahead. It seems surprising that the works of Motor Rail Simplex was not coerced into doing this if it was to be done.

At the beginning of 1961 some form of settlement seems to have been made with Lenning although details are not known. The South African subsidiary was operating at a loss, its premises at Booysens Reserve, Johannesburg was under-utilised and Motor Rail was short of funds. This precipitated a decision and on 1st August that year Dowson & Dobson Ltd took over the agency for Simplex locomotives, and the plant of Motor Rail Simplex (Pty) Ltd, together with the stock of spare parts, was transferred to their works at Krugersdorp from which a few locomotives were produced. For the time being, at least, this appears to have been the end of Motor Rail's association with Lenning in South Africa. Possibly the only plus factor in all this convoluted story was a discount on the price of new engines negotiated with Dorman's following that firm's appointment of Lenning as a direct agent in South Africa.

# 7

# Post War Boom

## 1945–1965

With the cessation of munitions orders production switched to more normal lines but sales remained subject to Government approval. The pre-war designs ranged from 8/12hp narrow gauge model to the 20 ton 65/85 standard gauge shunter, with the plate frame 20/28 narrow gauge diesel being by far the most popular as well as being the workhorse supplied to the War Office. In December 1945 the company was approached by the Ministry of Supply regarding the disposal of its large stocks of locomotives and spare parts. A similar approach was also made to the other suppliers of diesel locomotives. This differed from the policy adopted after the First World War when it had taken much longer to commence the process and all disposals had gone to tender or auction. Profiting from past experience the Government had decided to come to an arrangement with each of its suppliers to buy back locomotives of their own manufacture for resale after any overhaul that might be necessary. By January 1946 Motor Rail had already ordered a dozen of these surplus locomotives with a further sixty-five bought in March. In addition to these locomotives their production plans then envisaged an output of twelve dumpers, four 32/42 and two 20/28 locomotives per month.

A new stores building measuring 112ft by 40ft was authorised in 1946 as was an extension to the steel store. In addition a new crane and machine tools were ordered. It should be noted that all machinery was in heavy demand and delivery times were often severely extended making production increases very difficult to achieve, which may have done nothing to help their problems in South Africa. Motor Rail was fortunate in its location in that Bedford had not suffered the war damage inflicted on London and other major cities. There may have been these problems on the production side but the sales office could sell everything that the works produced with little or no effort needed. Official encouragement was being given to exporters and during the next five years the emphasis was to be very much on overseas markets. By the early 1950s Motor Rail was exporting around 80% of a

89. A typical light railway scene in the later years of British industrial railways, in this case with J. & A. Jackson, brick and tile manufacturers, at their Rixton works, near Manchester in 1961. A 2½ ton 20/28 with a home-built cab and a couple of wagons. From the yoke brackets on the body these look as though there may be a rope worked incline somewhere in the system and is that a Motor Rail dumper in the background?
*Courtesy Frank Jux*

much-expanded locomotive output in contrast to 10%–20% before the war.

One of the major factors in this expansion was the demise of the German firm of Orenstein & Koppel who had supplied the world's light railway market before the war. The devastation of their country and its partition into East and West Germany had broken their grip on the market, not least because their main locomotive works had fallen within the communist Eastern Bloc.

Railway, Mine & Plantation Equipment Ltd was formed by A. Gloster (see Appendix VI) and first registered in 1945. His early activities in the field of light railways is unclear but certainly he was agent for Orenstein & Koppel. RMP and Lenning in South Africa soon began to appear as increasingly large customers for Simplex locomotives. Home sales were not ignored and the company obtained its fair share of orders for narrow gauge locomotives together with a small number of standard gauge shunters.

The Second World War, like its predecessor brought changes in its wake. Among the problems was the run-down state of the coal industry together with labour unrest following its nationalisation. This allied to increased demand for electricity brought power cuts and the company congratulated itself on having bought an emergency generator. With the employment of women in factories during the war conditions had changed and better amenities for workers was seen as necessary. Among improvements at Bedford was the opening of a canteen in September 1949 and heating and other facilities in the works were improved. The canteen gained an enviable reputation for the meals it served. With the emphasis on exports there was also a national awareness of a need to seek improved methods of production. The Americans had imported equipment into Britain during the war – such as paving machines and bulldozers used in airfield construction – that made the engineering industry rethink its attitude to its production methods. A British Productivity Council was set up and arrangements were made in 1950 for representatives from diesel locomotive manufacturers to visit the United States and study methods of production there. Their report encouraged firms to look critically at their own operations and to consider using work study methods (then a new concept) together with modern developments affecting fabrication, such as flame cutting and welded locomotive frames.

In general the industry felt that American manufacturers had the advantage of a larger home market where locomotives could realistically be produced on mass production lines that did not apply in this country where locomotives were more varied and custom made. Many components such as engines, wheels, castings and forgings were in any case bought in from outside suppliers and not made in their own works. In fact Motor Rail were probably ahead of their competitors in this respect as they had standardised designs which were built on something approaching production line methods. A reflection of the difficulties of British industry even in 1951 was the ordering of a milling machine at a cost of £1,727 with delivery promised for 1954!

J.D. Abbott became ill in 1948 and was given leave of absence that extended for twelve months into 1949. He seems to have returned to his duties after this and maybe it was indifferent health that caused him to take a further three months leave in December 1951. T.D. Abbott was Managing Director and in February 1951 he went on an extended visit to Africa which was expected to last six weeks. The company had exhibited at the Utrecht Fair in 1947,

possibly hoping to pick up some business in the reconstruction of Europe. Through RMP, J.D. Abbott had been deputed to report on potential business in Jamaica in 1948 but the directors do not seem to have acted as their own overseas salesmen and instead preferred to rely on their appointed agents to promote sales.

This was the normal method of operation for British firms at the time and Motor Rail/Simplex stayed with the system right to the end of their existence. It had the merit of making sales easy in that all the company had to do was to deliver the locomotive to the docks emblazoned with the right shipping mark, together with the right paperwork and then it became someone else's problem! The down side was that they often had no idea who the end user was, had no control over end prices and, perhaps most important, had no rapport with that end user. Thus the agent could (and not infrequently did) find an alternative supplier from whom he obtained a better price for his customer or a better mark-up for himself! Then the company suddenly lost sales in a particular area without ever really knowing why. There were also complicated sales agreements covering different 'territories' (or countries to most people) and for Simplex it came down to Wigglesworth for the East African countries, a few stated agents such as Carl Strom handling Scandinavia, Glastra, South America, Parry for the Indian sub-continent and with RMP covering the rest of the world. Indeed it is not now clear just where RMP and Lenning began and ended in South Africa. Despite always apparently wanting to 'play it by the book' as far as Motor Rail were concerned, RMP were not above playing one agent off against another within the same country! This was in direct contrast to the intense pre-war sales activities of Orenstein & Koppel who established their own branches in many overseas countries where stocks of their products were held. Motor Rail could not, of course, compete with this as they only built locomotives whereas O & K could, and did, supply the complete railway.

The company had now expanded greatly with output at three times its pre-war level. With J.D. Abbott perhaps looking towards retirement and there being a need for access to greater capital it was decided to convert the company from a private to a public company as from 26th April 1951. In June 1951 the share capital of £125,000 in £1 shares was subdivided into shares of 5 shillings (25p) each and an application was made for listing on the London Stock Exchange. Particulars were published in *The Times* and *Financial Times* on 30th July 1951. T.D. Abbott was given a service agreement as Managing Director for a minimum of five years, T. Beighton appointed Assistant General Manager, R.F. Williams as a Director, with the firm of Kimber Williams & Co. as the company registrars. The accounts for the year ended 20th March 1951 showed a profit of £21,099 with output a record in the history of the company. The listing particulars also gave details of the works and property, which were recorded as a single-storey factory with a two-storey office block and three dwelling houses all on a three acre site. In October 1952 it was decided to extend the main works buildings to a size of 78ft 6ins by 43ft 6ins at a cost of £5,650, and in November to buy a 15ton overhead crane for £3,638 with delivery promised in 44 weeks. (Whether this latter actually happened is debatable as for all those who were there it was always only a 10 ton crane and this produced some interesting logistics with larger locomotives in later years.) The board of directors remained as before comprising J.D. Abbott, T.D. Abbott, A.H. Brown and R.F. Williams, with a

J.A. Pullinger as Secretary and T. Beighton as assistant Secretary and, whilst the status of being a public company may have brought new responsibilities, the running of the business continued as before. In 1953 Pullinger resigned as Secretary due to ill health and Beighton took over the position; he was later to become Managing Director. Also during 1953 it was decided to relocate the canteen and Shell-Mex were given notice to vacate the garage rented to them so that this could be renovated and utilised. Shell did not move out until September 1954 when it was decided to add a dining room and ladies toilet to the plans.

One of the side effects of two world wars had been to increase the realisation in the Colonies and Dominions that it would be desirable for them to become much less dependant on imports and to increase production in their own industries. As early as 1926, Frank Saunders Ltd, Motor Rail's agents in Australia, had asked if they could be licensed to manufacture Simplex locomotives there, but this approach came to nothing. In June 1953 their then

agents in Australia, Marine & General Products Ltd, advised that they believed duty barriers might be imposed by the Australian Government in order to encourage local manufacture and asked whether Motor Rail would consider such a move. In the fullness of time such barriers were indeed imposed and anyone wishing to import goods to Australia had to prove that such goods could not be obtained locally. However, the company took the line that in view of the small number of locomotives exported to Australia they would decline any such proposition preferring to concentrate their activities in one place.

In April 1954 their Australian agents again brought the matter up and suggested that the frames, wheels and axles could be made in Australia. They would then assemble locomotives using other parts sent from Bedford. This suggestion followed the local manufacture of Jenbach locomotives by the Bundaburg Foundry with at least twelve units having been sold to the Queensland coal mines over the previous two years. Motor Rail seem to have conceded the fact

# DUKE & DUCHESS of GLOUCESTER TOUR FLOODED FEN DISTRICT ON TRAIN HAULED BY "SIMPLEX LOCOMOTIVE" 30ᵗʰ March 1947.
AP Photo.

90. This is another picture that was displayed in Motor Rail's offices for many years and again with Alan Keef Ltd. The East Anglian floods of 1947 were severe in the extreme and I remember as a small child being taken on a daily basis to see just how much nearer to home the water was going to come. The caption says it all, with the Duchess, a feather in her hat, to the right of the second wagon and the Duke in a flat cap to the right on the third. Motor Rail only built twenty-three of these 8/12hp locos, of which this is one of eight purchased by the Great Ouse River Board.

segmenttion

62    MOTOR RAIL LTD

91. In 1955 Sir Robert McAlpine Ltd were working on a marine test tank for the National Physical Laboratory at Faggs Rd, Feltham, London. Here are MR 5865 of 1934 and MR 8725 of 1941, both new to McAlpine, with two bogie well wagons, one of which is loaded with what is probably an empty concrete skip. *Courtesy Frank Jux*

that some steps were necessary to protect their overseas markets but, although they accepted this proposal in principle, again nothing seems to have come of the project. The record does not state if it was Bundaburg Foundry that was to make the Australian Simplex locomotives, but that company's relationship with Jenbach was fraught with many problems. They did, however, go into locomotive manufacturing in conjunction with Hunslet Engine Co. to build bogie locomotives for the Queensland cane fields in competition with the local firm of E.M. Baldwin Ltd. (Coincidentally this was at the time when Hunslet Engine Co. itself was being taken over by Jenbach!) These also had their problems and the firm later moved to converting both 3ft 6ins gauge and standard gauge locomotives of 700hp plus to 2ft gauge for cane haulage. In this they were much more successful. It seems that if and when a small locomotive was required the users preferred to buy direct from either Jenbach or Motor Rail.

In July 1953 the competition from G.W. Bungey Ltd was considered and the possible acquisition of that firm debated. Bungey was a dealer with workshops at Heston Airport, near London, who had an extensive trade in secondhand and reconditioned locomotives predominantly of either Ruston & Hornsby or Simplex manufacture. It appears that he had been exporting locomotives to South Africa via National Engineering (Pty) Ltd who were a subsidiary of A. Oppenheimer & Co. Ltd of London. It was thought that if the company was acquired it would allow Motor Rail to control sales to South Africa. It could also have been used as a United Kingdom sales agency, again using an agent rather than doing it themselves! Bungey would also take over the hire fleet, which in 1947 stood at twenty-seven locomotives, together with the overhaul of secondhand equipment. Negotiations continued for about nine months until an accountant's report on G.W. Bungey's trading results served to decide Motor Rail that such an acquisition would not be advantageous. In fact the use of narrow gauge diesel

locomotives in Britain had passed its peak and rail haulage was shortly to decline further in favour of conveyor belts and rubber tyred transport. Therefore Bungey's business, based on the demand for secondhand locomotives which had been strong since the War, declined with it. The firm had been a good customer of Motor Rail for spare parts and the contacts thus made resulted in Bungey erecting a few new Simplex locomotives in 1954 for export to South Africa. The exact circumstances are not known but it may be that the work done was to offset sums owing for spares. Certainly an insurance policy was taken out to cover credit advanced to Bungey.

There was an interesting contrast between Motor Rail's attitude to repairs and that of Bungey whose work was rather decried at Bedford, where the locomotives he sold were described as having been 'Bungeyed'! Motor Rail would, if asked, quote for an overhaul, but expected to return the locomotive in 'as new' condition – whereas Bungey would make no bones about the fact that he was offering the locomotive as secondhand. It had been overhauled and he would not replace any parts still considered serviceable. Similarly, locomotives would be re-gauged on their existing axles whilst Motor Rail always insisted upon supplying new axles.

An almost identical situation presented itself some thirty years later when Alan Keef Ltd appeared on the scene (see Chapter 11), including the building of two new locomotives. However, on this occasion the boot was then on the other foot and it was Alan Keef Ltd that took over Simplex Mechanical Handling Ltd, successors to Motor Rail Ltd. Even at this earlier stage it is apparent that Motor Rail were not geared up for, and did not really want, to get themselves involved in anything other than the building of new equipment. Had they been so inclined and willing to widen their horizons as to potential business then this history might have been very different.

Meanwhile in Bedford an order was given to an outside firm – Weldall & Assembly Ltd of Stourbridge – for the supply of sixteen

92. Taken in 1956 this is one of very few pictures of the works of George W. Bungey Ltd, Heston. In the foreground is an 8/12 model fitted with an Ailsa Craig engine and a large tank for cooling purposes. This would appear to have been bought from the Great Ouse River Board and is recorded as being with Boothby Peat Co. in Carlisle later that year. It is the same type of locomotive as that in Plate 90. The other locomotives are all 20/28s. There is no means of telling them apart but all have interesting histories. MR 8724 was new to Sir Robert McAlpine & Sons Ltd in 1941. MR 8992 of 1946 was a rebuild of MR 8888 (originally built for the War Office in 1944) for McAlpine, later reconditioned by Bungey in 1956 and sold to Diesel Loco Hirers, eventually going on to Furness Brick & Tile Co. in 1961. MR 8994 was a rebuild of another War Office loco, MR 8618 of 1941, again for McAlpine and again reconditioned by Bungey and sold to Diesel Loco Hirers. Perhaps selling locos to Diesel Loco Hirers was another means of Bungey paying his bills! *Courtesy Frank Jux*

93. Joseph Arnold & Sons Ltd, Leighton Buzzard, in 1955 with a very tidy 20/28, probably MR 4708 of 1935 (originally petrol but converted to diesel in 1945), their No. 33, at Billington Road washing plant. The wagon on the upper level has been interestingly modified and this is no doubt part of the washing process. *Courtesy Frank Jux*

94. These two pictures show the only 9 ton loco built for use in this country: MR 9010 of 1949 of 2ft 11ins gauge for London Brick Co. Ltd. The upper picture shows the locomotive when new at Stewartby works coupled to a pair of transporter wagons. These carried 2ft gauge wagons loaded with 'wet' bricks which were hand pushed on temporary tracks into the kilns where they were stacked for firing. *Courtesy Bedfordshire Archives*

95. The lower picture shows the locomotive in 1962 after transfer to Peterborough No. 1 works doing the same job but at an intermediate stage of development. Here the wagons have been floored over and the 'wet' bricks loaded on pallets so that they can be placed directly in the kiln without manual stacking. In due course forklifts took over the whole job and the railway was redundant. Perhaps ten years later Alan Keef bought a number of locos from LBC and always regretted not buying this one, but at the time did not realise its significance! *Courtesy G.P. Roberts per Frank Jux*

9 ton frames at £300 each. This may have been Motor Rail's first venture into welded frames and must have proved satisfactory as this was followed by the purchase of a Yates rocking type welding manipulator to allow welded manufacture in house. Employed by the company since 1940, B.J. Tysoe was then its Sales Engineer and it was decided that he should now concentrate on overseas sales with J. Stanway appointed for home sales. It was also decided to add another storey to the drawing office at a cost of £9.000. The company already owned some of the adjacent houses and in 1956 added to these with the purchase of 12 Elstow Road.

In July 1957 J.D. Abbott resigned due to ill health. Although his father had set up the company he was probably more active in the practical development of the original tramcar designs. His brother T.D. Abbott had borne the brunt of the day-to-day management at Bedford since the end of the First World War and now became Chairman. Beighton was appointed a Director in addition to his duties as Secretary and indeed was General Manager as well for a short period.

Competition was intensifying and further efforts were again made to set up some arrangement for local manufacture in Australia.

96. (*Above*) Works No. 8696 was built for McAlpine in 1941 and was rebuilt by Motor Rail in 1949 for onward sale to the Standard Bottle Co. Ltd, New Southgate, London. It is here seen on what seems to be a very cold December day in 1954, so much so that the radiator is covered over to keep the engine, and perhaps the driver, warm. After various vicissitudes it wound up back at Motor Rail by mistake. They were by then in no mood to rebuild it again and Alan Keef Ltd bought it from them. It was then fitted with a Deutz engine and went to White Moss Peat Co. near Liverpool.
*Courtesy Frank Jux*

97. This is possibly the last of this type of standard gauge locomotive built by Motor Rail with its direct links back to the 40hp tractors of the First World War. Works No. 9009 was built in 1949 for Tweedales Smalley (1920) Ltd of Rochdale, Lancashire, fitted with a 3DWD engine and classified as 40/56hp. Here it is preserved with the East Lancashire Railway Preservation Society at Bury.
*J.A. Peden. Collection Industrial Railway Society*

98. Motor Rail were a bit lacking in publicising themselves but they did produce this Christmas card (main image). It features the then new 50hp locomotive (later to be the 60S), the first four of which went to Eastwoods Ltd for both clay and 'wet' brick haulage at their works at Orton, near Peterborough and Kempston Hardwick just outside Bedford. Included inside is a dumper for good measure. The artwork, printed in black and dark green, is a stylised copy of photographs in contemporary sales leaflets!
*Courtesy Frank Jux*

Proposals here advanced to encompass agreement in principle to allow Commonwealth Engineering (Queensland) Pty Ltd to manufacture locomotives under licence. That none of these 'agreements in principle' for Australia resulted in locomotives being built there may be either that there was an adequate home supply with the Jenbachs mentioned above, or that the sugar cane industry in particular was moving rapidly on to locomotives far larger than anything Motor Rail could contemplate. Similarly in Brazil, proposals were made in 1958 for their local agents, Parsons & Crosland to build locomotives in that country. These were followed by an agreement with Parry for manufacture in India. Although there was little practical result from any of these efforts, the late 1950s and early 1960s were a critical time for the British locomotive industry. It was faced with a tide of change sweeping the world railway equipment market as emerging countries became industrialised and fostered local industry by raising tariff barriers.

A further indication of the pressures on the industry as a whole was an approach to Motor Rail early in 1959 from their competitors F.C. Hibberd & Co. Ltd offering to sell their business for £60,000. Under the 'Planet' brand name they had been more successful in developing standard gauge shunters than Motor Rail, whilst in addition they also produced industrial road tractors and their designs would have broadened the company's product range. They were also very much more in the 'build anything we are capable of' mould than were Motor Rail, including such possibilities as rebuilding steam locomotives with diesel engines. However, agreement could not be reached on price or on the alternative of a merger, and the two firms continued as before until Hibberd built their last locomotive in 1965, although the company was not wound up until 1979. This may or may not have been another missed opportunity. Coincidentally, Alan Keef Ltd acquired all the Hibberd drawings shortly after the take over of the Simplex business!

The position at home had also deteriorated as the post war boom receded into the past and competition increased both from other

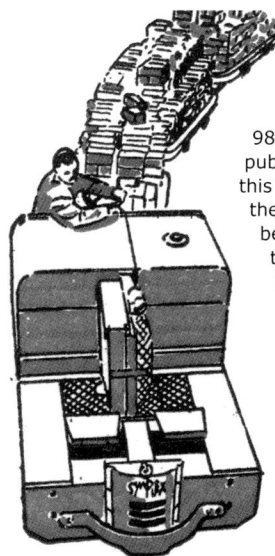

manufacturers and from alternative means of haulage. As Lenning had pointed out in 1951, there was increased price competition from Ruston & Hornsby in South Africa and this was reflected at home where, if anything, Ruston products had become cheaper. With their entirely hand operated controls, Ruston locomotives had the additional purely practical advantage in that they could be driven whilst the driver walked alongside. Not something one would want to do nowadays perhaps, but it did save on labour costs. The question of price is reflected in notes taken at a sales conference in 1960 when the following comments were made:

- 30hp locomotives. Demand not great and at least three orders lost on price, e.g. Leeds Corporation bought a Ruston for £1,254 as against our quote of £1,400.
- 50hp narrow gauge locomotives. Demand fallen off except for an order expected from Pilkingtons.
- 50hp shunter. Enquiries good and have not lost an order but demand limited for this size of loco.

99. This standard gauge shunter, MR 5766 of 1963, was ordered by C.A.E.C. Howard, a local firm of road hauliers who had many other interests, for a site at Tolworth Station in Surrey. It was presumably sold on by them to the National Coal Board who used it for the Coal Concentration Depots at Crawley and Southend-on-Sea before moving it on to Seaham Wagon Works in Northumberland. On 20th March 1987 it is seen with the last three wagons to be repaired at Seaham and it was scrapped there later that year. *P. Dawe, Colin Mountford collection*

- 14 ton shunter. Price too high at £5,530 as compared to other manufacturer's models with fluid couplings upon which customers now insist. Hibberd 77hp loco costs £6,300, Hunslet 71hp 13 ton model with hydraulic coupling, electric start, lighting and Westinghouse air brakes quoted at £5,300, Ruston 88DS 17 ton machine costs £6,000. Our locomotive too small for future requirements and needs upgrading.
- Dumpers. Salesmen like the MR4 model but the price is too high on the MR350.

Interestingly, and in the same year, the aforementioned M & R 3½ ton 'Simplex' locomotive, which is comparable with the first item on this list, was priced at £1,875 but at face value appears to be of a lesser specification, for example sanding gear is extra. This supports the notion that South Africa was prepared to pay more for home produced products.

This all reflected the rapidly changing market in the United Kingdom, which was in turn followed by similar conditions in the export market thus forcing the company to review its future. In time this led to a search for new products but by 1960 its continuing association with RMP was bringing in substantial orders from overseas, with Borneo and Malaysia becoming important markets. Despite this, total sales continued to decline to a level half that of the post war decade, in a trend that was shared with Ruston & Hornsby.

In May 1960 T.D. Abbott and the company's Chief Engineer, J.R.S. Lewis visited the works of Spoorijzer NV at Delft in Holland to examine the hydrostatic transmission used on locomotives being built by them. The visit was probably arranged through RMP who

had recently sold a Spoorijzer locomotive to Borneo. This firm also produced an 11hp locomotive with four or five being under construction at the time of the visit. However, the hydrostatic transmissions were used in larger locomotives that were fitted with Deutz engines up to 50hp. It was proposed that Spoorijzer fit one of their transmissions into a 20/28 Simplex locomotive which would then be sent to South Africa for tests but, as usual, nothing came of this. This may have been a sop to Lenning because one would have thought that it would have made more sense to have trialed such a loco nearer to home at, say, Leighton Buzzard. They may also have felt, probably rightly, that hydrostatics had nothing to offer over their tried and tested gearbox in this size of locomotive. Nevertheless one is left to wonder if there was any connection between this visit and the later production of the 12hp and G series locomotives, not to mention the eventual use of the Deutz engine as standard in most models.

Changes at home included a reduction in the working hours, with the works being reduced from 44 to 42 hours per week and the office staff from 39½ to 38½. Both worked a five day week with the works being open from 8.30am to 5pm, except on Fridays when work ceased at 4.30pm. The offices worked 8.30am to 5.30pm from Monday to Wednesday, and to 4.45pm on Thursday and Friday. Prices were also increased following a 7½% price rise for Dorman engines. However, as always, spares were the highest earner since they carried a higher profit margin.

The bi-annual Public Works Exhibition in November 1960 saw Motor Rail in attendance with their by now customary stand but there was little interest in their two locomotives and only the Lister engined dumper attracted any attention. Truly the era of being able

100. An unknown 32/42, of probably 1950s vintage, at Kiberanga sisal estate, Tanzania, in 'undressed' condition in 1990. This shows the principle of the Simplex locomotive that endured for so many years. The Dorman 2DL engine is obvious and as the fuel pump is missing one can assume that it is away for repair. The flywheel, which has the clutch inside it, can be seen, as can the belt drive to the radiator fan. The round fuel tank is prominent and the gearbox is below but not visible. The air cleaner rests on the locomotive behind and the drivers pan seat and cab floor, which are easily removable to give access to the drive chains below, are against the pillar. The bronze bearings in the axleboxes are part no. 30 in a list totalling some 200,000 items, so they have stood the test of time! The style of the fold-over engine covers are typical of the First World War 20hp tractors and suggest that this locomotive may have been supplied without a cab and that this is a later, local addition. Certainly the mesh cage on the roof, in which to carry tools etc. is not part of Motor Rail's remit. As the Tanzanian sisal industry, and particularly its railways, was in near terminal decline at this time the overhaul may never have been completed.

101. (*Above*) Large numbers of the 5½ ton 50hp locomotive (later the 60S) were sold through Wigglesworth to their own and other sisal estates in East Africa. This one is setting off on what could be a 10 mile haul at Lugongo Estate, near Tanga. These locomotives had the ability to haul more sisal but were particularly brutal to the lightly laid track and among many other factors contributed to the demise of the East African sisal railway. Alan Keef went to Tanzania a good deal in the early 1990s at the invitation of Wigglesworth and others to see what could be done to revive the rail systems but nothing significant came of it.

102. (*Left*) This plate came off a locomotive in the scrap line at Lugongo Estate and indicates how big a swathe of East Africa Wigglesworth served. Whilst the plate does not include a works number it makes clear as to where a customer should go for spare parts.

103. (*Left*) This photograph of a 12hp locomotive was used extensively for leaflets and publicity is well known, but its location at Bedford Silica Sand Mines Ltd at Heath and Reach on the outskirts of Leighton Buzzard is rather less so. We can presume that this was the prototype being trialed as the buffer is a fabrication and the locomotive itself seems to have been photographically touched up. Being unsprung these locos were not entirely suitable for the inevitably lightly laid track for which they were intended.

104. (*Below*) As proof that some of these 12hp locomotives were built, this one, MR 26014 of 1967 of 2ft 6ins gauge, is at the Solway Moss of Richardson's Moss Litter Co. Ltd (a peat operation) at Gretna, near Carlisle. Being hand start, audible warning in the form of a large gong may be a way of using up old stock from East India Tramways! Re-gauged to 15ins, this locomotive is still in use at the Perrygrove Railway in Gloucestershire.
*Courtesy Frank Jux*

to sell pretty well anything they made had come to an end. Ruston showed their LBU locomotive with exhaust quencher that was being featured in their South African advertising.

Following the resolution of the problems with South Africa generally and Lenning in particular, by 1961, and in the spirit of this rapprochement, most M & R locomotives appeared amongst the specifications offered by Motor Rail. The similarities are striking, as has been remarked in the last chapter. Most included torque convertor drive which it was claimed reduced chain wear due to lack of snatch loading. Whilst it seems that M & R used Perkins engines by choice, those offered from Bedford used the ubiquitous Dorman 2LB and 3LB. There had been at least some lateral thinking at M & R as evidenced by a very tidy 3½ ton design with longitudinal engine and only 3ft width. Around this time, perhaps again in the spirit of cooperation, Motor Rail tended to offer their locomotives as MR type 40 or 60 – or maybe it was done to confuse or encourage customers into thinking that it was all one outfit!

All this did little to immediately improve the company's finances. As a consequence, staff reductions together with a cessation of overtime were the order of the day with even the closure of the canteen being proposed in order to effect economies. The order situation was unsatisfactory with often barely enough orders in hand to cover a month's production which averaged £26,100 in 1962. General inflation did not help the company in world markets creating the need to constantly increase prices. With the aid of outside consultants the search for new products to manufacture under licence continued, with proposed lines including American floor washers, vibrating compactors and an Italian designed crane. The first positive steps towards the manufacture of other products came in the same year, when it was decided to import a Corvette industrial sweeper from Balayeuse Mathieu of Toul in France and to enter into a licensing agreement for their manufacture in Bedford (see Chapter 13). With all these other possibilities being

considered, the design of a hydrostatic drive locomotive (for which the company seems to have had little enthusiasm) was again deferred and, although occasionally mentioned, did not ultimately come to fruition until after a change of ownership.

The hire business had also declined and efforts were made to effect a merger of this department with an outside plant hire contractor. This was achieved in 1964 when Bedford Plant & Crane Hire Ltd was formed (see Chapter 12).

Some of the old wood and corrugated iron buildings formerly used as stores were demolished as being no longer required as the company shrank in size. Production for 1963 ran at about £28,000 per month, although this increase may have merely been accounted for by inflation. Despite this the future remained uncertain and a further firm of consultants was called in to recommend changes. Whilst it was a fashionable course of action at that time, it has to be debatable whether any outside firm could solve the problems facing Motor Rail. The company was tied to a declining industry although it is certainly doubtful if that was clear at the time. Since becoming a public company in 1951 it had been successful and had paid dividends up to 1959, but not since. Being relatively small it was in no position to raise new funds. The share capital was £250,000 that included £125,000 capitalised since 1951. What was needed was a major change of product and Motor Rail had neither the resources nor the expertise (nor, possibly, the will and imagination) to design and develop new products on its own. The main result of this consultant's report was a further round of redundancies.

The management in 1963 comprised T.D Abbott as Chairman, T. Beighton, Managing Director, A.J. Holley, Secretary and J.R. Abbott, Production Manager. Up until this time T.D. (Tom) Abbott had been actively involved in the management of the works despite his advancing years. Many employees had been with the company for decades, and as was traditional at the time, had brought their sons into the works for training. There was a strong family feeling between management and employees and it was intensely upsetting to have to make so many redundant; so much so that it is reputed that T.D. Abbott never visited the works again, leaving the day-to-day management entirely to his son. This may be one of those myths that arise in all businesses as there is correspondence dated to 1965 apparently signed by him.

On the locomotive side a small 10hp design was produced in 1963. This initially used the Lister SL2 engine with later versions using the SR2 of 15hp. Some twenty of these locomotives were built for a wide variety of UK and overseas customers. However, they were unsprung and therefore not ideally suitable for the uneven tracks they were likely to encounter. The design metamorphosed into the G series, which was altogether a more workmanlike design. The first fifteen of these, in 18ins gauge, went via RMP to Ghana State Goldmines and hence, reputedly, the G designation. Initially they were fitted with 17hp Enfield engines that apparently had very low emissions making them ideal for underground work, but later almost exclusively with Petter engines of 20hp. These locomotives achieved worldwide sales through RMP and some eighty-five were built.

105. (*Above*) There are a goodly number of pictures of the two G series supplied to Severn Trent Water for their Stoke-on-Trent sewerage works, some of which were used in publicity leaflets. This shows one of the locos a short while after delivery; it has had time to get dirty and have the headlight position changed, perhaps in 1978. See also Chapter 14.

106. (*Right*) In later years RMP had these plates fitted to not only Simplex locomotives but also to those they sold built by Baguley. Not very distinctive but maybe sufficient to point customers in their direction when spare parts were needed.

SUPPLIED BY

RMP

RAILWAY MINE & PLANTATION EQUIPMENT LTD

ROYAL LONDON HOUSE
22-25, FINSBURY SQUARE, LONDON, E.C.2.

In 1964 it was decided to develop a remotely controlled driverless locomotive and an outside firm – Tele(Techniks) Ltd – was engaged to undertake the necessary work with a light 20hp locomotive being loaned to them for the purpose. It is not clear just what market this was intended to tap and it may have been undertaken in an attempt to anticipate future developments. It probably came too late to make any significant difference, in much the same way as the development of the Hydrotip wagon by Alan Keef Ltd. (This latter used the locomotive hydraulics to tip the wagons in the train behind it.) The sum of £2,000 was voted towards the project in 1964, this being increased to £5,000 the following year. These were substantial figures and in today's term represent £34,000 and £82,000 respectively. Presumably this was justified by proposals put forward by T.D. Abbott for a wholly automated railway for Eastwoods Flettons Ltd, initially for their works at Kempston Hardwick, conveniently close to Bedford, but also for the works at Peterborough. It seems that two locomotives that do not appear in the records were used as guinea pigs for this project (24511 and 12061, 40hp and 60hp respectively), and that practical on-site experiment reached the point of the project being approved by the Mines and Quarries Inspectorate. The system was intended to supply 150 tons of clay per hour to the works and was thus necessarily elaborate. It included a road crossing, presumably internal, and was to have up to five trains in operation at any one time. Allowance was made for insertion of driver operated trains into the system to cope with surges in production if required. In this instance the electronics were developed by Telearchics of Gloucestershire. Sadly it come to nothing as the result would have been impressive and it was perhaps T.D. Abbott's swan song for Motor Rail. It was also one of the few attempts by the light railway industry to fight back against other forms of materials handling but, even then, was customer rather than industry driven.

However, the idea did not die there and offers were made to the Ministry of Defence for standard gauge target trolleys using the driverless system thus developed. This also came to nothing but the idea was continued into the mining industry as will be seen in the next chapter. Much later the Catron system of remote control was used by Alan Keef Ltd for passenger trains to obviate the necessity of running the locomotive round its train at the terminus of a single track line.

Meanwhile, circumstances in South Africa had not improved. The original agreement with Dowson & Dobson had been extended until the end of April 1964 but it did not result in any great change to Motor Rail's fortunes in that country. Dowson & Dobson appear to have mainly sold spares and a few locomotives that may have already been in the country. Sales of new locomotives virtually dried up in the face of competition from Lenning and other local manufacturers. The relationship with Lenning seems to have changed as Motor Rail's position weakened. In September 1963 it was proposed that a joint company be set up to handle Simplex business in Rhodesia and this was later formed as Northland Engineering Co. Ltd. This was followed in March 1964 by an agreement for Lenning to once again take over the spares agency and to buy the stocks of spare parts held by Dowson & Dodson. This may have reflected Motor Rail's precarious financial situation. It must have been humiliating to be forced to accept, as a condition of this agreement, that they would withdraw from the South African market in respect of sales of new locomotives and spares for

a period of fifteen years, thus locking themselves out of seriously important business. One has to ask how Motor Rail got themselves into this position where Lenning seem to have had total control over them. Blackmail in some form hardly seems too strong a word! Like the proverbial bad penny, whatever they tried and however they tried it, Lenning always appear to have been in the frame somewhere.

It was accepted that new designs were needed and both T.D. Abbott and the drawing office staff were asked to submit proposals. Lenning (again!), and its chairman B.T. Tessel, had big ambitions that were perhaps justified in the rapidly expanding South African economy. Despite these ongoing problems, fluorescent lighting was installed in the fitting shop together with the purchase of spray painting equipment and other items of machinery. Even as the diversification programme proceeded (see Chapter 13) things were still not going well and the Chief Engineer, J.R. Lewis was given notice.

It was decided not to produce any more dumpers unless specifically authorised by the directors, this despite the fact that dumpers appear as a significant source of revenue in a spreadsheet of 1966. Once again it is difficult not to be critical. As established manufacturers of what generally appears to have been a successful machine they were in an ideal position to enter a whole new market for dumpers large and small, particularly the latter for the growing building and hire market. This was of course done by the likes of Benford and Thwaites. They probably viewed the market as being for the bulk transport of materials and, if they had wanted, that market could have been available to them also. Alternatively, it may well be that they were mentally unable to scale down the quality of their products for a short life and a gay one, with replacement being made after only a few years use rather than an ongoing supply of spare parts.

107. It is by no means certain just when this style of logo was introduced, but early 1960s is best guess. It is certainly quite inspired and was used on leaflets and locomotives for a considerable time after Motor Rail itself had ceased to exist. There were indeed some around at the time of the final auction but they did not appear in it.

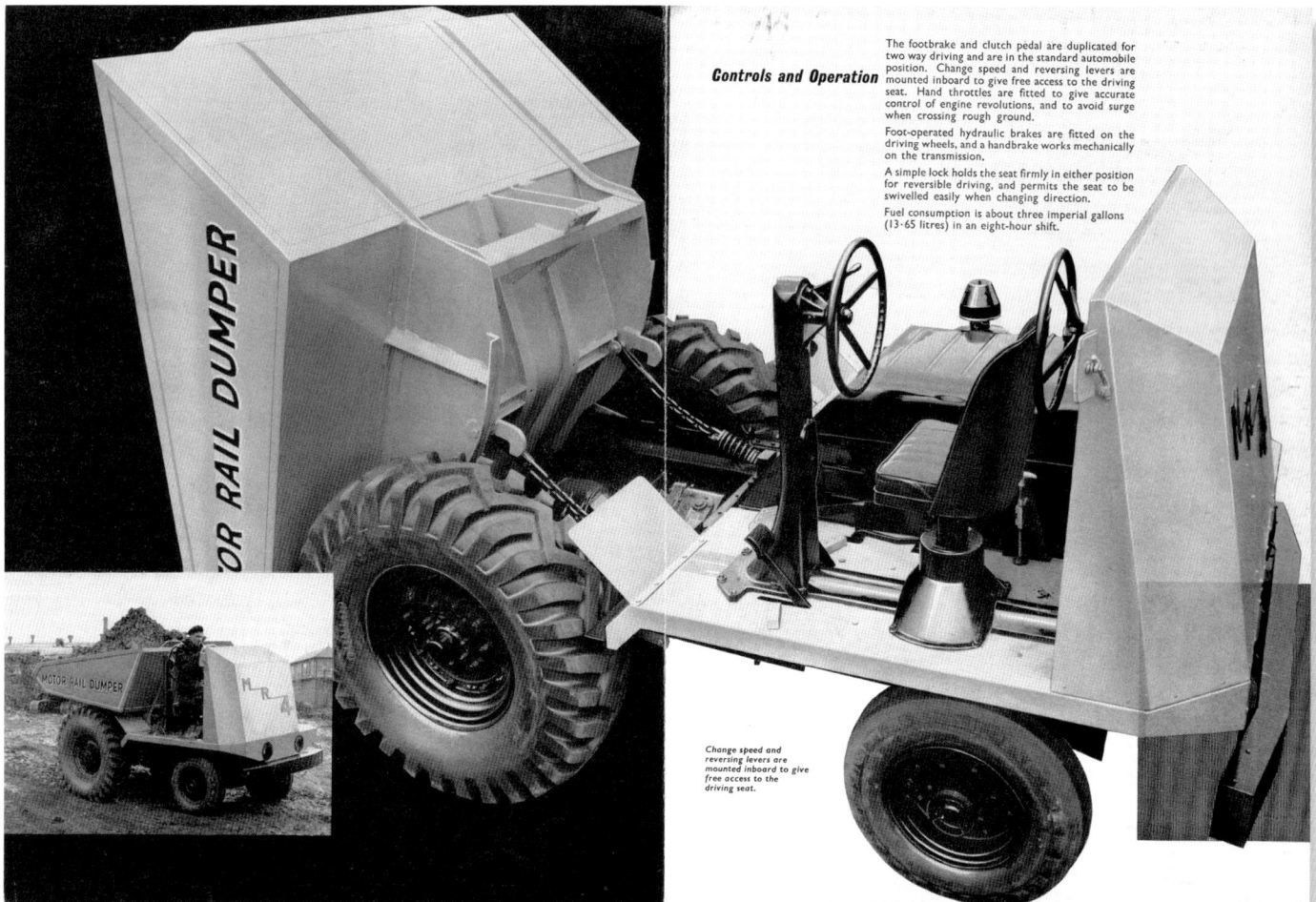

**Controls and Operation**

The footbrake and clutch pedal are duplicated for two way driving and are in the standard automobile position. Change speed and reversing levers are mounted inboard to give free access to the driving seat. Hand throttles are fitted to give accurate control of engine revolutions, and to avoid surge when crossing rough ground.

Foot-operated hydraulic brakes are fitted on the driving wheels, and a handbrake works mechanically on the transmission.

A simple lock holds the seat firmly in either position for reversible driving, and permits the seat to be swivelled easily when changing direction.

Fuel consumption is about three imperial gallons (13·65 litres) in an eight-hour shift.

*Change speed and reversing levers are mounted inboard to give free access to the driving seat.*

108. The MR 4 was the workhorse of dumper production at this time and the nature of its construction and arrangement of the controls can be gauged from this leaflet dated for 1959. The usual Dorman air cleaner cowl confirms it is fitted with a 2LB engine together with the standard Simplex flywheel/clutch assembly and 3-speed gearbox. The vertical steering wheels and reversible seat are very prominent. With no steps, getting in and out of the driver's position would have required some agility!

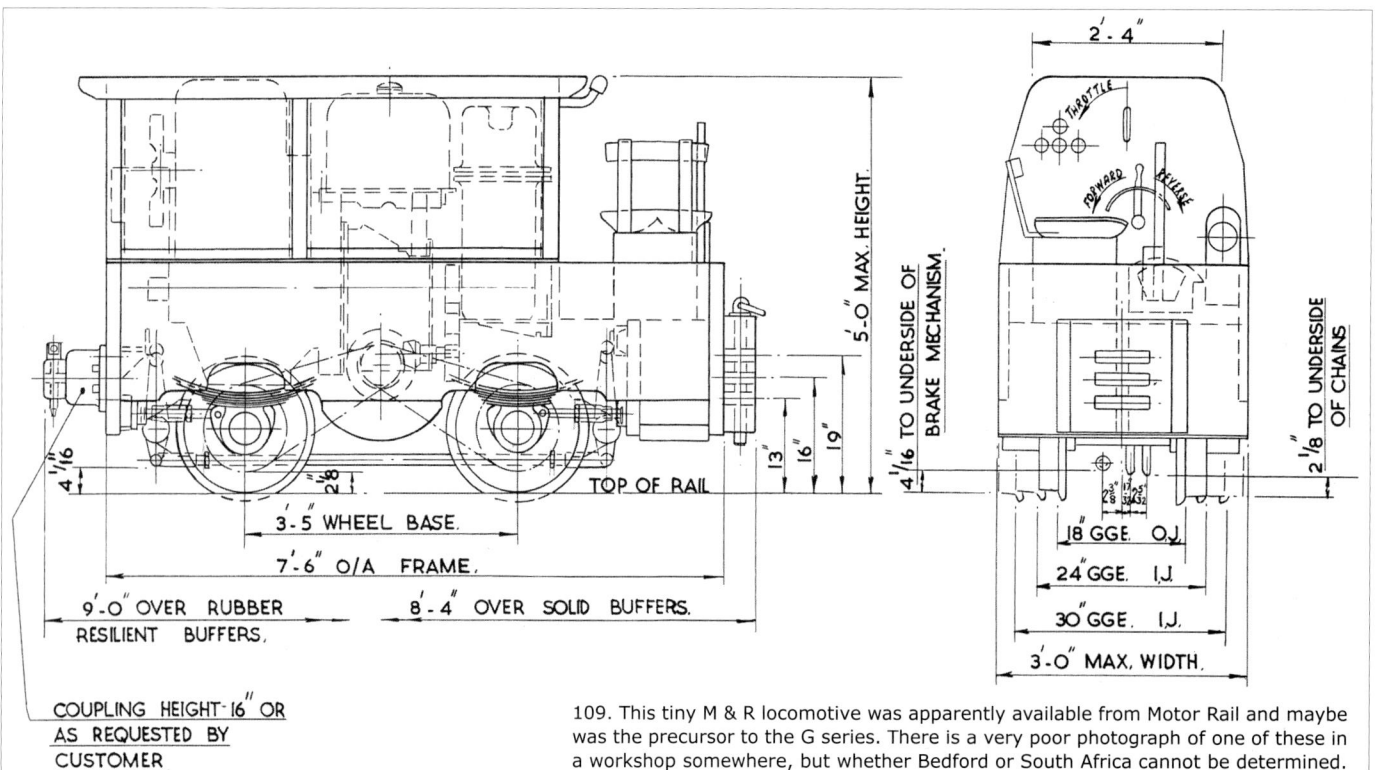

109. This tiny M & R locomotive was apparently available from Motor Rail and maybe was the precursor to the G series. There is a very poor photograph of one of these in a workshop somewhere, but whether Bedford or South Africa cannot be determined.

# 8

# New Owners

## 1965–1972

The value of the company's shares had slumped and in March 1965 an offer to acquire a controlling interest in the company at a price of 4s 6d (22½p) per share was received. This was from a firm named Loco Holdings Ltd, registered in Dublin but in fact controlled by Lenning. Whether they knew this fact at the time or not, the approach was accepted by the directors and the offer then extended to all shareholders. The directors and their families held some 455,000 of the one million shares issued and the offer was also accepted by the owners of over 150,000 shares held outside the family. This enabled the offer to be made unconditional and J.D. Abbott, J.R. Abbott and R.F. Williams resigned, thus terminating the Abbott family's connection with the company they had founded. The directors of the South African subsidiary also resigned with both companies thereafter being controlled by Lenning. Although this does not quite fit with Dowson & Dobson having taken over the activities of Motor Rail Simplex (Pte) Ltd it does seem that the latter was kept as a non-manufacturing entity in an effort to protect Motor Rail's interests in South Africa. To fill the vacancies, N.F Benjamin (Lenning) and P.W. May (a former Sales Director of RMP) were appointed as well as R.V. Wood of Noble, Lowndes & Partners. T. Beighton continued for a short period as Managing Director but was soon replaced by R.A. Wenham (a former Sales Director of the locomotive builders W.G. Bagnall Ltd, but who came to Motor Rail from David Brown Industries Ltd).

The effect of the new ownership was immediate. It would seem that Lenning viewed their new acquisition as a means of allowing them to break out of the strictures of South Africa onto the world stage. Unsurprisingly, the new locomotives envisaged followed the lines of their M & R designs and included the products that they had been trying to get Motor Rail to build over the past many years. Lenning's Managing Director, W. Hoadley, was present at the planning meetings held at the beginning of both June and July 1965 and their chief engineer, George Webster, was sent to Bedford to take charge of the drawing office. As recorded in the minutes, their deliberations may be summarised as follows:

- UNILOK. Following a visit to Hugo Aeckerle in Hamburg by Mr Hoadley, it was believed that the Unilok locomotive had a large potential in the UK and the possibility of manufacture should be followed up. RMP had the sales agency for this country and Motor Rail was trying to get them to relinquish this. At this stage the Unilok may have been something new to Lenning although they went on to build over 250 of them under license in South Africa between 1966 and 1982 (see Chapter 13).
- LENNING LOADERS. An assessment of the UK market for these was to be made.
- CLARKE PRODUCTS. The agreement with Studebaker International was considered burdensome and should be

110. At the other end of the scale, this design came with the Lenning takeover and was theoretically offered as the K series. It was obviously intended for the South African market as it was only available from 2ft to 3ft 6ins gauge. The Motor Rail design of 15–20 tons and 150hp was smaller but otherwise identical to this Lenning beast that tipped the scale at 28 tons and 269hp. Three were built by them and this one is at the BCL Selebi-Pikwe Nickel Mine in Botswana and at the time of writing is still in use.
*Courtesy John Middleton.*

111. One of the main thrusts of the Lenning takeover was the production of a hydraulic drive locomotive and the first was built a year later in 1966 and went to Canada. A year after that MR 114U004 was despatched to Ulu Remis Estate, Layang-Layang, Johor, Malaysia for hauling palm oil fruits. The establishment was a Ruston & Hornsby stronghold and this was obviously an attempt to break in. As a consequence this 700mm gauge locomotive was fitted with a Ruston 3YDA engine of 61hp but as this was the only one of its type built one must assume that the experiment was not successful. The picture is undated but from appearances one can assume a few years after delivery.

112. This is one of a series of Motor Rail pictures taken on an unidentified palm oil estate in Malaysia. The locomotive is a 2½ ton 40S, possibly of 1969 vintage. For this purpose it is slightly unusual as most palm oil estate locos were weighted to 4½ tons to give better adhesion on tracks that were inevitably covered in oil! The overall roof may be original but is more likely added locally. The track looks good with what appear to be concrete sleepers. These railways still exist and some claim to have no less than 500km of track attached to them.

renegotiated. In due course it was probably terminated as sales of Corvette sweepers proved simpler and more profitable.
- HIRE FLEET. To be sold off gradually. How this decision fitted with the formation of Bedford Plant & Crane Hire Ltd the previous year is unclear.
- NEW DESIGNS
  - A prototype hydrostatic loco to be built by October 1965. Up to £1,000 was allocated for use of an outside drawing office to develop the design. One presumes that the company had insufficient staff to achieve this within the required time frame. According to Motor Rail lore they only concerned themselves with the aesthetics of the machine leaving the mechanical design to Motor Rail's own staff!
  - A prototype battery loco to be built by November 1965.
  - The driverless locomotive project to be continued.
  - A Mark 2 version of the Corvette sweeper to be produced. It never was.
  - A flame proof 56hp loco to be produced. It never was.

- The 12hp design to be converted to hydrostatic drive. It never was.
- A cheaper version of the MR375 dumper to be developed. No serious effort was put into this and the decision to abandon dumper production held – up to a point.
- New plant and tooling to be purchased including welding sets and metric tooling for Matisa products (see Chapter 13).

The problem with the Lenning loading shovels was that they were generally very similar to the much-used Eimco product. These were used in both tunnelling and mining work and were operated by compressed air from a trailing air hose. At the 'end of track' the bucket was driven into the pile of blasted rock and the machine effectively 'threw it over its shoulder' with the contents going into a wagon standing behind. They could also slew sideways in both directions to clear a wide enough path for locomotives to follow. In the confines of a small tunnel they can be an alarming machine to watch in use, not to mention the noise that goes with them!

The only known user of Lenning loading shovels in Europe was Mogul of Ireland Ltd at Silvermines in County Tipperary for which a pair of 3ft gauge U series locomotives were later supplied. Virtually all the other underground rail equipment at this mine, including locomotives, had been supplied by Lenning. It was intended to design a machine with a higher capacity than the Lenning unit but with no first-hand experience of mining machinery this would have proved a difficult project. With Eimco already well established in Great Britain for a market which was limited by the very small amount of either rock tunnelling or hard rock mining taking place, to have broken into that market would have been nigh impossible. Thus rocking shovels did not become a line of production.

Before moving on to the new locomotives developed under the aegis of their new owners it is necessary to distinguish between the two drive arrangements used by Motor Rail. Both tend to be described as 'hydraulic drive' but are in fact very different. These were classified as hydrostatic and hydrokinetic and either could be supplied in both the U series and the later T series to suit customers preferences.

The hydrostatic drive is, as its name suggests, a hydraulic system usually configured with a variable pitch swash plate pump driving a fixed displacement motor which in turn operates whatever is required, in this case driving a locomotive along the track. The driver has control of the amount of oil the pump passes which in turn controls the speed of the motor and thus the train. Power from the engine is added to start the load, climb a hill or simply travel faster. In this form Motor Rail used a Dowty variable displacement pump (as did Ruston & Hornsby), initially driving a Ruston hydraulic motor with Staffa later becoming the standard. The final drive to the axles was with roller chains from the motor shaft, normally with at least a 2:1 reduction ratio. As mentioned previously, they had considerable problems with the Ruston motors (of which more in Chapter 10) and several different makes were tried.

The hydrokinetic system was basically what Lenning had been clamouring for all along and consisted of a fluid flywheel attached to the engine flywheel which gave a 'soft' take-up allied to engine speed driving a 2-speed Twin Disc transmission unit with reverse to both gears. A drop box of Motor Rail manufacture was fitted behind the Twin Disc unit with a cardan shaft drive to a right-angle

113. Charlcote Gravel Pits, Warwickshire. For environmental reasons this traditional gravel pit railway lasted until 1977, much longer than most of its kind. This undated shot from the Motor Rail archives shows two trains passing at an intermediate loop. The left hand loco is a rare 3½ ton Perkins engined 40SP and the other a 20/28 that has been re-engined with a Deutz air cooled engine. From the cloud of exhaust the latter would seem to be in need of some attention but it does at least suggest that the train is being pushed!

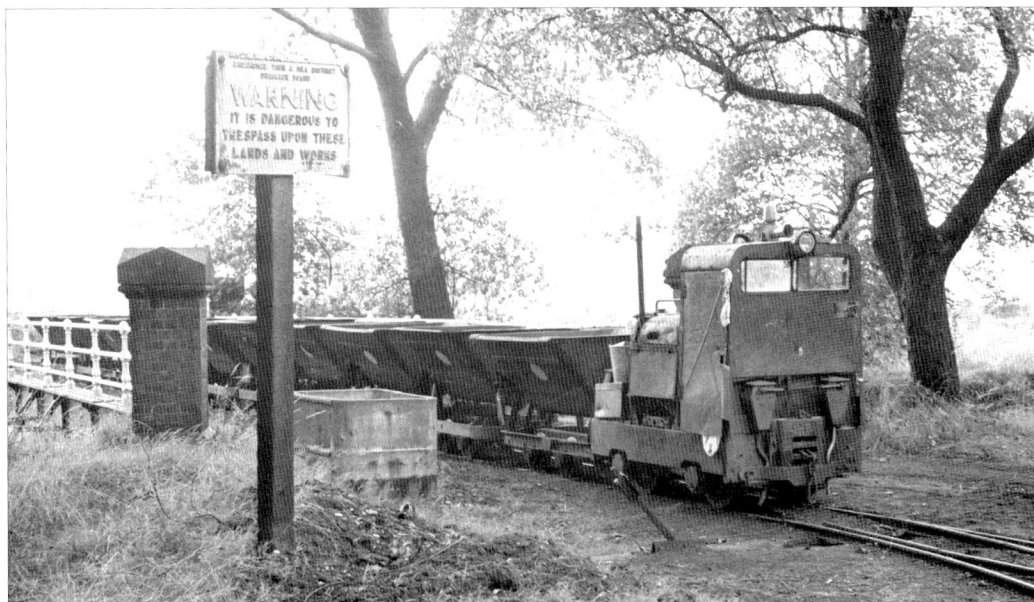

114. MR 22221 of 1964, a 2½ ton 40S, with a train of empty wagons photographed in 1976 in an apparently rural situation, but actually on the edge of Birmingham. This was the very extensive system that served the settlement beds in the sewerage works of Birmingham, Tame & Rea Drainage Board but by this time was part of Severn Trent Water. This organisation was possibly Motor Rail's largest regular UK customer for new locomotives at the time.
*A.J. Booth. Collection Industrial Railway Society*

115. This works photograph of a nearly completed H series locomotive demonstrates how it was intended to 'fold up' for lowering down a mine shaft. It was of 3ft gauge, weighed 3½ tons and was despatched to the Canadian nickel mines in 1969. The insulated exhaust pipe can be seen above, and the catalytic exhaust conditioner below the alternator of the Deutz engine.

drive box (again of their own make) and their well tried chain drive to the axles. Certainly in the T series at least, this right-angle drive box was the Achilles heel of an otherwise good locomotive in that the fixing to the frame was insufficiently substantial for the power of these larger locomotives and it tended to work loose with potentially disastrous results.

The use of the term hydrokinetic for this type of drive seems to have been restricted to Motor Rail (M & R termed it 'hydro-dynamic') whilst hydrostatic was, and still is, a normal term for that type of hydraulic transmission. In the case of the hydrokinetic transmission there does not appear to have been any attempt to use a drive box on each axle with shaft drive direct to them. There are occasional instances of the U series being offered thus, but it was very half hearted. This arrangement was later developed by Alan Keef Ltd and would transform the hydrostatic T series locomotives supplied to East Africa.

A further Lenning innovation was a change in the numbering system of locomotives and other products. Each model was given a category followed by the number within that category. Thus, for example, what was the 20/28, by this time fitted with the Dorman L series engines of up to 48hp became the 40S and later the 40SD when Deutz engines became standard, even though the numbering remained consecutive. There were many variations of the U series in particular.

The first prototype hydrostatic drive locomotive was not finished until December 1966 and was classified as the 40H. It had an in-line Dorman 4DA engine and the conventional chain drive to the wheels. From photographs it may have been slightly narrower than the conventional 20/28, which would have been a wish of Lenning's for underground working. It was sold through Carl Strom AB, the Motor Rail agents in Sweden, to Nya Asfalt AB for a tunnelling contract in the north of that country. It was the only one of its type to be built, and therefore not to be confused with the later

H series. These were a very compact mining locomotive arranged so that the driver's compartment would fold over the engine covers to allow the machine to be dropped down a very small mine shaft. Four were built with Deutz engines and all went to International Nickel in Canada. One other was built for the Lochaber Railway of the British Aluminium Co. Ltd and was arranged to use the hydraulics to drive a ballast tamper. The experience thus gained was subsequently developed into the U series locomotives proper.

No battery locomotives were ever produced although the company dallied with the idea on a continuous basis over many years. The reason was no doubt fundamentally commercial and not dissimilar to the problems with loading shovels. There were basically three builders of battery locomotives in UK: Greenwood & Batley (later part of Hunslet), Clayton Equipment, and Wingrove & Rogers (BEV). Greenbat had the market for the military and the National Coal Board, while Clayton and Wingrove competed for the UK tunnelling industry with Clayton probably in the ascendant. Wingrove also had a large market in the South American mining industry, to the point that most of their sales literature was also in Spanish! Thus Motor Rail would have had to break into a market that was already well catered for and possibly already had a surplus of production capacity. As will be seen, the South African market was already well supplied so there was no point in Lenning trying to export into their own home market.

Despite this, the driverless locomotive project went ahead and by August 1971 a prototype radio control system had been developed. Initially this was in conjunction with their consultants, Humphris & Hughes, but was actually brought to fruition by their own employee, Chris Bashford.

The locomotive was controlled from a unit carried by the operator who obviously did not need to ride upon it. Because of the twisting nature of mine tunnels the signals were carried by a guide wire laid alongside the track and picked up by a unit on the locomotive.

116. Remote control locomotive 123U117 on trial at Leighton Buzzard in June 1973. Here it is carrying out the sort of duty for which it was intended, pulling wagons under the loading conveyor as required. In this case it is probably being 'driven' by the person standing at left, but in practice it would have been moved forward by the operator of the conveyor system. The locomotive is very shiny and new but the idea came too late to have an impact on the light railway scene.

117. (*Right*) The remote control prototype was ultimately converted to metre gauge and used at Newport sewage works in South Wales. From there it went to Talywain Garden Centre & Building Products for use on a passenger railway. It is doubtful if this ever operated but it at least got as far as this. It is believed that the locomotive still exists buried under a heap of scrap in the same locality!

118. (*Below*) Mr Glastra and Mr Wenham in the latter's office at Bedford in February 1970. Glastra were Motor Rail's agents in Argentina and when, in 2000, Alan Keef Ltd supplied a tourist railway to the Iguazu Falls, that company laid the track. The world of small railways is very small indeed!

119. This aluminium works plate would have been fitted to locomotives supplied to Glastra with the works number stamped into the raised middle section. On the back of this plate are written instruction of exactly where it is to be fitted.

This latter is believed to have been a commercial decision because whilst straight radio control would have been possible, it required considerable further development at that time. To have to lay another wire alongside or above the track was a considerable expense for users that would tend to annul any advantages gained, not to mention the cost of maintenance and protecting it from damage. U series locomotive 121U117 was fitted with this equipment and the system was successfully tested in 1972 on very steep gradients at the Blackdene fluorspar mine of the British Steel Corporation during the mine's annual shutdown. All concerned were impressed with the results achieved. Tests were also carried out at Leighton Buzzard where the tracks of the sand companies and of the Leighton Buzzard Light Railway had been made available to the company for the testing of new locomotives over many years. (Less than 20 miles from Bedford this was something of a Simplex 'stronghold' with well over a 100 locomotives having been in use there over the years.) However, despite their best endeavours no locomotives of this type were ever sold and the test locomotive was finally sold as a standard model without its radio control equipment and after conversion to metre gauge went to Newport Sewage Works at Uskmouth, Wales.

An interesting venture at this time was the production of an illustrated in-house journal entitled 'On the Track'. The first edition appeared in April 1968 and erratically thereafter until December 1972. Its purpose is now a little difficult to divine but it was probably intended as a morale booster after the turmoil of recent years. Whilst it did contain relevant information about the doings of the company, most of its content was chatty comments about the staff and quite lengthy details of some of their holidays. All the same, there is some relevant information to be gleaned from its pages. For instance:

| | |
|---|---|
| April 1968 | 35 locomotives on order. |
| August 1968 | 27 locomotives on order and the takeover of the Low Loading Trailer Co. is announced. |
| December 1968 | 16 locomotives and 1 dumper on order, plus trailers to the value of £52,000. |
| May 1969 | 26 locomotives, 1 Thumper, and trailers valued at £27,500. |
| August 1969 | 27 locomotives, and trailers valued at £30,000. This was the year the company achieved its |

120. This is either MR 22031 or MR 22032 of 1959, with both having been part of a batch of nine 4½ ton locomotives for Mitchell Construction. They are believed to have been used on the Morar Dam in the far north of Scotland. However, in 1972 they were still together and at work with A. Waddington Ltd on a drainage contract at Farningham, Kent in what is a typical contractor's scene of the period.

121. Standard gauge 8 ton shunter SMH 9933 was supplied to Booker Sugar, Guyana in 1974. In 2014 it was still doing its job of hauling containers of bulk sugar to the jetty for shipment. These containers are there lifted off their wagons and emptied into storage bins to await the arrival of a ship. This sugar mill is unusual in that the cut cane is brought to it, not by rail but by small barges known locally as punts.

*Courtesy Thomas Kautzor*

Queen's Award to Industry for Export Achievement and this issue is, understandably, largely taken up with that.

December 1969  21 locomotives on order. Trailer sales not recorded. It also records John Palmer joining the company from Brush; he went on to work for Alan Keef Ltd until his retirement.

April 1970  No sales records at all but the takeover of manufacturing fork lift attachments from Oldham & Son Ltd is announced.

April 1971  38 locomotives and 100 trailers on order.

August 1971  Locomotive orders described as 'substantial' together with 100 trailers and fork lift attachments beginning to come to the fore.

June 1972  41 locomotives, 250 trailers and 540 attachments recorded.

December 1972  (The last issue.) No specific record of orders but the spotlight placed very much on trailers.

It would be unkind and unfair to say that the figures were massaged but the numbers of all products probably included those that had not been completed from the previous issue; for example, the twenty-one locomotives given for December 1969 may well have included any not completed from the twenty-seven in August 1969. Nevertheless, a good indication is given of just how the business of the company was changing away from its roots in narrow gauge diesel locomotives.

After Ruston & Hornsby ceased building locomotives the company claimed to be the world's largest producer of narrow gauge locomotives, a claim that is debatable, to say the least! Nevertheless the search for new products continued.

A licence from an American firm to produce a road breaking device known as the 'Thumper' was agreed and a number of these were produced and sold (see Chapter 13). In the same year, 1968, the locally based Low Loading Trailer Co. Ltd, with offices in Dean Street, Bedford, was acquired (see also Chapter 13). The company also undertook development work on brick handling equipment for London Brick Co. Ltd who were at that time considerable users of Simplex locomotives.

Certainly under Lenning's control the range of locomotives had been modernised and upgraded, the culmination of which was without doubt the 10-14 ton T series of up to 120hp. Although obviously intended for the mining market, none of the locomotives of this type built ever worked underground! There are also drawings for a proposed K series locomotive of 150/200hp and 17/20 tons weight. Curiously, this was envisaged as only being built up to 3ft 6ins gauge and not as a standard gauge shunter, although Lenning may have seen it as that for South Africa where the main line system is of that gauge. It could be supplied in either 0-4-0 or 0-6-0 configuration. Whilst it is in the Simplex files, this locomotive also appears in an M & R specification book rated at 27 tons and 270hp, and Lenning themselves did in fact build a few for the South African market. It was obviously one of their products that had strayed to Bedford.

However, whilst the company was busy, it never produced large profits and at the height of a stock market boom in 1972 an approach was made to buy Lenning's controlling interest. They agreed to sell.

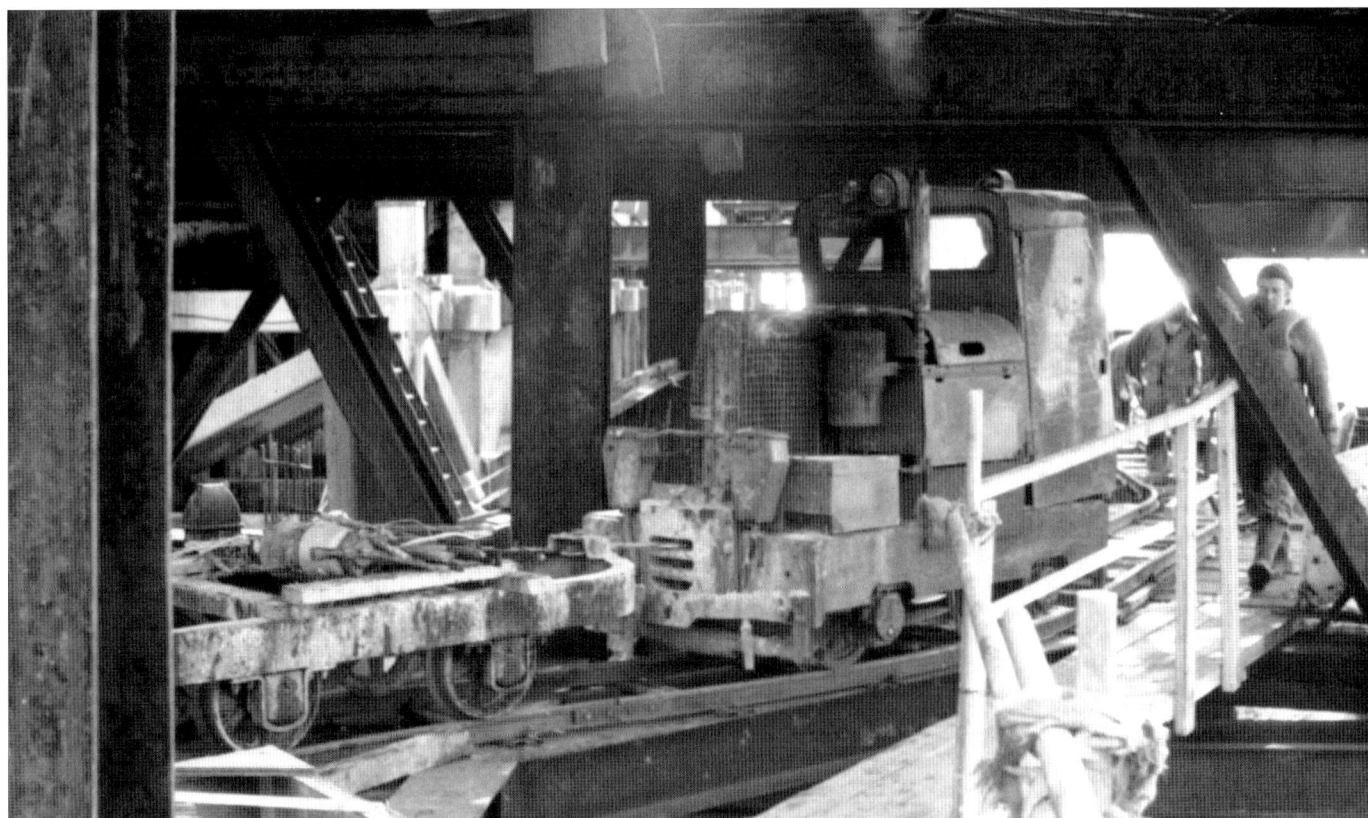

122. This is either MR 22237 or MR 22239 of 1965 working on the rebuilding of Bournemouth Pier in 1979 for the contractors Christiani & Nielson and on hire from Alan Keef Ltd. Both were originally built for Severn Trent Water Authority. One went on to a similar contract in the North East for May Gurney and the other was sold to a peat operation in Denmark.

# Plan of Motor Rail Works, Bedford

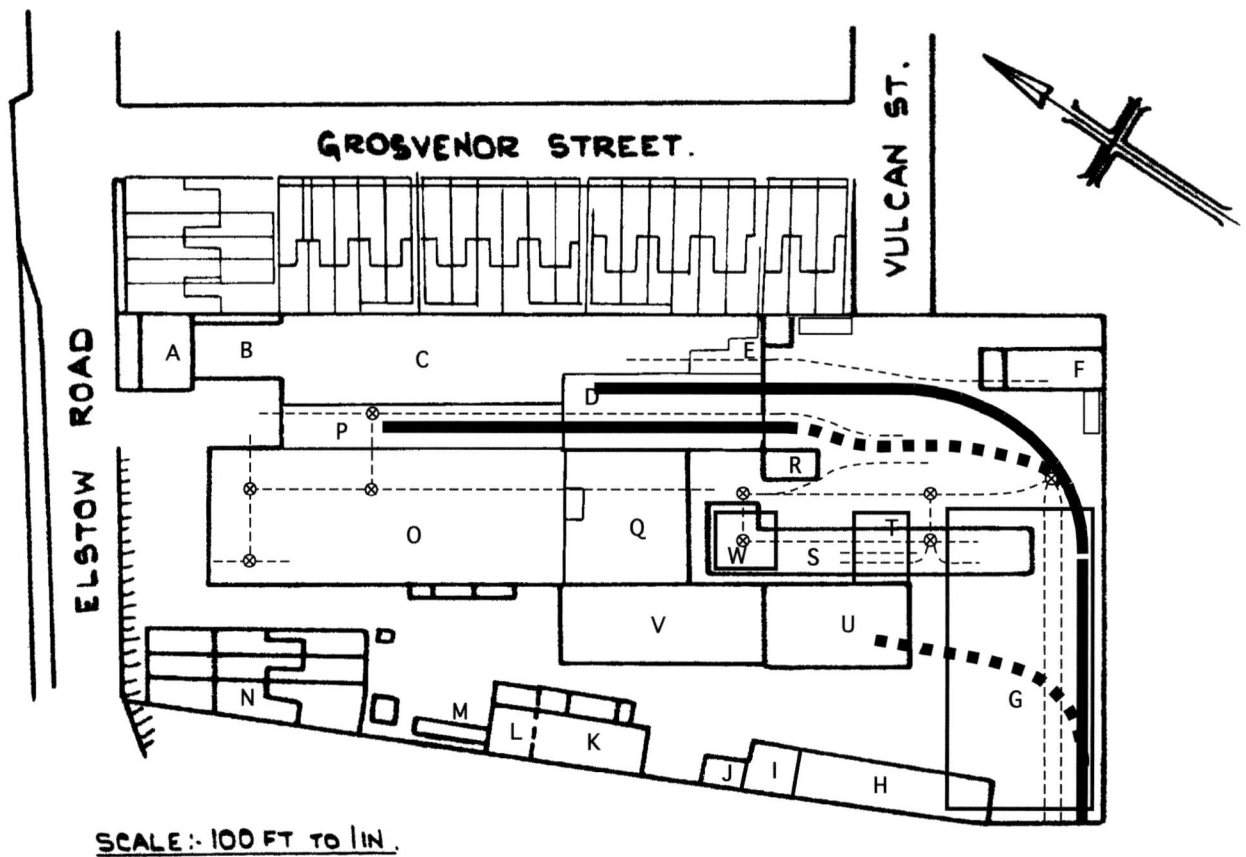

GROSVENOR STREET.

VULCAN ST.

ELSTOW ROAD

A  B  C  D  E  F  P  O  R  Q  W  S  T  V  U  G  N  M  L  K  J  I  H

SCALE :- 100 FT TO 1 IN.

| | |
|---|---|
| ▬▬▬▬ | Multi-Gauge Test Track |
| - - - - - - - | 2ft Gauge Internal Tramway |

A  New office block erected in 1938.

B  Original offices of Simplex Works.

C  Original Simplex Works, a former Laundry. Used initially for locomotive assembly, then later for gearbox, clutch and cab manufacture. In 1952 this single storey building was extended to three floors. The ground floor eventually became the parts store, the rear became packing and then goods inwards. There was a chimney towards the rear which was demolished in 1928.

D  Extension built in c.1926. It became an erecting bay by 1967 and by 1974 was in use as a packing area.

E  1920 extension to the original Simplex Works.

F  Pre-1926 building which was originally a paint store, was refurbished prior to 1967 and then let to Matisa as a store. It had been demolished by 1974 and the area was in use as a steel store.

G  New assembly building for fork truck attachments erected between 1971 and 1974. In the 1980s it was let to the local authority education department as a store.

H  Garages built in 1920s or 1930s. By 1974 they were in use as a storage area for wheels, axles and patterns. Partially demolished to free space for building G.

I  Early stores dating back to before 1919.

J  Extension to Stores, added prior to 1941, demolished by 1972 and this area used for managers' car parking.

K  Formerly Gowers' Works in 1919, before this part of the site was acquired by Motor Rail. Later used as a garage until converted into the works canteen in 1955.

L  Extension to Gowers' Works in 1919, before this part of the site was acquired by Motor Rail. Later used as a garage, converted into a works canteen by 1955 and by 1986 in use as the company's offices.

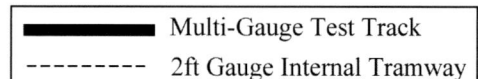

M  Cycle sheds.

N  Houses. Demolished by 1974 and area in use as a car park.

O  Original Slogger Engineering Co. works, acquired in 1920. Latterly used for the machining and sheet metalwork shops. The front part of this building was let out to Caslake Ltd in the 1970s.

P  Original cartway between the Simplex and Slogger works, acquired in 1920. It was arched over in c.1921 to become the heavy erecting bay for locomotive assembly. Equipped with travelling crane, it was used as such until closure.

Q  Extension built 1934.

R  Post-1926 boiler house. The roof accommodated a cast iron rain water storage tank. Demolished between 1967 and 1971.

S  Built between 1926 and 1934. Demolished in 1966. This consisted of a variety of structures. The top end contained a 'plonker' where hardening was carried out. Lower down the 'letter store' accommodated obsolete records.

T  Erected post 1966 as a crane bay. In use as a paint shop by 1971.

U  'High Bay' for erection of 9 ton locos. Built 1952 it was fitted with a 15 ton travelling crane. By 1966 it was divided into welding booths and areas for general fabrication.

V  Built during the Second World War for manufacture of parts (probably tank gearboxes) for the War Office. Later in use as a stores building, it became an area for welding and cutting by 1966. In use as welding booths by 1972.

W  Temporary wooden building erected c.1972. Purpose unknown.

*Courtesy Moseley Railway Trust*

# 9

# The Struggle for Existence

## 1968–1987

Burnholme & Forder Ltd, the purchaser of the company in 1972, was a very different kind of outfit to Lenning. For a start they had no connection with the railway industry, rather the reverse if anything. When the Abbott family had control, Motor Rail had retained the characteristics of a family business and they would, no doubt, have been reluctant to give up their connections with the locomotive business. Whilst Lenning apparently owned Motor Rail Ltd, in fact 51% of the shareholding was held by Loco Holdings Ltd which was controlled by the family trusts of B. Tessel who was in turn Lenning's Managing Director and its main shareholder.

During this period R.A. Wenham had continued the search for new products with considerable success and, whilst at the same time the locomotive range had been updated, the emphasis had transferred to other products. The major lines involved had become fork lift truck attachments and road trailers, but in the drive for survival any engineering work was considered. Sales agencies for a variety of products were also sought as a means of generating income.

Burnholme & Forder Ltd had originally been formed in 1964 to take over three road haulage companies. By the time it came into contact with Motor Rail it had come under the control of a new

123. Curiously, MR 9931 does not have a build date recorded for it but is probably about 1968. As a metre gauge shunter it stands at the end of the 1½ mile long Kahe branch of Tanzania Railways in the sugar mill of TPC Ltd whose locomotives are described elsewhere in this book. As seen in 1989 it is as built with a Simtran gearbox and Dorman engine. Later Alan Keef Ltd fitted a Perkins engine and Spicer pre-select gearbox, in which form it carried on working the branch for many years until that power unit was somehow fitted into a U series locomotive!

124. Photographed in 1971, MR 60S364 of 1968 was close to being new to the Campbell Brickworks of the Stanton & Stavely Iron Co. in Derbyshire. Track condition may not be so good, however, as the locomotive has been fitted with crash bars to prevent it dropping too far in the event of derailment! It does not appear to be overloaded even if the wagons are of at least 2 cu. yd capacity.
*A.J. Booth. Collection Industrial Railway Society*

125. SMH 40SD516 of 1979 stands in the Lagoon Workshops of Severn Trent Water Authority for what would appear to be routine maintenance. As neither loco is on rails one can presume they have been put there by overhead crane. With the fitting of air cooled Deutz engines Simplex extended the covers to the front of the locomotive. This, however, left nowhere for the second man to ride, so immediate modifications were done upon arrival together with the high handrail. Judging by the lawn mower and headlight tester this workshop maintained all types of equipment.
*J.A. Peden. Collection Industrial Railway Society*

board of directors led by a Chartered Accountant, L.E. Scruton. It was not the intention of the new board merely to operate in the mundane world of road haulage, or even locomotive building, but to obtain interests in property and other businesses thought to be more profitable. Motor Rail's status as a publicly quoted company would make it easier to acquire assets in exchange for new Burnhome & Forder shares. Since the Tessel trusts wished to sell for cash, a purchaser had to be found for these shares and Victor Industrial Securities 'squared the circle' by finding a buyer. These transactions took place in June 1972 and Motor Rail Ltd was afterwards turned into a holding company for various engineering interests transferred to it from Burnhome & Forder. It thus became a vehicle for the complicated manoeuvres of its principal directors and shareholders, all of which led to its demise a few years later. The report of the Department of Trade inspectors into the affairs of Burnholme & Forder Ltd and Brayhead Ltd (both of which held large interests in Motor Rail Ltd at varying dates) are not part of this story but, shall we say, make interesting reading.

Fortunately for the core business, one of the first changes made by Burnholme & Forder had been to transfer the business previously carried on by Motor Rail Ltd to a new subsidiary company, Simplex Mechanical Handling Ltd (hereinafter SMH), as from October 1972, with R.A. Wenham remaining as Managing Director. At first he was also a director of Motor Rail Ltd but in December 1973 he was asked to transfer his service contract to Simplex Mechanical Handling which was done in April 1974. Unfortunately, far from gaining the possible advantages of being part of a larger group, SMH was soon to be wholly on its own again, this being brought about by the collapse of the parent company.

Despite Wenham's considerable efforts the company remained unprofitable and at a shareholders meeting of Motor Rail Ltd held in January 1976 a proposal was put forward to sell SMH to its directors who appear to only have been R.A. Wenham and C. Trupp, as from 1st August 1976. The consideration for this was the repayment of an outstanding loan of £160,000 due to Motor Rail by SMH and the acceptance of responsibility for the overdraft

of £140,000 owed by SMH to its bankers. To obtain finance for this Wenham sought and obtained backing from the Wemyss Investment Trust Ltd who thus effectively became the business's next owners. This concern had industrial railway connections in that it had originally been formed in 1894 as the Wemyss Coal Co. Ltd in Scotland and its activities had included the operation of the Wemyss Bay Private Railway. Following the nationalisation of the coal industry its interests had broadened to include the operation of tea estates in Kenya amongst other ventures. It had need of engineering capacity and its acquisition of SMH brought useful and different work to help utilise the works' capacity.

Although the firm now had another new owner its operation continued very much in the former tradition under the continuing management of R.A. Wenham. The number of locomotives built began to decline rapidly and so the emphasis was placed even further on other lines of production. From a financial standpoint the making of trailers, forklift attachments and other products had a number of advantages. In the main these products were sold in Britain and in consequence did not have the problems of payment that can be associated with overseas markets. Neither did they require the keeping of large stocks of spare parts, although the obverse of this was that there were not the high margins to be made on spares sales. Similarly they did not require large costs for bought-in components. Thus, despite the railway market being in decline, a large new building was erected at the rear of the works site in 1972 that was intended primarily for trailer and forklift attachment production. In the event it was only used to a minimal extent before being leased to Bedford Borough Council for storage purposes.

Under Wemyss control the range of products was broadened to service the interests of the parent group whilst agencies continued to be sought for the sale of other manufacturer's products. Some large items were produced for the Wemyss tea estates including a travelling gantry to spread tea on drying floors. Production of this equipment continued elsewhere after the closure of the Bedford works. Another successful venture was the manufacture of beer

126. (*Right*) SMH 60SP756 was the last locomotive to be wholly built at Bedford and left the works in August 1986. A very few years later it lies in abandoned condition at Kikwetu Sisal Estate in southern Tanzania. Whilst the 60S was always offered with the alternative of a Perkins 4.236 engine, this was the first example to be actually so produced. It seems from subsequent experience that this particular engine set up vibrations that the engine mountings could not withstand; hence its abandonment.

127. (*Below*) SMH 60SD757 of 1986 was a 6 ton 60hp locomotive fitted with a Deutz F4L912 engine. This engine only just fitted into the standard 60S frame so note the cover over a frame cutout and the slightly widened side panel. This locomotive was built by Alan Keef Ltd with the work starting at Bampton and being completed at Lea. It is here seen loaded on a lorry for transfer to Bedford for the fitting of buffers, final testing and export packing. It was of 3ft 6ins gauge, ordered by RMP and destined for Ghana Bauxite.

128. (*Below right*) With their Works No. 43 of 1992, Alan Keef Ltd built what will probably prove to be the last traditional Simplex locomotive. At the Skeldon Factory of Guyana Sugar Corporation it is here seen out of use after the factory in the background was replaced with a new one in 2009 that is not rail connected. Note the double tropical roof and the track gauge of one metre. It was used for the transport of bulk sugar. *Courtesy Thomas Kautzor*

barrel and crate handling equipment with some 200 'Cellar Drop' units being made before closure; these also continue to be made. Extending masts for forklift trucks to an Italian design proved successful although they were not without their problems. A good deal of prototype work was undertaken that did not proceed to quantity production, the most obvious of which was the brick handling equipment.

The Wemyss group had no interest in the railway side of the concern per se and undoubtedly viewed it as an encumbrance to their efforts to create a modern forward-looking business out of what they had bought. Effectively they wanted the locomotive business to die off completely, something it steadfastly refused to do! Arrangements were thus made with Alan Keef Ltd, with whom the company had a long-standing business relationship, for the latter to build any locomotives for which they should unfortunately receive an order, and also to manufacture spare parts if and when required. As previously touched upon, two locomotives were built under this arrangement and a third was to have been, but SMH decided to make that one themselves. Also, provisionally, it was agreed that Alan Keef Ltd would at least assemble, if not wholly manufacture, a batch of twelve locomotives, out of thirty-five, for Bord na Móna

in Ireland if the order should materialise, which in the event it did not (see Chapter 10).

Despite all this activity to find alternative employment for the works and its staff, there was a fundamental flaw in the structure of the company. As early as 1970 the freehold of the works and its undeveloped land had been sold to a property company who had then leased it back on a 99 year lease to the then owners, Motor Rail Ltd. This was, and no doubt still is, a common method for a company to ease its financial constraints by releasing the cash value locked up in freehold property. However, somewhere along the way – possibly in the liquidation of Motor Rail or as part of the Burnhome & Forder debacle – the site was sold to the Post Office Pensions Fund. Thus SMH came to have only a 25 year lease that was due to expire in September 1987. Arithmetically these dates do not tally but it was, nevertheless, the *de facto* situation. One must also presume that, surprisingly, SMH did not have the right to renew or that if they did it was at a rent that would not have been viable to the business as it then stood. Alternative premises were sought but it was deemed that the sheer cost of removal made the project unviable. Thus the decision was made to cease manufacturing and rely on subcontractors for any business offering.

With that decision made, it was time to split the assets up to the best advantage. The locomotive business was sold to Alan Keef Ltd and transferred to their works at Ross-on-Wye, Herefordshire. The forklift attachment side was sold to a new company, Simplex Attachment Spares Ltd, that was set up by two former employees primarily to service existing equipment. However, as it turned out, some new items were made and sold as and when ordered, including a container handling toplift. The items of interest to the Wemyss group, the tea estate machinery and the beer handling equipment, continued to be dealt with from the Bedford office until that closed.

Alternative premises were found in Kempston, with manufacture being done by sub contractors. SMH continued to exist and be operated by the company's accountant from his home address in Kings Langley.

It might be of interest to take what I wrote for my autobiography, *A Tale of Many Railways*, about this. It should be borne in mind that Alan Keef Ltd had only moved to Ross-on-Wye less than a year beforehand from their previous site near Witney, Oxfordshire. Here it is verbatim:

*Matters with Simplex were looking good too when they obtained an order for a 40S locomotive from what became Butterley Brick Co. Ltd for their Star Lane Brickworks, near Southend. As agreed we started building it although they actually made the frame. When it was about half-complete I had a phone call from Martin Everitt, the managing director, asking to come and see me. In six words, 'Did we want to buy Simplex?' In principle at least there was only one answer! In practice we were only interested in buying the locomotive side of the business, others were going to take on the fork lift attachment work which would be primarily spares only. [My late wife] Susan and I took a trip to Bedford to try and see what sort of deal we might expect and also to see what we might be going to get for our money. I, quite obviously, had enormous enthusiasm to take it on; it perhaps meant that Alan Keef Ltd had finally arrived on the railway scene. Martin Everitt and especially his accountant, Cyril Trupp, had equally obviously done their homework and they quite rightly saw us as possibly the only buyer. Between them they had worked out a deal by which I bought the business effectively on hire purchase. The story was that the lease on the Bedford premises had nearly run out and the parent company did not consider the business sufficiently viable to make it worthwhile renewing. Simplex Mechanical Handling Ltd was to remain in business to receive payments from me and to act as a buying house for the Wemyss' family tea estates in Africa. The purchase price was £100,000 of which £70,000 was to be paid off in monthly instalments over ten years.*

129. The End. Alan Keef sits at the auction when the contents of the works were sold off on 15th September 1987. This photograph was taken by Peter Cross who, having worked there all his life, knew more about Motor Rail than anyone else before or since. He should really have written this history!

130. *Cheyenne* for Wicksteed Park at Kettering was Motor Rail's only serious attempt at something for the leisure market. MR 22224 of 1966 was a standard 2½ ton 40hp machine that was given a quite satisfactory steam outline. The carriages were supplied at the same time but whether Motor Rail built them is not known; the wheels and axles were from Allens of Tipton. It was delivered with a fanfare of 'Wild West' cowboys and the regular driver seems at least amused by the whole performance although the passengers appear wholly indifferent.

*For that we got all the drawings, manufacturing records, patents, the jigs and fixtures for manufacture, all the spare parts currently in stock, fifty-two boxes of nobody knew quite what which had been going to be exported to South Africa but never was, the gear cutting machinery, foundry patterns, the choice of any staff who would make the move and finally anything that we liked to buy in the disposal auction. All in all it added up to another eight 40ft lorry loads to the works at The Lea! On the staff front, John Palmer, who was assistant design engineer came permanently, at last I had a properly qualified engineer on the strength. Peter Cross, who probably knew more about Simplex than anyone then living, came for a period of about three months to teach us how the spares system worked and one of their machinists came for a week or two to teach us about gear cutting.*

*It was all very impressive but there was one ingredient missing which I did not immediately realise, indeed did not properly appreciate for some years. There were no customer records. For the last twenty years or so most of their production had been sold through agents, of whom Railway, Mine & Plantation Equipment covered the bulk of the globe, although there were a few others such as Wigglesworth in East Africa, Carl Strom in Sweden and Glastra in Argentina, but Simplex themselves kept no records of the end users. Thus we were unable to do a mailshot to wave the*

*flag and say, 'Here we are now, we can supply any spares or new locomotives that you need.'*

*It all worked something like this. Simplex kept records of their locomotives by works number and in about three different systems. The drawing office had the technical and build details together with any variations from standard, sales kept a record of type and some basic information such as engine number and the accounts people kept detailed customer and financial records. All this was then paraphrased onto a record sheet that included customer – normally the agent only except for the UK where they did deal*

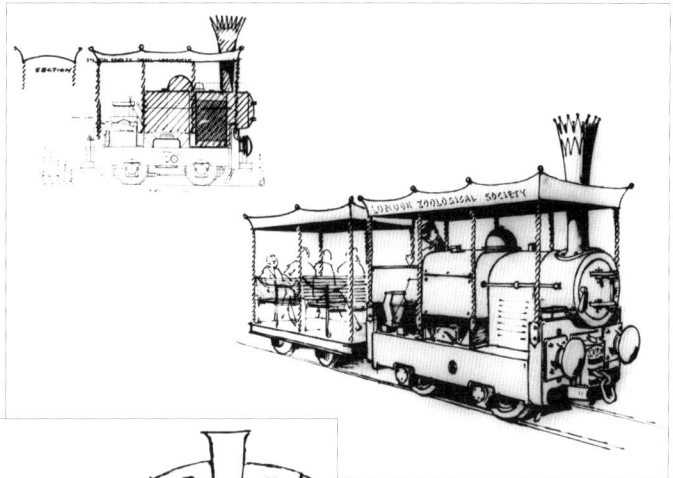

131, 132. Maybe a precursor to *Cheyenne*, these two concept drawings are drawn around a 4½ ton locomotive so perhaps serious gradients were involved. The one with the overall roof is lettered London Zoological Society so were these for either Whipsnade or London Zoo? If the latter, did they have to compete with the Far Tottering & Oyster Creek Railway conceived by Rowland Emett for the Festival of Britain in 1951 at Battersea Park, and hence their whimsical nature.

133. As the concept of the leisure railway began to take off a good many Motor Rail locomotives were given a steam outline look. MR 9978 of 1954 is one of the more attractive efforts and was carried out by Track Supplies & Services of Wolverton who were the franchisees for this railway at the Cotswold Wildlife Park, Burford, Oxfordshire. By the time this shot was taken in 1982 the 2DWD engine was getting worn and smoky, which was at least appropriate!

*direct – basic details of type, weight and rail gauge, how it was despatched and, of all things, the shipping marks. The latter did at least tell one to which country each locomotive went to but precious little else. When RMP effectively collapsed a year or two later, by slightly devious means I came by their records that were something of an eye opener. They kept a similar card index that again detailed their agent as the customer and in turn, often, but far from always, the agent's customer. Even then it was usually very brief such as Kalimantan Timber Co. or Benguela Railway. It looked good but in practice it was not. The most astonishing part was that although RMP were always most insistent that they should be sole agent for a particular country they themselves were quite happy to deal with two or three different agents within the same country and occasionally deal direct with the end user as well. However, none of this helped us greatly even if it made fascinating reading.*

*To complete this story it is necessary to move forward a year or so to the point where RMP, quite suddenly, ceased to be the firm they were. Again it was said to be a case of a lease running out on their sophisticated offices in Finsbury Square. Again I took advantage and took into my employment Dennis Wilby, who I had known for many years as I had, latterly at least, bought most of my new rail through RMP – this being easier than dealing with either*

*Raine & Co. or British Steel. I had long thought that to employ somebody to promote and handle sales would be a good thing as I just did not have time to get round my customers as I felt I ought. In addition, more sales were needed to carry the additional costs of moving, Simplex, better premises, etc. In the event I was proved wrong; either Dennis was the wrong person or my type of business does not lend itself to being 'sold' by anyone other than a principal. In reality there must have been some of both but I think more of the latter. He was with us for about two years and we all parted amicably enough.*

After the factory closed the remaining contents were sold by auction on 17th September 1987. Many parts of the premises had been sub-let including the main office building after SMH moved their offices into what had been the canteen. All of these buildings were subsequently demolished and the site redeveloped for housing. Today there is no indication whatsoever that this was once the location of a busy works whose products were known, and are often still in use, across the globe. The only slight reflection of its industrial past is a cul de sac within the development named 'The Sidings' – and even that is largely on the land of the old Hitchin branch and what was Grafton Cranes. The world had changed and an era had passed.

134. (*Above*) From 1966 to 1970 over sixty 8 ton 3ft gauge U series locomotives were supplied to Jarvis Clark for INCO, Canada. It was this series of orders that precipitated the Queens Award for Export Achievement in 1969. This is believed to be an INCO publicity shot of one of these locomotives working underground. A very few spares have been supplied for these locos of recent years.

135. In late 1970 two lightweight U series were supplied to S.N.A.I. in Somalia. Of 600mm gauge and only 5½ tons weight they were fitted with Deutz F4L912 engines down-rated to 48hp. This one has had the cab modified and heads a train of sugar cane.

# 10

# 1968 to the End

## 1968–1987

The sales files from about 1968 onwards came to Alan Keef Ltd and to read through them is to have an insight into what was a very busy, very buoyant but not very profitable time for Motor Rail Ltd and its successor Simplex Mechanical Handling Ltd. For instance there is a letter in August 1968 to Guthrie & Co. concerning the possible cancellation of an order for two locomotives for Malaya that says:

*Currently we have going through our shops fourteen locomotives of different types and a further batch of 26 locomotives scheduled for production during September, October and early November. As you can appreciate, with two locomotives in part completed condition, with in addition stock space being tied up with engines and torque convertors, we are finding that the lack of decision for the two locomotives for Oil Palms of Malaya is causing us some considerable embarrassment at this moment, and this situation will unfortunately get worse because of our present order book.*

In the early years of the 21st century the mind boggles at the necessity of having to produce at least two or more locomotives per week! However, reading the files suggests that all was not what it should have been and that these apparently good times may have been the precursor to the firm's ultimate demise.

As has been recounted, one of the main requirements of the Lenning takeover was the design and production of a hydraulic drive locomotive. Whilst Lenning's main concern was for the South African mines, the locomotive was intended as a mining locomotive for worldwide sale and, indeed, it did achieve just that, not to mention a Queen's Award for Export Achievement for the company – no small accolade. This was presented to Mr Wenham by the Lord Lieutenant of Bedfordshire, Major Simon Whitbread.

The initial U series locomotives supplied to Canada were of the hydrokinetic type using a Brockhouse transmission unit and these were very successful but suffered from the fact that the drive unit was only single speed. When the hydrostatic version appeared in 1968 it again proved successful. On test the locomotive was able to haul fifteen 140 cu ft loaded wagons upgrade and round a curve as opposed to ten wagons hauled with their existing locomotives.

However, even if the mining industry was clamouring for a hydraulic drive locomotive it is doubtful if their respective maintenance departments and operating staff were ready for the niceties of this type of transmission. This was especially true in the necessity of keeping all components clean and free of dirt. Also, the principle drive components, pump and motor, could not be made in Bedford and had to be bought in. Although Motor Rail bought what were probably the best units available at that time neither they nor their suppliers really realised what they were up against in putting these units into a railway vehicle. This was aided

and abetted by the decision to only have one design of locomotive, the U series. The result was that what had to be a cramped design for underground use became quite unnecessarily so when called upon for surface operations. The narrow tapering cab supplied for the latter use also made it look faintly ridiculous.

If it had worked faultlessly all this might have been forgiven, but it did not. The files make depressing reading and whilst it is probably true that not all of these locomotives misbehaved themselves the appearance is that they must have been a nightmare for all concerned. In fairness it was a long way from all being Motor Rail's fault and a great deal of the problems seemed to revolve around the Ruston hydraulic motor that was used. A very hard hitting and technical report sent to that company in 1971 sums the situation up for the locomotives supplied through Jarvis Clark to Inco in Canada:

*The whole position from Motor Rail's point of view is disastrous. In previous years there has always been an order from Canada on our books at this time of year for ten to fifteen locomotives. At the present moment there are no orders for Canada and Canada will not be ordering further locomotives until they are sure that the motor problems have been solved. This means that Motor Rail will have to build a locomotive incorporating all the various modifications, test it thoroughly here and then supply this to Canada for site testing before further orders can be realised. The cost to Motor Rail of this is in effect the loss of production of at least five locomotives per month for a period of not less than three months. This is quite apart from the fact that Jarvis Clark are withholding payment of their account amounting to the sum of £40,000, have submitted warranty claims in excess of £7,500*

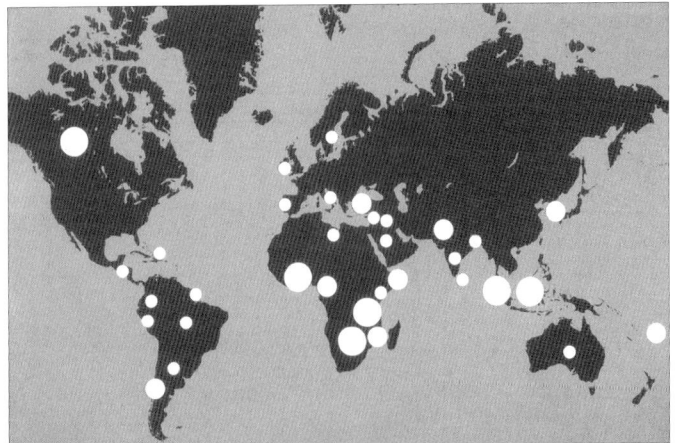

136. This and the previous two pictures come from a few slides thought to be part of a set for a talk or presentation. This one obviously shows the spread and density of Simplex/Motor Rail customers around the world.

*and Motor Rail is committed to an expenditure of £5,000 relating to modifications of the 25 locomotives in the field.*

And it would appear that Ruston & Hornsby could not have cared less. In today's terms those figures are eye-watering and represent £588,000, £110,000 and £73,500 respectively.

It could be said with a good deal of justification that the machines were ahead of their time and had all the problems associated with prototypes. It could also be said, and was at the time, that the users were not playing fair with the new technology. There were also considerable problems with engines, both Dorman and later Deutz. Both were air cooled and the former had serious problems with overheating in hot conditions, whether on the surface or underground; the latter were better but had other problems. Some customers truly were ignorant of the most basic knowledge of this type of hydraulic drive. Further faults came with the control systems which consisted of external valves, springs and levers and was largely dreamt up by the Bedford drawing office. Again, in fairness, this was no mean achievement, but local fitters were not aware of the significance of a spring requiring adjustment (or dropping off

altogether) – the loco simply did not work. If the warning lights came on (and this is a well attested fact), the operators would take the bulbs out, throw them away and then wonder why something more serious happened! Hydrostatic locomotives do not tow easily and many a broken-down locomotive was further damaged whilst being towed out of the way. This also seemed to coincide with a period when contractor's plant generally was treated with brutal disregard for its care, maintenance, or future longevity. In the mining industry the situation was even worse, exacerbated by the fact that production was, and still is, the be all and end all of the operation.

The result of all this was a continuous succession of designations for the U series as each of its problems was resolved. One can only but be surprised that so many were sold (nudging 200) and that customers kept on buying them despite the problems. One also wonders why Motor Rail did not make a clean start with the benefit of their experiences rather than continue to make do with what they had. Maybe they really were the only people building a hydraulic drive locomotive that actually worked – most of the time. For instance, at the silver mines of Mogul of Ireland the U was

137. Cameroon. This is one of a batch of five 118U series (8 tons and 87hp) supplied to Cameroon Development Corporation through RMP in 1968. This one is working a service train at Tiko which is the main depot for the extensive system serving both banana and rubber plantations.
*Courtesy Frank Jux*

138. One of the problems with the U series locomotive was that its hydraulic controls were all external requiring cleanliness and precise adjustment, something that was largely not understood in the mining industry of the time. This is the servo mechanism to operate the swashplate on the Dowty pump; at top a new unit and below one taken off a locomotive from Mogul of Ireland!

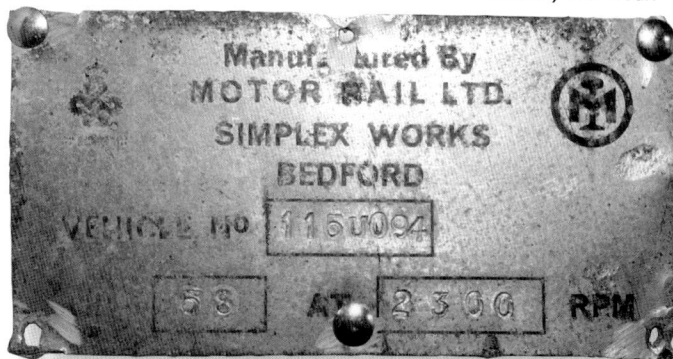

139. By 1970 works plates had been downgraded to engraved aluminium sheet with the works number stamped in, as indeed it had always been. MR 115U094 was one of those supplied to Mogul of Ireland and, aside from having the fixing rivets ground off, seems to have had a hard life anyway.

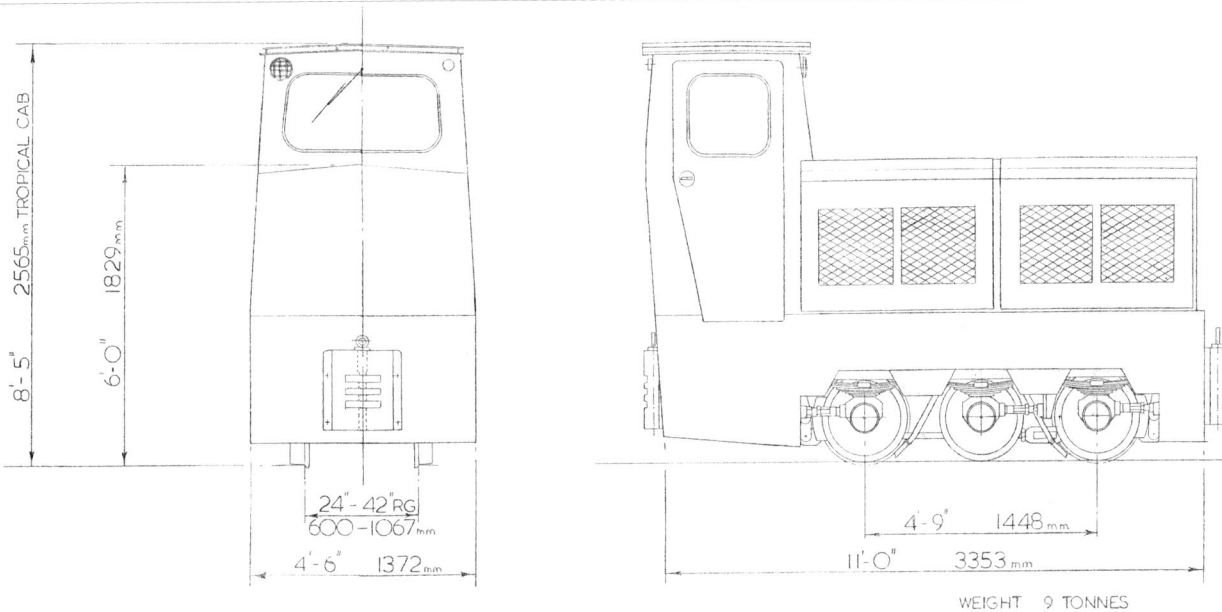

| DRAWN | J.P. | SIMPLEX MECHANICAL HANDLING LTD | DIESEL HYDROKINETIC LOCOMOTIVE | P/2 291 |
|---|---|---|---|---|
| ISSUE 1  DATE 10·4·78 | SCALE 1:16 | BEDFORD    ENGLAND | TYPE  O-6-O | |

140. There was a good deal of discussion about the possibility of building a six-wheeler version of the U series and this at least got to the stage of a preliminary drawing. These were always known at Bedford, and still are with Alan Keef Ltd, as a P over 2. Whilst conceptual from a customer's point of view, enough work has been put into the design that it can be built if necessary! Alas this one almost certainly never saw the light of day.

considered a far superior locomotive to the M & R locomotives they already had. Certainly they were cheaper than what competition there may have been. One case is quoted of being some 20% cheaper than the equivalent Clayton, and that machine was far from reliable. Also, as compared with the Hunslet and Hudswell Clarke mining locomotives of the era they were not as massively constructed but were only half the price. Some would have said that they were only half the locomotive as well! Driver comfort was very low on anyone's priority list at that time and Motor Rail may have had a very slight advantage there.

Much the same situation applied when the T series came into being in 1972. Again it was designed as a mining locomotive although none ever worked underground. The powers that be steadfastly refused to allow it to be built as a proper surface locomotive with full height cab and width to match. An attempt was made with one for Indonesia but it was a poor substitute for what could have been. Those subsequently rebuilt as a 'proper' diesel locomotive by Alan Keef Ltd have proved the point handsomely.

The U was offered quite frequently as a tandem pair or as a locomotive and slave (as occasionally was the T series), although it appears that none was sold in either configuration. Some were also offered with the option of cardan shaft drive although it has to be said the offers were a bit half hearted in view of the considerable design work that would have been needed. More intriguingly, the U was several times offered, and there are drawings to go with it, in the form of a six-wheeler, or 0-6-0 as Simplex always termed it.

141. Under an evening sun, and with a plume of white exhaust, a 7 ton 60S starts a train of stone away from Takerghat Limestone Quarry in Bangladesh. Shipped in 1972 and carrying RMP plates, this is one of seven locomotives (SMH 60S405-411) supplied to this project. This came at the time when East Pakistan became the independent country of Bangladesh, which created a few problems at home with export guarantees and made this industrial line possibly unique in having a customs post between the two countries partway along its length! The man under the shelter operates the winch to bring trains up from the quarry until locomotive power can take over. This railway is somewhat 'in the middle of nowhere' with access being only by water.

There is no specific mention of one being built but Alan's father went to Bedford to collect some spares on one occasion and came back with tales of having seen an 0-6-0 locomotive in the works. There is a good deal of correspondence with RMP in 1979 for such a machine for new sugar mills in Indonesia but by 1983 Tony Wenham is saying that they would only build the design if there were a reasonable number to be made. Regretfully one probably has to conclude that it never happened, although it is quite credible that such a machine would have been just another one going through the works and no particular note made of the fact. Even more surprisingly there were suggestions of building an equivalent Orenstein & Koppel locomotive under licence!

On the positive side, and presumably paying all the costs incurred by the above problems, there was a continuous succession of 40S and, particularly, 60S sales to all parts of the world. These were not wholly without their problems either, especially when it came to fitting the Deutz engines.

Nevertheless they proceeded through the works at a steady rate with very little hassle. These were sold largely through RMP and

142. A rare example of lateral thinking at Bedford. When the Wolverton Carriage Works of British Rail required a small shunter for moving single carriages and wagons, Simplex came up with a modified G series locomotive. Known locally as 'Titchie', SMH 103GA078 of 1978 is, at the time of writing, still in regular use doing what it was bought for.

143. (*Right*) Three 14 ton T series of 2ft 6ins gauge and 112hp (SMH 101T018/19/20) were built in 1979 for the Ledstone Luck Colliery of the National Coal Board to work a surface line of some length. With good reason Simplex were proud of them even if locomotives were in decline at the time. 101T018, the first of this batch, was later given a complete rebuild to become Alan Keef Ltd's 59R, *Beaudesert*, for the Leighton Buzzard Railway in Bedfordshire, making it the precursor to 78R to be seen in Plate 226.

144. The trio were bought by Alan Keef Ltd when their work with the NCB ceased and this is SMH 101T018 rebuilt and re-gauged to 900mm ready to depart for the Channel Tunnel contract in 1989. It and its sister were used to shunt wagons through the wagon repair and maintenance workshops. Having been cannibalised for spares whilst with the Coal Board, SMH 101T019 was ultimately scrapped.

their network of agents. The table of prices in Appendix III gives an indication of just how far flung this network reached. They came up against some interesting commercial problems such as seven 60S locos all set to go to East Pakistan which suddenly became Bangladesh and would the British Government, who was financing the project, continue to do so? It did. And there were problems with

shipment due to strikes in the docks; something we have almost forgotten about nowadays. It was also a time of very high inflation, reaching 26% per annum at one stage and any delay in the planned production, shipment and payment could have a very serious effect. This was also a time when their spares prices were being increased by 2½% per month!

145. (*Above*) Little and large. A G series alongside a T series on the multi gauge track in the works yard with the rear entrance into Vulcan Street in the background. There is no information about this photograph but the T could be the first for Tanganyika Planting in Tanzania and the G one of the last to be supplied to Ghana State Goldmine.

146. (*Left*) SMH 101T017 was an attempt to provide a more appropriate cab and bonnet line for a surface locomotive. Sold through RMP and despatched to Indonesia in 1979 it was of only 9 tons weight with the Perkins 6354 engine downrated to 94hp. Gauge was 700mm (common in former Dutch colonies). It is also on the multi gauge track, but this time inside the works.

147. (*Below*) Photographs of the many G series locomotives sold overseas by RMP are rare but this is SMH 103G058 of 1975 at the entrance to the drift coal mine of Tire Linyit in Turkey about twenty years later. The operation has since closed and the locomotive presumably scrapped.

A side light, no more, on all the above is the curiously formal arrangement that existed with RMP. One is aware that it was a much more formal age, but considering the amount of business that the two companies did together it is surprising that most correspondence begins 'Dear Sir', with only the occasional 'Dear Tony' to Mr Wenham. In fact it seems to have got worse in later years. It also appears to have been something of a love/hate relationship depending upon whether delivery times were being met and made worse by the problems with the U series locos.

In the period 1981-83 the company put an enormous amount of effort into an enquiry from Bord na Móna for no less than thirty-five 5 ton locomotives. This was a follow up on twelve locomotives supplied in 1979/80. These were very different from the norm, being fitted with Lister HA3 air cooled engines, a soundproofed fully enclosed cab and a brown and cream paint scheme. They obtained finance to cover the costs of construction until payment started to materialise – some £250,000 at what was at that time considered a very satisfactory interest rate of 14%! Late in the tendering stage it became apparent that Bord na Móna wanted some Irish input into the machines and various possibilities were investigated but all to no avail. In the event the order seems to have gone to a joint venture between the Italian firm of Gleismac and Dundalk Engineering Ltd; and then not for the full quantity of locomotives. The end results were not entirely satisfactory either.

As part of these negotiations, and with perhaps a foretaste of what was to come, detailed negotiations took place with Robert Hudson (Raletrux) Ltd for them to part-build these locomotives using frames, wheels and gearboxes from Bedford. This was possibly in part to reduce SMH's risk and financial commitment to the contract but also with the longer term view of Robert Hudson taking over the whole locomotive business. For the record, SMH were very concerned as to whether Hudson were capable of building locomotives to Simplex standards of quality. This came to naught largely because Robert Hudson kept 'moving the goal posts' every time a new agreement was produced. This may have also been because, despite appearances, they were in no position to take on the financial commitment as it was not long afterwards that they closed down themselves. It may have been when this all fell through that there were discussions with Alan Keef Ltd about a joint operation to build them.

Although Simplex locomotives had been supplied to Bord na Móna before, they were not wholly satisfactory largely because the company was unable, unwilling or both to adapt it's designs to suit the precise needs of a specific customer, even when thirty-five locomotives were involved. Because of that Simplex may never have been in the running anyway. Either way, it must have been a huge disappointment for all concerned and at the same time dealt a near lethal blow to the company.

148. SMH 60SL742 waits quietly in the sun while the crew have a tea break on the Cashel Bog of Bord na Móna's Coolnamona system in Ireland. These locomotives were largely used for service purposes, as here taking fuel and oil to other machinery out on the bogs. Built to 3ft gauge and fitted with Lister HA3 engines they were different from most 60S locos, but the process was not fully worked through, which may have had a bearing on why a further order for thirty-five locomotives was not obtained.

149. Whilst the 60SL locos were largely used for maintenance and service purposes they occasionally got to hauling peat and here is SMH 60SL740 with a train of empty wagons also on Cashel Bog. The scale of Bord na Móna's operations is immense; for instance they have more miles of track than the Irish national railway system!

# 11

# Alan Keef Ltd

## 1972–2016

Having got this far with the Motor Rail/Simplex story it is necessary to backtrack a bit and describe where Alan Keef Ltd (AKL) appeared from and how it came to be in a position to take over what was patently a much larger concern. I make no apology for writing this chapter largely in the first person as to do otherwise could make it very cumbersome. The use of 'we', generally refers to Alan Keef Ltd as an organisation. I tend to describe how I came to be in this business as 'a hobby that got out of hand' but it must be borne in mind that there are small railways in the blood. My great grandfather put a 2ft gauge railway in the garden for his children to play on about 1870. There's nothing new! According to family lore a steam locomotive was planned for this line but perhaps unsurprisingly it never happened. My father and his brother had a fairly extensive '0' gauge garden railway, most of it Bassett Lowke, in the early 1920s and took a lively interest in the lesser known railways of this country. So it is perhaps not surprising that I should follow suit, but on a larger scale.

The Wemyss organisation's lack of interest in locomotives was a reflection of the times when rail haulage became very much out of fashion, a situation that remains to this day although there are signs that opinions are changing. This has been exacerbated over the years by the activities of organisations such as the World Bank who fail to look at the lifetime cost of the components of transport systems. With the rise in the use of rubber tyred vehicles, conveyor belts and other methods of materials handling, the use of narrow gauge railways had shrunk considerably, not only in Great Britain but also in the rest of the world. Their main use remained in specialist applications together with the tunnelling and mining industries where rail has considerable advantages. Although even here rubber-tyred equipment is often used where constraints allow.

The demise of steam traction across the world has given rise to the railway preservation movement. Now termed Heritage Railways, these in turn have become a considerable industry in their own right. No longer is it 'oddball' to work full time for a preserved railway, be it either standard or narrow gauge, and there is a generation of railwaymen arising who have never done anything else. Allied to this is the rise of small railways, a mile or so long, in theme parks, safari parks, zoos, garden centres and the like, not to mention private estate railways in larger gardens built purely for their owner's pleasure (shades of my great grandfather!).

In 1972, several years before it became a limited company, I started the business as a one-man show. At that time there were still a fair number of industrial railways in this country and there was a living to be made from buying and selling secondhand light railway equipment between the existing users. This also included dismantling lines that had closed and passing the material on to new users. Shades of George Bungey, so looked down upon by Motor Rail!

All businesses have major turning points and the first of mine was obtaining the maintenance of all the railways in Butlin's holiday camps. (The second was buying Simplex!) At that time they had six substantial railways, mostly in 2ft gauge that they described as miniature railways and eight 'railway' amusement rides also in 2ft gauge. The former, especially, needed major work to bring them up

150. There are four locomotives in this picture, three Simplex and one Ruston, and the owners were intending to bury them! Although this is taken very much later, buying a lot like this is how Alan Keef Ltd started. They were refurbished, re-engined as necessary, tidied up, painted and sold on. At the time there was a seemingly insatiable demand for such locomotives in the Far East for logging operations. Of the four here only one was scrapped!

151. In 'the good old days' RMP used to maintain a stock of locomotives, mostly 40S and 60S, at Bedford so that they could offer more or less immediate delivery if required. In 1977, with the decline in light railway use worldwide, this policy was abandoned and the stock locos offered for sale. Quite by chance Alan Keef Ltd had an order for a passenger train on a jetty for the Imperial Iranian Navy and snapped up two of them. Here is either 40SD505 or 506 re-bodied and air braked with two of the carriages supplied. Astoundingly, one of these locomotives reputedly turned up in Damascus a good many years later!

152. The enquiry for these two U series locomotives was with SMH at the time of the takeover. As AK24 and 25 of 1988 they are here seen being loaded onto a container flat for shipment to the Kyung Dong coal mine in South Korea.

to a standard that would be acceptable to HM Railway Inspectorate who had just started to take an interest in this sort of railway. The 'ride' type of railway was outside the scope of HMRI but all needed considerable attention. It was work for Butlins that precipitated AKL into the manufacture of new equipment instead of just being a dealer. This was primarily new carriage bogies and in due course carriages as well. It also involved contract tracklaying; work that has continued ever since.

The first diesel locomotive was built for use on one of the peat mosses of Richardson's Moss Litter Co. Ltd near Carlisle. This was built at their request using ideas that they had for such a machine. It was to be used as a replacement for the ageing Lister locomotives on the temporary tracks used for harvesting peat. It was basically successful and subsequent models, designated K12, were refined and several sold to them and other users. This was followed by the K30 design of a 2½/3½ ton locomotive that was offered in direct competition with Simplex. Again these were sold to various customers but the crunch came with the sale of four, in two batches

of two, to ICI Nobels Explosives in Scotland. SMH also tendered, and I could be wrong, but I have always felt that it was the loss of this order that decided them to get out of the locomotive business altogether.

Previous to this RMP had always held a number locomotives in stock at Bedford in order to be able to offer immediate, or at least prompt, delivery of standard designs. But it was obvious that this was no longer viable and I received a circular from Bedford offering both 40S and 60S locomotives at very competitive prices. Quite by chance this coincided with AKL receiving an order from the Imperial Iranian Navy (this was in the days of the Shah) for a railway on a jetty to carry personnel from a ship to be used as barracks moored at the end of it. I snapped up two of these 40S locos which allowed very prompt delivery. With my experience at Butlins this train was to be fitted with fail safe air brakes. Typically, Simplex said it was not possible to fit air brakes to a 40S. It was actually very easy and led on to my fitting air brakes to some 60S locos for them! It was a measure of the state of British industry at the time that this contract

153. AK 26 of 1988 was supplied to Butterley Building Materials Ltd for their Star Lane Works near Southend-on-Sea. In order to provide a more comfortable and commodious cab this 40SD has reverted to the 20/28 frame but lengthened at the cab end only. Beginning to look scruffy it is heading a train of empties for the clay fields. Literally so, as this operation took a few feet of clay off the top of the surface rather than have the conventional clay pit.

154. AK 28 of 1989 was also supplied to Butterley Building Materials Ltd for their Cherry Orchard Works at Southend-on-Sea and is seen shunting loaded wagons into the tipping shed. In this case the full length 20/28 frame was used and both included the traditional screw-down handbrake.

comprising two locomotives, three quite sophisticated carriages and 800yds track, turnouts, etc was completed in a mere eight weeks! I have reason to believe that one of the locomotives later turned up in Damascus, of all places!

As stated in Chapter 9, a 40S was in build at the time of the take-over. This and the previously built 60S were included in the SMH works lists and numbering system thus meaning that Alan Keef Ltd have built two more new locomotives than its own numbers suggest. For the record, I did see the last locomotive to be built at Bedford, a 60S, in Tanzania some years later where it was derelict having suffered a problem with its Perkins engine that struck us later on and to which we never really reached an answer. This last 40S was built for Butterley Brick Co. for their works near Southend and we went on to build two more for them. For these we reverted to the 20/28 frame which gave a considerably more convenient cab size.

SMH had the enquiry before the takeover, so that in due course we received an order to build two U series locomotives for a coal mine in South Korea. In its way this was something of a coup as most trade with South Korea is the other way round. These were required to be of the hydrostatic variety and we had some considerable redesigning to do as many of the components in the original design were by now obsolete. It is sobering that these locomotives suffered many of the problems that Motor Rail had with the U series, again in part due to the external adjustments to the pump. We just could not stop the users fiddling with them! This was followed by rebuilding an early 60S to 3ft 6ins gauge for shunting main line wagons in Nigeria which in turn was followed by the supply of a new locomotive of the same type to the same customer. A year later we redesigned the Simplex 9 ton locomotive and supplied one for shunting the same customer's wagons in Port Harcourt Docks. In 1992 we built a metre gauge 60S for Guyana Sugar Corporation and this is almost certainly the last traditional Simplex that will be built. That is unless someone, somewhere, decides they want an original one built as a replica – and stranger things do happen! The truth of the matter is that by using the virtually indestructible JCB powershift transmission with shaft drive to our own design of axle-mounted final drive unit we can build a better locomotive cheaper than by sticking with the admittedly well proven Simplex designs.

At the time of the takeover we were told that we could expect at least two very large spare parts orders per year and for a while this did indeed happen. Aside from that the trade in spare parts has been considerable over the years but has inevitably tapered off as

155. In an attempt to bring the ubiquitous 20/28 up to date this one, 9543 of 1950, was rebuilt with a Deutz F3L912 engine and a Lipe automotive clutch. As can be seen the bodywork had to be widened by a couple of inches to get it all in but that was not a problem with Midland Irish Peat at Mullingar. In addition this locomotive was fitted with solid rubber tyres in order to increase adhesion. These worked well, even in wet conditions, and had a surprisingly long life before renewal was needed.

locomotives have been scrapped and rail systems closed around the world. At one stage we sold large numbers of spares to the Zambia copper mines but there seemed to be no logic to what they ordered unless they were actually building new locomotives themselves, and even then it didn't make much sense. From our point of view it had the further snag that we only got paid when the price of copper was high! We used to supply large numbers of spares to the UK peat industry until the environmentalists destroyed that industry and it moved to places where they are not so petty about these things. Over the years we have carried out major rebuilds and re-engining of Simplex locomotives, including a rebuild of a First World War armoured Simplex repatriated from Antigua. Perhaps surprisingly, two major rebuilds have been done for heritage railways, these being the T series locomotives mentioned previously that are now virtually unrecognisable as having come from Bedford. Similarly we supplied new engines and transmissions for some of the first T series locomotives to be built and supplied to a sugar estate in Tanzania. To see these in action with over a hundred wagons of cane behind them is a sight to gladden the enthusiast's eye.

However, we live in an age where everything is getting bigger all the time in order to take the so-called advantages of scale. This is as true of small railways as it is of the local supermarket. Aside from what are technically narrow gauge railways but are the national systems of most of Sub-Saharan Africa, for example, most of the remaining large systems are dealing in locomotives of 200hp plus (the Queensland sugar cane lines reach 750hp!) and as such left Motor Rail Ltd and its successors behind many years ago.

Which leaves the question. Why? In their early years as Motor Rail & Tramcar Co. Ltd they were well ahead of their time. They

156. In 1988 Alan was invited to Tanzania by Wigglesworth with the idea of resuscitating some of the 500 plus Simplex locomotives that had been supplied to East Africa. The only place where anything significant happened was at the Dutch-owned Lugongo Estate where two 3½ ton Simplexes were re-engined with the idea of using locomotives better suited to the light track in use. Here *Kidau* brings a train of sisal leaf in towards the mill. Shortly afterwards a change of management reverted to a 'big engine' policy that paved the way for replacement by tractors and trailers.

were innovative and willing to take on any work offering in their line of business. It could quite reasonably be said that they were at the cutting edge of the technology of the time. They had an absolute bonanza with the First World War and rose to the occasion with an ability that is mind blowing to look back upon. Their success with the Karachi trams and their designs of the various railcars they built were well ahead of their time. Indeed it is possible that they were too far ahead of their time and the world was not yet ready for the petrol or diesel railcar. They had built themselves a reputation that would have been the envy of any business but, perhaps on the strength of it, they seemed to vegetate from there on. As has been detailed, they seemed, as though with deliberate intent, to misjudge situations and therefore miss opportunities that could have kept them as a household name in their field of operations. In many ways maybe they had it too easy. Between the wars any material to be moved tended to mean movement by rail. The Second World War brought its deluge of work, although nothing like the time before. And whilst RMP kept locomotives rolling out of the door for perhaps thirty years, the company itself did not have to think very hard about it. It did not have to design new machines for new markets, and whilst it dabbled in the upcoming leisure market it did not take it seriously. In truth it should never have let Alan Keef Ltd get on its feet!

\* \* \* \* \*

Motor Rail's only significant entry into the leisure market was the provision of a 40S locomotive in 1966 dressed up to give it an American appearance together with four carriages for Wicksteed Park at Kettering. It may be doubtful whether they built the carriages themselves, certainly the wheels and axles were from Allens of Tipton. This was a very presentable train set and could have been a precursor to more business of that nature. There is, however, correspondence about supplying bogie carriages and for these they proposed to use 40S frames and wheels as bogies! Not surprisingly it became wildly expensive. There are doodles of a cosy little futuristic locomotive wrapped round a 40S which might have had a future. And of course, but nothing to do with them, there were at one time a goodly number of Simplex locos dressed up to look vaguely like a steam locomotive, or not, operating on park railways around the country. The ultimate in this direction has to be the conversion of a 20/28 into a vertical boilered steam

locomotive – and very successful it is too! Of the hundred or so locomotives built by Alan Keef Ltd, over sixty, and all the recent ones, have been for the leisure industry. Carriages to go with them are a substantial business and we must have built in the order of a thousand carriage bogies by now. As an example, at the time of writing we are building a fleet of eight carriages for a park in Belgium, these are large by park railway standards and cost in the order of £50,000 each. Motor Rail's insistence on a high quality job could have come into its own because some of these 'little railways' that they were inclined to laugh at work very hard indeed. The replacement train at Wicksteed Park, for example, carries at least 250,000 passengers in a season, which by any standards is an awful lot of people. However, this is totally dwarfed by the trainsets we supplied to the Iguazu falls in Argentina which have worked no less than 37,000 engine hours each since delivery in 2001 and handle some 1.5 million passengers per annum. The JCB transmissions are just in for their first overhaul! There would not have been enough business to keep a works the size of Elstow Road going but could they have reinvented themselves to supply some of the other components of the entertainment industry? Who knows.

157. The Motor Rail 9 ton design was resurrected to produce this 3ft 6ins gauge shunter, AK 37 of 1990, for Chemicals & Fertilizers Nigeria to use for shunting wagons in Port Harcourt docks. It is here seen on test at Lea Line prior to shipment. It was supplied without couplings which were to be fitted on arrival, presumably salvaged from redundant Nigeria Railways stock!

158. The first T series locomotives were supplied to the sugar estate of the Tanganyika Planting Co. (TPC) in Tanzania, although the hydraulic drive was not ideal for African conditions. Alan Keef Ltd re-engined four of them with 125hp Perkins engines and a JCB transmission unit with shaft drive to the axles. Thus transformed they were quite able to handle a train of over a hundred 3 ton cane cars. This is one of them but no-one has got round to painting it or tidying it up! The locomotive behind is a U series into which the engine and transmission from a metre gauge shunter (also Simplex) have been shoehorned! Bundles of cane can be seen being loaded in the background and over the head of the man sitting on the second locomotive is the snow-capped summit of Mount Kilimanjaro.

159. Commonly known to all concerned as the 'Steamplex', this is a rebuild of 20/28 MR 5877 of 1935. The boiler came from a steam boat and the non-reversing engine was either a ships generator or barring engine. As a consequence this drives through the original gearbox giving two speeds in either direction. The whole assemblage is described by those who use it as '*a wondrous thing that outperforms all our original expectations*'! As AK 93R of 2013 it can be seen on the Groudle Glen Railway on the Isle of Man.          *Courtesy Neil Hay*

160. Motor Rail's *Cheyenne* remains as a spare to AK 85 of 2010 at Wicksteed Park, Kettering. The four carriages in this train were also built by Alan Keef Ltd. Although only using the one trainset, this is one of the most heavily used railways of its type in this country carrying in excess of 250,000 passengers per annum.

161. (*Left*) In the spirit of quality that was the hallmark of Motor Rail, Alan Keef Ltd supplied this trainset to the Tren Ecologico de la Selva (Ecological Train of the Jungle) at the Iguazu Falls in Argentina in 2001. This railway works every day of the year, including Christmas Day, and by 2015 the two locomotives, AK56 and 57, had each clocked up no less than 37,000 engine hours of use, which equates to 7 hours for every day that they have been there!! Also in the spirit of Motor Rail these locomotives are radio controlled and can be driven from either end of the train. This obviates the locomotive running round its train at each terminus, creating a 3 minute turn-round time and thus 1.5 million passengers are carried each year.

# 12

# Other Business

## 1936–1970

This chapter covers the products that might be regarded as Motor Rail's 'own', as opposed to those built by concerns they took over, built under licence or simply bought and sold-on in this country. Those are covered in the next chapter.

## Petrol Loco Hirers Ltd

This company was set up as a completely separate entity as a partnership between J.D. Abbott, T.D. Abbott, G. Gale and A.H. Brown in 1921. Despite belonging to much the same people it was financially separate from the Motor Rail & Tramcar Co. Ltd, although it doubtless relied on the main works for overhaul of its fleet of locomotives.

Early records are sparse but by 1924 it was reported that:

- Five reconditioned locomotives had been bought from the MR&T Co. at a total cost of £1,000.
- The available hire fleet consisted of sixteen 2½ ton 20hp locomotives of which eleven were out on hire and five in stock.
- Of the locomotives owned since the commencement of the business six had been sold.

The business had particular relevance to the construction industry where plant was required for short periods only during work on specific contracts. Locomotives were often hired out with an option to purchase, which gave potential customers a chance to try them out and assess suitability for purpose before committing themselves. It did buy secondhand locomotives in its own right and no doubt relied on the main works to undertake any necessary overhauls. It also exhibited locomotives and its services at various trade exhibitions but it is not clear whether it did this in association with MR&T Co. or on its own account. The former would seem the most logical.

The business was acquired by Motor Rail & Tramcar Co. Ltd in 1930, with its partners being bought out for the sum of £12,400, and from then on operated as a department of the main business. To prevent a similar trading title being registered by someone else it was decided to form two limited companies, Petrol Loco Hirers Ltd and Diesel Loco Hirers Ltd, both as subsidiaries of Motor Rail Ltd (as the main company had now become) and these were registered on 24th April 1935. Neither of these companies actually traded.

In the process of the disposal of the hire business the names become convoluted. It seems that Petrol Loco Hirers Ltd became Dumpahirers Ltd to reflect the change in the business, although again it possibly never traded. The company then became Simplex Crane & Plant Ltd and there is a photograph showing a pickup truck signwritten accordingly, before ultimately becoming Bedfordia Cranes in May 1969.

Diesel Locomotive Hirers went through a similar process when Bedford Crane & Plant Hire Ltd was set up in conjunction with W.J. Billington Ltd and, initially at least, may have continued to hire out locomotives. It then became Bedfordia Plant (Earthmovers) Ltd in 1969 and Bedfordia Earthmovers Ltd in 1970.

The records suggest that this must have been a fairly substantial business in its own right and no doubt lucrative with it. Initially, locomotives were bought from MR&T Co. at a 15% discount with payment deferred for three years, for which privilege interest was charged at 5% per annum. If this continued into more recent years, and in view of the numbers involved, it must have put a considerable strain on Motor Rail's finances, always difficult at the best of times. The peak period was the first half of 1931 when there were no less than seventy-seven locomotives out on hire. This was more consistently equalled in the run-up to, and the first years of, the Second World War when the figures range from fifty-six to seventy, plus six to thirteen dumpers as well. The intervening years were very quiet indeed. There were generally a number (around ten but it could be into the thirties) of locomotives held in stock ready for immediate hire or, presumably, to cover for any breakdowns. The numbers were kept in line with need by selling off locomotives from the hire fleet, often to customers who had initially hired one for the purpose of trying it out. For full details of the numbers in the hire fleet at any one time see Appendix V.

The actual day-to-day operation of such a fleet must also have been considerable with the necessity of keeping track of all those locomotives, not to mention despatching them and retrieving them before the advent of today's crane-fitted lorries. In turn they must have had to be maintained and serviced both on site and on return from a period of hire, or reconditioned for subsequent sale. It must have provided a steady workload for some sections of the works. It also makes it all the more surprising that Motor Rail

162. Possibly the only tangible evidence remaining of either Petrol Loco Hirers, or its namesake, Diesel Loco Hirers Ltd, is this nameplate. It makes it clear that DLH is a subsidiary of Motor Rail and came to Alan Keef Ltd amongst the oddments of the takeover.

163. Most of what can be said about this product has been deduced from this picture and is detailed in this chapter. The inclined engine carries a plate from W.H. Dorman Ltd but is more reminiscent of Ford practice. Although apparently designed for electric start it has in this instance a starting handle of typical Simplex design. The components would be distinctly chunky to carry about but with a few simple tools the whole unit could be assembled.

164. This is an MR450 dumper packed for export. Dumper records cease to be useful after about 1950 so one cannot even guess where this unit may be going. It would be fitted with the Dorman 2LB engine and a modified locomotive 3-speed gearbox giving a road speed of up to 16mph. With 5 tons capacity and reversible controls it may have closed many a light railway!

(and its successors) were never interested in repairs and overhaul of locomotives either for their regular customers or for purchase and resale. They were quite happy to let George Bungey and latterly Alan Keef do it instead, and then grumble about them! There were of course many other firms in the scrap metal and plant dealing business who no doubt bought and sold Simplex locomotives as the occasion arose, such as George Cohen Ltd and T.W. Ward Ltd to name but two.

There is very little record of hire rates, but in 1924 it was decided that the rate for a 20hp petrol locomotive would be £5 per week although experience later reduced this to £4 per week. The hire fleet was retained into later years with a record of there being sixteen 20/28 locomotives available for hire as late as 1954.

## Portable Arc Welders

The Sure-Arc Electrode Co. Ltd were formed in 1932 and the minute books record an agreement to manufacture their portable welders signed in July 1933. Following this the two companies had a joint stand at the British Industries Fair of 1933. After that the record fades except that the company is listed in *The Aeroplane Directory of Aviation & Allied Industries* for 1937 as being based at 14 Lloyds Avenue, London EC3 but this was almost certainly just the registered office.

The units produced were petrol driven welding sets with AC/DC capacity and also arranged so that two operators could work from the same set, all of which was quite advanced for the period. Just how many of these units were made and over how long a period is unknown.

Some useful information can be deduced from the photographs. The radiator is pure Simplex but under a magnifying glass has THE SURE-ARC ELECTRODE CO LTD cast into the top tank and thus one can perhaps assume that the overall design was done by Motor Rail. As to whether Motor Rail had any financial stake in the manufacture of these units is unknown. Some intelligent guesswork suggests that this company later became part of Lincoln Electric Co. Ltd, a well-known name in the arc welding business. The radiator appears to have the top and bottom tanks cast in aluminium, presumably to save weight. Judging from the detachable handles attached to the components, the whole unit could be dismantled and manually carried to anywhere that two, or possibly four, men could walk. Trailer mounted sets were also available and it is likely that all concerned may have hoped for orders from the military as by then war was at least on the horizon.

## Dumpers

At risk of repeating some of what has already been said, Motor Rail were in the right place at the right time when they decided to produce a dumper design in 1936. They had major customers in the construction industry and preparations for war with Germany were about to become a reality even if they may not have been fully aware of that. Certainly by the time the first production units came along in 1938 rearmament was a reality. Also the decline in the use of temporary light railways for the movement of material was beginning to seriously bite into locomotive sales. They must have foreseen big things for the product to order an initial batch of twenty-five from the works. This confidence was indeed born out by subsequent sales, which by the war's end envisaged a production of twelve dumpers per month.

Motor Rail dumpers were massively built and utilised the engine, clutch and an only slightly modified gearbox as fitted into the 20/28 and 32/42 locomotives. From the sales leaflets most seem to have had the 3-speed gearbox giving speeds up to 15mph. They were also fitted with a reversible driving position as the locomotive gearbox gave equal speeds in either direction of travel.

165, 166. These two pictures taken from a sales leaflet for the MR450 dumper show the machine being loaded from a dragline bucket, common before the days of the hydraulic excavator, and fitted with an enclosed cab. The full cab with its bulbous door was designed to allow the driver to reverse his seat and stay in the dry although it might have been susceptible to passing damage.

The skip was gravity tipped and returned, and Motor Rail seriously investigated the possibility of hydraulic tipping, so as to give the driver better control of how much he tipped at any one time. This never went into quantity production and can only have exacerbated their problems in loss of market share. The skip seems to have been classified as of 3 cu. yds capacity in all cases although the struck capacity is given as 3¼ cu. yds and heaped as 4½ cu. yds with a gross load of 5 tons. They were intended for the serious movement of material.

Most were fitted with the Dorman 2DWD engine and later with the Dorman 2LB. As was the way with most contractors and agricultural machinery of the time the driving position was open to the elements. The MR450 could be fitted with a fibreglass cab with a bulbous door allowing the driver to reverse his seat position without getting wet. The windows look small but it was claimed the cab did not impair the driver's all-round vision.

The MR375, which the sales leaflets suggest was introduced in 1960, was a leap into a more modern era. It was fitted with a Lister HA3 air cooled engine driving through a Borg & Beck automotive clutch and gearbox and was classed as forward control as it could not be driven at all speeds in both directions. However, it compensated for this by having a top speed of all but 20mph.

It is difficult to judge just how many were built as the numbers run into 500 plus up to 1942, with only odd ones recorded thereafter. It is hard to believe that the trade just stopped, especially as they saw fit to redesign the machine in 1960 as the MR375 described above. In similar vein, they must have considered there to be a future because also in 1960 their dormant company Petrol Loco Hirers Ltd had its name changed to Dumpahirers Ltd.

On the basis of their own statistics the decision was made in 1965 not to produce any more dumpers. In spite of this an order was accepted and presumably built as late as 1968. It would seem more likely that the will to totally redesign the product so that it met the now changing market was simply too much effort. In any case locomotive sales had risen with the introduction of the hydraulic drive locomotives and the future may have seemed rosy without dumpers.

Many of the big contractors of the era bought them, often in very large quantities. W.C. French took no less than forty-eight in 1945 alone. A.M. Carmichael bought sixty-three over the wartime period, presumably for contracts in Scotland, whilst Glasgow Corporation Housing Department found use for forty-four. McCormick took thirty-five to various destinations in Ireland. Not many went abroad although Gloster bought a few for South Africa. It is believed that only one survives in preservation (see Chapter 14). Sometime around 1980 Alan Keef Ltd bought the remaining spare parts and drawings. None was sold as such but some were used for other (locomotive type) purposes.

The following table covers percentages of sales of different categories of product and gives a good idea of the spread of the business. Presumably it was figures like these that precipitated the decision to cease dumper manufacture.

| YEAR TO 20 MARCH | LOCOS | DUMPERS | SPARE PARTS | REPAIRS | OTHER |
|---|---|---|---|---|---|
| 1954 | 50.9% | 13.6% | 33.7% | 1.7% | 0.1% |
| 1955 | 42.7% | 10.9% | 44.9% | 1.4% | 0.1% |
| 1956 | 41.5% | 8.1% | 48.6% | 1.6% | 0.2% |
| 1957 | 49.4% | 5.1% | 44.1% | 1.4% | – |
| 1958 | 54.9% | 4.3% | 39.3% | 1.4% | 0.1% |
| 1959 | 41.6% | 11.0% | 44.5% | 1.5% | 0.1% |
| 1960 | 47.2% | 4.9% | 44.5% | 2.8% | 0.6% |

As in so many matters Motor Rail, they had hit the market just right before the war and then missed the opportunity at this later stage. Thus they could have seen off the challenge from upstarts like Thwaites and Benford, or even given the big boys like Volvo a run for their money. In this latter connection there is hearsay evidence that a 6 ton prototype was built but that it ended up languishing in T.D. Abbott's hedge from whence it was no doubt scrapped.

MR 375 the dumper with the AIR COOLED ENGINE

and these BIG ADVANTAGES

- will operate in *all* climates
- air-cooled diesel engine eliminates radiators and liquid cooling problems
- wide skip area for easy loading
- tough rolled steel frame takes every type of terrain in its stride
- twin ratio gearbox—sticky conditions present no problem
- spring loaded check chains prevent chassis damage while tipping
- fuel consumption only 2½ gallons per 8-hour working day

DESIGNED AND BUILT BY

MOTOR RAIL LIMITED

167. The MR375 was the machine that caused some excitement at the 1960 Public Works Exhibition and had moved the product into the modern era. It was fitted with the Lister HA3 air cooled engine, Borg & Beck clutch and gearbox. This had three forward and one reverse with high and low ratios; as a result, the dumper was uni-directional from a driving point of view but a road speed of all but 20mph may have compensated for this. The decision to cancel dumper production therefore becomes all the more surprising.

# 13

# The Search for Other Products

## 1965–1987

As recounted heretofore, the search for other products to make or to sell had started before the Second World War and was unrelenting from about 1960 onwards. Motor Rail had varying degrees of success in these ventures, tending to be less successful when it came to making the various products themselves. This may have been due to their regimented system of mass production which precluded lateral thought (LoLode Trailers), or through circumstances completely outside their control (Matisa). It may not have helped that they did not really have a sales office in the accepted sense of the term. In effect one or two people looked after sales of all sorts: up to the 1960s it was B.J. Tysoe and his assistant J. Stanway, followed by Roger Parsons, who regrettably died unexpectedly, and then John Hulme into the 1970s. These largely

dealt with UK sales, with overseas sales coming through RMP and other agents. After this date sales were handled by the managing directors, Tony Wenham and later Martin Everitt. Locomotive spare parts sales were dealt with by Peter Cross, who probably came to know more about Simplex than anyone before or since, with attachment sales handled by Don Skevington. Inevitably there was considerable overlap between all these people.

Although it came a little later in the day than some of their projects, this chapter starts with the fork lift attachment business (often shortened to FLA) as this eventually became the mainstay of the business and accounted for its change of name to Simplex Mechanical Handling Ltd.

168. This photograph sums up this chapter. Taken at The International Construction Equipment Exhibition at the Crystal Palace, South London 2nd-7th October 1967 it shows a 3ft gauge 110U series locomotive of 8 tons weight fitted with a Dorman 4DA engine ready for despatch to INCO in Canada. Centre stage is a Clarke sweeper (with attendant glamour!) and to the right a Thumper mounted on a Ford D series chassis. Somewhat lost behind the mast and the surrounding girders is a full cab for the operator from which could not only Thumper itself be operated but the vehicle be moved forward as well. Note also the caravan office and the MR roundels on the locomotive and the chain fencing. This would have been a costly exhibition to attend.
*Courtesy Bedford County Record Office*

## Forklift Attachments

It is recorded that in 1970 Motor Rail took over the manufacture and marketing of the forklift attachments made and marketed by Oldham & Son Ltd of Manchester, although in turn that company seems to have originally manufactured this equipment under licence from Little Giant Products Inc. from Illinois, USA. There is no doubt that when SMH came under Wemyss control this was the sector that that organisation wanted to keep and expand.

Oldham's aim was to concentrate on their core business of making batteries and Motor Rail took on their attachment business in its entirety to include stocks of spare parts, drawings, customer details, etc., etc. This was followed by a licensing agreement with the Californian firm of Brudi for the manufacture of similar equipment, particularly side shift units which sold 'in their hundreds'. Indeed there were proposals to have much of this equipment made in Korea at greatly reduced cost and simply import it to sell in this country. This never happened. In similar vein, side shifts and clamps were made for the Dutch company of Mandigar, but whether this was simply sub-contract work or for Motor Rail to sell is less clear. In times of high workload at Elstow Road forklift masts were bought in from Italy but created problems as, whilst notionally the same, there were subtle differences that made them incompatible.

Also at this time a night shift was set up to manufacture complete forklift trucks for Lancer Boss of Leighton Buzzard. All parts were to be supplied so it was, in theory, simply an assembly job. However, due to lack of management control at night it became something of a fiasco and came to an untimely end. Reputedly the staff were repairing their own and other people's cars when they should have been assembling forklifts!

Probably the largest items in this business were sophisticated container handling attachments for 20ft to 40ft containers. These were designed by an outside designer, one Eric Salmond, and proved successful to the point that some were made and sold after the closure of the Elstow Road works. As a measure of the scale of this part of the concern, 'On the Track' records the sale of 540 attachments in 1973 and a catalogue produced in 1987, their last year in business, lists some twenty-five different product lines with innumerable sub-categories for most of them. However, and for all that, it has been said that at best the manufacturing business only broke even, with profit being generated by the sale of spare parts, mostly locomotive.

This part of the business was sold off to a company, Simplex Attachment Spares Ltd, set up by two former members of the staff and still continues to supply spare parts as and when required.

169. From the photographic evidence it seems that side loaders were the principal items made for Lancer Boss and here is one (conceivably the first?) beside the front gate in April 1970, with both company's names to the fore. It is destined for Rijeka in what is now Croatia.

170. (*Above*) The apogee of SMH fork lift attachments were these container top lifts. This one is designed to handle 40ft containers and is shown upon delivery to Tilbury Docks in 1971. Note the size of the forklift required to use it.

171. (*Below*) Almost certainly the same toplift leaving the Elstow Road works with the main office block in the background.

172. A tyre manipulator from 1971. From other pictures of this attachment one can deduce that it could handle tyres of considerably larger diameter than that shown; it could pick them up from lying flat on the ground and then sideshift and rotate them to line up the wheel nut bolts. Although taken in the works yard, the forklift is badged for Taylor Woodrow Construction so perhaps this unit was made for them.

173. In similar vein pictures from 1973 show this pipe handler with a capacity of 10 tons. At that time the civil engineering industry was busy with replacement and new sewers in new towns such as Milton Keynes so this sort of equipment would have come into its own.

174. Barrel handling was always a significant sector of the Fork Lift Attachment business and here we see the sequence of operations for clamping and lifting a group of nine barrels. The barrels could be of 10, 18 or 36 gallons capacity. 1973.

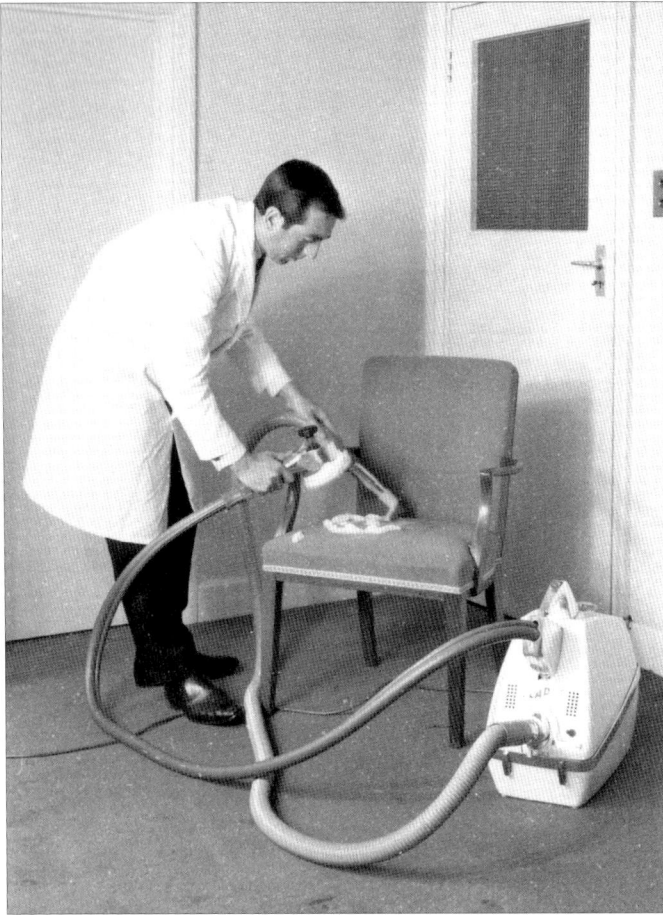

175. Apart from photographs of a consignment damaged in transit, this appears to be the only available picture of anything in the sweeper/ cleaner line that Motor Rail sold. This is the Clarke Shampooer-Vac being demonstrated in Mr Wenham's office and seems an unlikely product for a company like Motor Rail to try and market.

176. The Mars Sweeper was classified as a forklift attachment and it is doubtful if these were ever built at Bedford but were simply bought in and rebadged. It was ingenious in that it attached to a standard forklift truck and swept into its own container which is here shown in the open position.

## Sweepers

Sweepers were the first items to be licensed for manufacture in Bedford from an outside supplier and in about 1960 arrangements were made with Balayeuse Mathieu of Toul in France for the making of their range of road sweepers. Apparently a very few were actually made in Bedford, but after that they were simply imported from France, had the works plates and decals changed, and then sold on. This simple operation created useful sales and profits for the company with minimum effort. The Corvette 50, which was the principle model sold, was a manually operated machine and there were proposals to either convert it into a driven unit or design something new altogether. These ideas were overtaken by the new designs of hydrostatic locomotives which in turn were better understood by Motor Rail and promised greater sales volume.

The sales of sweepers seems to have quietly died away, possibly due to apathy as much as anything, as the French company is still in existence and still making sweepers! The only remaining record seems to be a tatty parts list for a Corvette 50 Industrial Sweeper. In similar vein, an agreement was reached with Studebaker International Corporation of the USA to sell their Clarkomatic scrubbing machines. Four were ordered in February 1965 but nothing more seems to be known about this venture. There is a picture of one on the stand at the exhibition the Crystal Palace in 1967 with a suitably glamorous girl in charge!

Whether it should be in this section or not is open to debate, but a MARS sweeper was sold, even if not manufactured in Bedford, to be mounted on the forks of a forklift. This not only swept but gathered the debris into a container that could then be emptied where required. This was more in the line of a road sweeping machine than the Corvette or Clarke machines.

## Thumper

Thumper was, and is, a machine for breaking up concrete roadways or floors, and also, with a suitable head, for compacting trenches. The principle of the unit was akin to a pile driver with a hammer head that could be individually controlled or set to give up to thirty strokes per minute, somewhat after the style of an out-size pneumatic hammer. The whole assembly could then be tilted down for transport on the road. Very little seems to be on record or known about this machine and indeed staff at Bedford seem to have treated it as something of a joke. Certainly the American-style leaflet with its overtones of Superman may not have helped and not been appropriate for this side of the pond. The units were manufactured in their entirety in Bedford and mounted on Ford D type chassis/cab units. As far as can be ascertained about a dozen were made and sold.

In April 1968 Mr Tysoe wrote to Mr S.W. Thieme of British Deutz Ltd, firstly about Deutz engines for a batch of fifteen locomotives for Cameroon and then, it would appear, about the possibility of using the Deutz network of agents for the sale of Thumper in Germany. In this instance the units would have been mounted on Deutz lorry chassis. This may be as much as we shall know of this product!

*In the meantime, I am enclosing two copies of our Thumper specification and this is the machine that we hope to introduce*

TRENCH CUTTING

SIDE TILT LEFT

SCREAMING STOPWATCHES – LOOK AT HIM GO!...

YEAH! WHEN THUMPER RACES TO THE RESCUE –THAT'S ANOTHER SCHEDULE SAVED!

ZOOM

motor rail ltd

simplex works bedford

Telephone: Bedford 56422.
Telegrams: Simplex Bedford Telex.
Telex: 82254 Simplex Bedford.

177. (*Above*) Taken from a Thumper leaflet, these three pictures explain what the machine was all about but the American gung-ho of the pictures may have tended to put off more conservative British buyers. Note the then new MR roundel logo on the back cover.

178. (*Right*) Thumper working alongside its competitor from Arrow Construction Equipment Ltd on the '*coast road between Newcastle and Whitley Bay*' in 1968. This was close to where the latter was made but why they are together is not recorded. Possibly as simple as that two machines were required for the job and neither firm had two available!

into Germany sometime during this year, but I am certain it will be necessary for us to mount the Thumper unit itself on a German chassis. My secretary will be sending you, within the course of the next two or three days, a specification of a Ford chassis, giving the modulus, so that your engineers in Germany can look into which of the Deutz lorries would be suitable for mounting the Thumper unit. To my knowledge, there is no other Mobile Hydraulic Hammer as yet produced on the Continent, and we are of the opinion that there is in fact a large market for this machine, particularly in the Common Market countries,

and as discussed, we shall be looking for a distributor who would be capable of taking the Thumper unit and mounting it onto a Common Market chassis, so that any help that Deutz can give us in this respect would be most appreciated.

In this country we are mounting the unit on a Ford D.550 chassis with a D.750 frame and the selling price for the complete unit is £4,750 plus £175 if a cab is required over the operator's console.

However, the Thumper Unit, on a sub chassis ready for mounting to a vehicle would be approximately £2,550, and it would be our intention to only offer this Thumper Unit through one main distributor.

There are a considerable number of photographs of Thumper in use in Bedford and in Northumberland. Indeed these include a photograph of Thumper working alongside a similar machine manufactured by Arrow Construction Equipment Ltd on the coast road near Blyth in Northumberland. This says it is near the Arrow factory although that company's business address was in London. Was there any tie up with America or was it a case of synchronicity of thinking? The pictures suggest that the machine is on hire, possibly through Diesel Loco Hirers. Thumper was exhibited at the International Construction Equipment Exhibition at the Crystal Palace in 1967 and again by McCormick at the Royal Dublin Show in May 1968. Technically, Motor Rail described it as a Hydro Hammer.

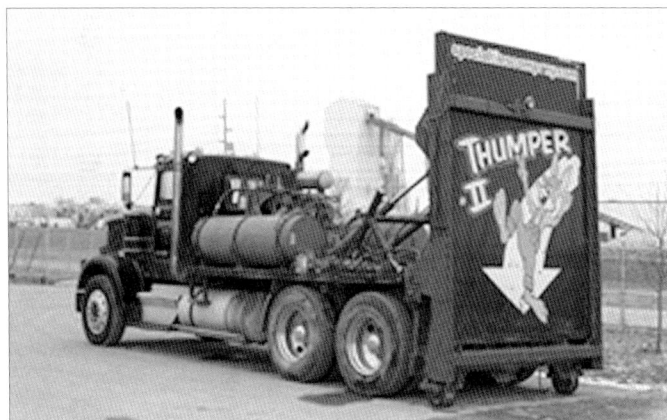

179. Taken from a modern website the Superman type image still exists. Even the website suggest that you will hear this machine in action before you see it!

180. This is close to being the only picture that shows the ingenuity of later versions of the LoLode trailer. By the use of a hand operated hydraulic system the whole trailer is lowered to ground level and whatever is on it, in this case a fork lift truck, can be driven off. Loaded or empty, the process was then reversed and locked in position at the correct ride height.                                    *Courtesy Bedford County Record Office*

181. This has to be a classic photograph from another era, but even in the early 1970s one might question using it on the front cover of leaflet about LoLode Trailers! A considerable number of these refuse trailers were supplied to the Cleansing Department of the London Borough of Tower Hamlets at that time.

The product is still manufactured and in use in the USA where it now has multiple heads to break a whole vehicle's width of concrete and as can be seen from the advertising photograph it still seems to maintain its 'Superman' image. The sales literature does say that you will probably hear the Thumper before you see it and from appearances that could be a considerable understatement!

## LoLode Trailers

The Low Loading Trailer Co. Ltd was founded by Major Cecil Vandepeer Clarke shortly after moving to Bedford in 1924. Having served with distinction in the First World War (he was awarded a Military Cross in 1918) he started by making his own design of car engine but gave this up when mass produced engines became available at much lower prices. His brother ran a large farm and he conceived the idea of making trailers of various types initially for farm use. In particular he thought that two-wheel trailers swung about too much when in use especially when they were horse-boxes.

In its shortened form of LoLode Trailers the business prospered and made a wide variety of trailers based on Clarke's design for a low slung chassis with four close coupled wheels and a particularly stable suspension system. Initially the company was based in Clapham Road, Bedford but later moved to Goldington Road. According to Wikipedia the company also made a name for itself in the design of purpose-built caravans that had facilities far ahead of their time. These included onboard batteries, petrol generators and a suspension system that allowed a passenger (this was permitted at that time) to pour out a hot drink at 40mph without spilling it. The designs also included a double deck vehicle with toilet, shower and

hot and cold water. Some of their more normal production may be seen in the photographs.

From the size of the buildings, of which parts can be seen in the background of some photographs, and emblazoned with their name, it seems that LoLode may have been a much bigger firm than Motor Rail. Intriguingly, also, there are some trailer sales leaflets that include the name of R.A. Wenham as a director. Perhaps there was an informal connection from long before Motor Rail took over the business of LoLode trailers in 1968 and transferred manufacture to Elstow Road. Whilst these trailers became a significant part of the business for a short period it was not as successful as might have been hoped. It seems that with the purchase came a three man team who built trailers to suit customer requirements very much on an ad hoc basis. This did not suit the establishment at Elstow Road where every last item had to have its part number and be itemised in the build list for each product. In order to take advantage of their mass production type of manufacture MR embarked on building a batch of 100 light trailers with the idea that every garage should have one to hire out to people with material to move. In their inimitable style they then purchased 100 of all the bought-in components, such as wheels and ball hitches, but only built about ten! The remainder went for scrap. Internally this was known as the UHaul trailer but whether there was any connection between this and the well-known American trailer manufacturers of the same name is unknown. Aside from this debacle it seems that the selling prices for trailers barely covered the cost of materials, never mind the actual cost of manufacture, painting, etc. Fairly rapidly it was realised that the trailers could not be manufactured profitably with this sort of system imposed upon them and the business was sold

# LO LODE Trailers for Highways and Industry
### 5cwt – 25tons

30 cwt. 2 wheel trailers for special application

4 Wheel Transporters 2½ tons. to 4 tons.

Special Trailers for your particular requirements

Cable Drum Transporters 30 cwt. to 6 tons.

7/15 cwt. Standard Tool Trailers

Tipping Refuse Trailers 2 and 4 wheels.

Tipping Hopper Trailers 225 gal. to 350 Gal.

12 ton. trailers with knockout axle.

182. This page from a leaflet of 1971 demonstrates the variety of standard LoLode trailers available with variations on every theme being possible. Interestingly, by this date the company's products are listed in order as being Simplex fork lift attachments, LoLode trailers and Simplex locomotives, and the leaflet arranged accordingly. How the world had changed!

183a, b. (*Left and above*) This is a modification of the U Haul trailer in 1971 to be used to carry demonstration welding equipment.

184. (*Above*) A trailer for HM Coastguard taken at Walton-on-the-Naze rescue HQ in 1973. Another very poor photograph shows a line-up of at least eight of these trailers.

185. (*Above right*) Also 1973, one of a large number of cable trailers built for the G.P.O. These suffered with problems of manufacturing quality and finish which meant that the order was not repeated.

186. (*Right*) There is nothing new in supplying your products in flat pack or knocked down form. Here we have a trailer for Iran cut down to the smallest possible volume in 1970.

around 1973. Motor Rail lore has it that the business was sold to a firm in Turvey but I have memories of seeing this type of trailer being made at premises in Kempston Hardwick, a few miles from Bedford. Certainly a firm called Eezion Ltd is recorded as trailer makers at this same address in 1976. It seems another suitable acronym for the Low Loading Trailer Company, but they may have gone out of business shortly afterwards.

The in-house magazine 'On the Track' provides the best guide to the extent of trailer sales, which tended to be given in value rather than numbers and averaged around £10,000-15,000 per month. There were peaks as in June 1971 when 100 trailers were on order and again in 1972 when 250 cable trailers were sold to the GPO. However, this latter customer had some serious complaints about the finish of these trailers and a plaintiff internal memo points out that they should try to do better as the gentleman concerned buys around £500,000 worth of trailers each year! Probably Motor Rail lost out.

## Unilok

As suggested in the planning meetings of 1965 after the Lenning takeover, it seems that Hugo Aeckerle of Hamburg headed the organisation founded in 1905 that now produced the Unilok tractor. This is a road/rail shunter and was well proven in Europe at the time. The unit is arranged to take some of the weight of the first wagon in its train in order to give it adequate adhesion for its relatively low weight and power to handle the loads intended. Problems arose, however, when a prototype was imported for trials and subsequent sale. This was given a works number, 13954, even though it was basically a German product. It was designed to shunt standard European wagons whose axles were nearer to the end of the vehicle than was the case with the British wagons. This altered the weight to point of balance ratio and resulted in a test rake of wagons slewing the tractor sideways and thus losing control of the load. Quite apart from the bad publicity of this incident a considerable

amount of design work would have been needed to make it suitable for British conditions and no further examples were either imported or made. Ultimately Unilok set up their own manufacturing facility in Galway, Ireland from whence they still operate.

Motor Rail produced a very professional glossy booklet that included their latest logo, explaining how the machine worked and including a number of interesting and excellent photographs. It is not entirely clear whether it was part of the original concept or whether it was Motor Rail having their own input, but it is certainly shown with a forklift mast and typical MR attachments are offered with it. One would think that it might have been an extremely cumbersome beast to use as a forklift truck. It was fitted with a Volkswagen four-cylinder petrol engine that from the pictures looks very reminiscent of the VW Beatle.

## Matisa

Matisa (UK) Ltd was a Lenning venture and by some means, possibly by their being agents for Matisa in South Africa, they had acquired the rights for Matisa products in the United Kingdom. At some point in the early 1960s they offered to sell these rights together with a licence to manufacture M & R loaders in the UK to Motor Rail. The offer was not accepted. However, even if not purchased, this company initially shared offices with Motor Rail.

Although British Railways used a number of Matisa ballast cleaning machines it is believed that by this stage they had decided not to adopt them as standard and therefore the available business was mainly for spare parts which were made in the works. Later, separate offices were provided in the form of 16 Elstow Road, one of the houses owned by the company, and this they continued to occupy after the sale of Motor Rail Ltd to Burnholme & Forder Ltd in 1972. Later still they had an office within the works complex.

This provided useful manufacturing business for the works but by the nature of the circumstances was a declining market from the start, although at the time Motor Rail were not to know this.

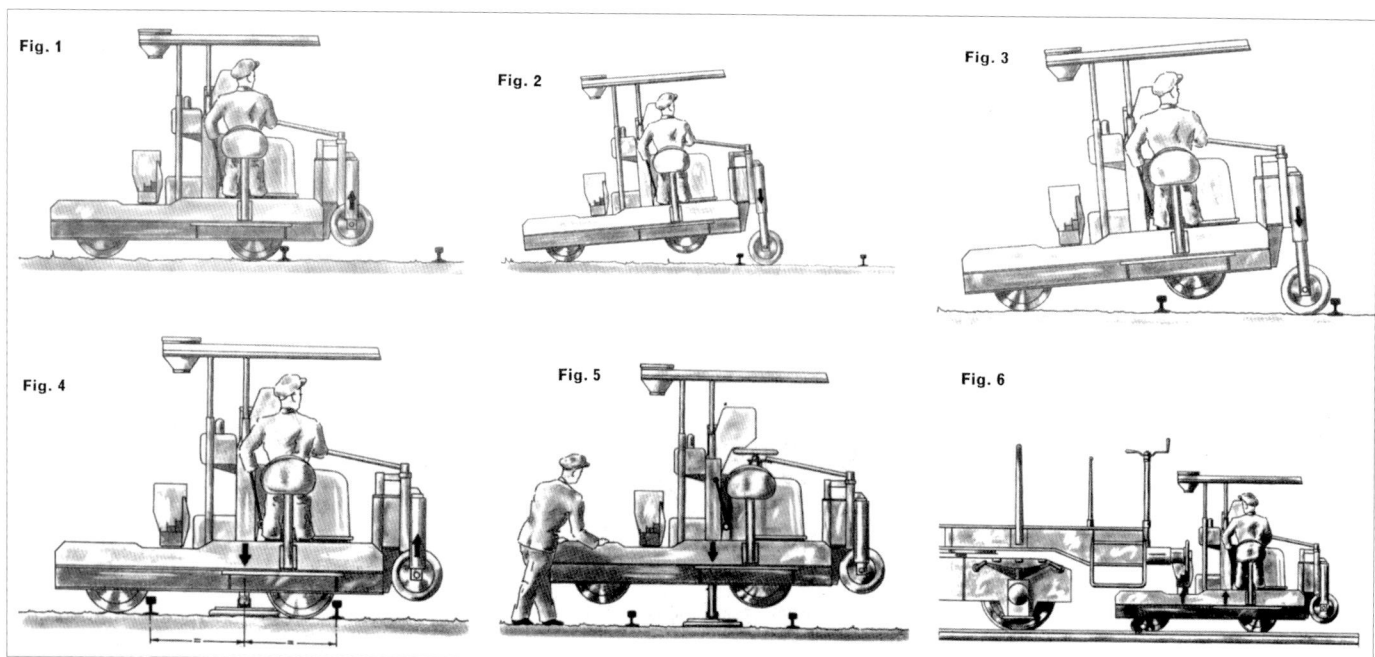

187. Taken from a glossy sales leaflet produced by Motor Rail, this shows the principle of the Unilok and how the operator got it onto the track. Up to six tons of weight was taken from the leading wagon in order to provide the necessary adhesion.

The Unilok does its work at one tenth of the operating costs of conventional locomotives.

Speed up and save with the Unilok system.
See it work.

**MOTOR RAIL LTD · SIMPLEX WORKS · BEDFORD**

TELEPHONE: BEDFORD 56422          TELEX: SIMPLEX BEDFORD 82254

188. From the same leaflet, the unit with a substantial train even if not the full 200 tons claimed. The solid rubber or neoprene tyres are very evident in this picture.

189. Unilok was offered with a fork lift attachment and this may have been part of its attraction to Motor Rail, but one cannot but think that it would have been a very cumbersome machine to use in this form. As can be seen the front wheels do the steering, the leading rail wheels are flanged but the rear ones are not and have a hydraulically raised guide wheel behind them.

190. A Matisa ballast cleaning machine probably somewhere in the Leighton Buzzard area. Motor Rail's involvement with these machines was to manufacture and supply spare parts for them. Despite the fact that Matisa had an office within the Simplex works complex up until closure these machines had ceased to be British Rail's preferred choice even before Motor Rail became involved. Thus through no fault of their own the business did not develop as might have been hoped.

## Lenze

For a period around 1970 Motor Rail were sales agents for the German firm of Lenze, makers of electro-magnetic clutches and transmission units. In this they were successful although as far as can be ascertained Motor Rail did not actually make anything themselves. Doubtless they lived in hope that ultimately they would do so. This was obviously set up as a no-cost experiment by the German firm and when successful they did not renew the sales agency but in turn set up their own manufacturing unit in Bedford from which they continue to be very successful. Indeed their website suggests that Bedford may now be their head office.

# 14

# Locomotive Histories

Much has been written about the types of locomotive built by Motor Rail Ltd and for more precise details the authors would refer the reader to *A Guide to Simplex Narrow Gauge Locomotives* by D.R. Hall and J.A.S. Rowlands. This, as its name suggests, covers their narrow gauge production in useful detail. For more extensive information of the early railcar production and subsequent development of standard and narrow gauge locomotives *The Early Years of the Motor Rail & Tram Car Company 1911–1931* by the late W.J.K. Davies can hardly be bettered. For details of what was built, when and for whom *The Motor Rail List* by Clive Walters and Robin Waywell is incomparable and has the merit of having been compiled from the official work sheets for each locomotive. All these have been invaluable in compiling this book.

Therefore, it is proposed in this chapter to deal with their products in a more 'personal' manner by detailing the history of individual locomotives from manufacture through the vicissitudes of their history with as many photographs as are obtainable. Inevitably there will be gaps and not all types can be covered, but hopefully this will be of more general interest than a collection of facts and figures. No apology is made for the fact that a large number of these locomotives have been altered or sold through Alan Keef Ltd. It is, after all, what that company does!

Except as otherwise detailed, all these locomotives are of 2ft nominal gauge, bearing in mind that First World War and MoD locomotives were of 600mm gauge so that they could be used on the enemy's tracks if appropriate. A part of the criteria for this section is that the locomotive in question still exists at the time of writing and is available to be seen. However, readers should be aware that there may well be restrictions on doing so where it is in commercial use or in private ownership.

## 1.   20hp Tractor MR 246 of 1916

Motor Rail, or more correctly Motor Rail & Tramcar Co. Ltd, works numbers start at 200. Possibly the earlier numbers were used on the Karachi tramcars or, more likely, they wanted to

191. 20hp tractor, MR 463 of 1917, *'somewhere in France'*. This is what 246 would have looked like and been doing during its spell in France. The crew look cheerful, so despite the devastation they may not be too close to the front. This is a good shot of the driving position of one of these locomotives. The driver has his foot hovering over the clutch pedal, with one hand on the screw handbrake, the other on the throttle and the gear change readily to hand.
*Collection Industrial Railway Society*

give a better impression of the quantity of their products sold! It was quite a common practice at the time. Therefore locomotive No. 246 can claim to be very early in their production and with a fair degree of certainty one can say that it is the oldest Simplex locomotive still in existence. It was delivered to the Ministry of Munitions for use in France in 1916, with no specific date being given. It was one in their Order No. DRT 824 for forty locomotives, which in turn was part of seventy-two locomotives delivered that year. It carried the running number LR246 which at that date followed the works numbers. Although not stated, it can be assumed to have been built to 600mm gauge and to have been fitted with a Dorman 2JO petrol engine.

Being very possibly one of the batch purchased jointly with

William Jones Ltd it went to Howden Bros Ltd of Larne, County Antrim, Northern Ireland in July 1921. This company were shipowners and coal and stone merchants, but also operated a granite quarry at Carnduff, where presumably the locomotive was used to haul stone from the quarry face to a crushing plant. A new engine was supplied for it in March 1927.

When this operation closed around 1950, it was sold to S. McGladdery & Sons Ltd for use at their Collin Glen Brickworks to the north-west of Belfast, from whence it was donated to the Belfast Transport Museum in 1971 and was put on display at their premises in central Belfast. In 1985 it moved to the new transport section of the Ulster Folk & Transport Museum at Cultra where it may now be seen.

192. With near certainty one can say that this is the oldest Simplex locomotive still in existence. Despatched to France in 1916 with no precise date given, it probably came back to Motor Rail in the combined purchases with William Jones Ltd before going to the granite quarry of Howden Bros near Larne in Northern Ireland. It then moved on to a brickworks before being donated to what is now the Ulster Folk & Transport Museum at Cultra.
*© National Museums Northern Ireland. Collection Ulster Folk & Transport Museum*

## 2. 40hp Tractor MR 435 of 1917

As recorded earlier, the 40hp tractors came in three forms, open, protected and armoured and this was one of the protected variety, recorded as being of the 'later protected type'. Just what this latter designation refers to is unclear but it may be the cooling arrangements noted in Plate 39. The typical heavy curved ends were not only protection but also served as ballast to help bring the locomotive weight up to 6¾ tons. It was one of four despatched on 1st September 1917, again to the Ministry of Munitions, France. It was fitted with a Dorman 4JO petrol engine and on these locomotives the driver sat on top of the engine with the gearbox under his feet with clutch and gear change controls thus very convenient for him.

Once again this locomotive must have been one of the 'buy-back' machines from the French Disposals Board as it was reconstructed to 2ft 6ins gauge in 1924, renumbered 3663 and sold through Henckell Du Boisson & Co., of London EC4 to St Kitts, part of the Leeward Islands in the Caribbean. Here it would have worked on the extensive sugar cane railways, a system that ultimately encircled the island and which became a Hunslet and Ruston stronghold when the power requirements outgrew anything Motor Rail could provide. With these increased power requirements the Simplex became redundant and along with other locomotives it became derelict until overtaken by the tropical undergrowth.

But all was not lost. In 2007 it was purchased by an English railway enthusiast who repatriated it. Alan Keef Ltd then set about restoring it to a near original condition that included replacement of some frame members and the curved ballast weights. It was re-gauged and fitted with chopper couplings to suit the Ffestiniog Railway where it joined its younger sister from the First World War, *Mary Ann*, MR 596 of 1918. As part of this rebuild it was fitted with a 4-cylinder Gardner engine that had been reclaimed from a Jaguar car!

193. This is not MR 435 but is typical of the condition of locomotives abandoned in Antigua following the cessation of sugar refining and at the time of writing is still there. This one has not only had large holes cut in the armour plate to give better cooling to engine and driver but had the armoured roof raised for the same reasons. It still retains its petrol engine and, remarkably, the Simplex silencer on the roof. These latter could glow red in the dark making an interesting target for enemy snipers!

194. In 2005 a lonely locomotive crosses the Britannia Bridge between the Ffestiniog and Welsh Highland railway systems in Porthmadog, North Wales. Note the addition of vacuum brake pipes for use on the Ffestiniog Railway.
*Courtesy Peter Johnson*

195. A good picture of the driver's position on a 40hp tractor. He sits on top of the engine casing, with his right foot on the clutch pedal and the hand brake wheel convenient for his right hand. The short lever between his legs is for forward/reverse and the longer one for 1st and 2nd speed. Fuel tank is to the left of the handbrake column with the radiator balancing it on the opposite end. Note also the vacuum brake valve behind driver's left arm and the position where a step would have been fitted.

196. This is not MR 2262, but its sister MR 2263 which went to Agwi Petroleum at Fawley in Hampshire. When sold from there it was used in the dismantling of the Ringwood to Salisbury line and is seen with a train at Breamore Station on that operation.

*Courtesy Stephenson Locomotive Society*

197. (*Below*) In the early days of the Foxfield Railway when the railway was operated from the upper terminus, *Helen* was used to shunt the train into a siding in order to allow the steam locomotive hauling it to run round to other end of its train. It is here seen performing that operation.

*J.A. Peden. Collection Industrial Railway Society*

## 3. 65hp Standard Gauge. MR 2262 of 1923. *Helen*

Whilst the standard gauge version of the 40hp tractor was a very successful design, it was felt that something larger was required. A prototype of a 65hp locomotive was sent to the Nitrate Railways of Chile and two further examples of the same design were built for stock. This example was sold to the Cornforth Limestone Co. Ltd for use at their quarry at Cornforth in County Durham, but not until September 1929. It was used to shunt the quarry and the lengthy siding leading to it. As far as sales were concerned they proved a singularly unsuccessful design with the sister locomotive remaining in stock for some thirteen years!

Although these machines looked most unlike anything that Motor Rail built either before or since, they were to the same basic design inside with the transverse engine and gearbox. The arrangement of the controls was taken directly from that used on the Karachi trams with forward/reverse and gear change levers working transversely from the driving position to the gearbox. These controls are duplicated so that the driver can always face the direction of travel and be on the left-hand side of the locomotive. Originally fitted with a White & Poppe petrol engine this was changed to a Dorman 4RBL in 1934 and eventually to a Dorman 4DL. This latter is recorded as having been a rebuild by Motor Rail but they could have supplied a kit of parts for it to be done on site. It then passed through George Bungey's hands in 1949 before going

to Dunlop Rim & Wheel Co. Ltd of Coventry a year later, again for shunting private sidings. In the mid-1960s this came to an end and the locomotive moved into preservation at the Foxfield Railway near Stoke-on-Trent in 1968. Here it was initially used to shunt trains until such time as a proper passing loop could be installed at the lower end of the line. It is not currently in operational order but at least it can be seen.

198. *Helen* looking a bit woebegone at the Foxfield Railway once her duties as shunter had been overtaken by a proper passing loop. A rebuilding project has ground to a halt with the loco now entirely open to the elements.

## 4.  40hp Standard Gauge.
## MR 2098 of 1924. *Rachel*

This was the typical early form of standard gauge locomotive that sold well and proved itself ideal for the private sidings with relatively small numbers of wagons to be moved. It was fitted with the well proven Dorman 4JO petrol engine driving through the equally well proven gearbox that had been fitted to the 40hp tractors for the First World War. It was supplied new to James Cropper & Co. Ltd for their Burneside Paper Mills near Kendal in what is now Cumbria. A later spares order suggests that this was a rebuilt locomotive, but no details are available unless perhaps the 'works' of a bought-back tractor were fitted into a new frame. Certainly if that was the case then Motor Rail would have given it a new works number.

In some respects this locomotive does not fit the criteria for this section in so far that it worked in the same place all its life until sold into preservation in 1973. It was not just a the odd siding that it operated on, however, but two quite extensive lines, one about half a mile long that served the company's main works, and indeed its current head office, but also another line a mile and a half or so in length that ran to a subsidiary operation at Cowan Head Mill. The former of these lines seems to have included some street running as well, although this may have been a private access road. There must also have been some very sharp curves for it to have been fitted with the extra large heads on its buffers. Whether these were from new is not known but from appearances they have seen some rough service over the years. The locomotive is reputed to have acquired its name from one of the owner's daughters who loved to ride on it as a child. It can be seen today at the Lakeside & Haverthwaite Railway not many miles from where it spent its working life.

199. Here *Rachel* is entering the Burneside Mills of James Cropper & Co. Ltd in 1950 and pushing some wagons before her. This is still the main access to the works and appears to have included a short stretch of street running.
*B Roberts. Collection Industrial Railway Society*

200. One man and his locomotive! A proud driver stands beside his machine in the exchange sidings at Burneside Station in 1951, on the track that leads a mile or more westwards to the subsidiary Cowan Head Mills.          *B. Roberts. Collection Industrial Railway Society*

201. (*Right*) Remarkably, a small section of the track to Cowan Head Mills remains in place under the tarmac at Burneside Station in 2015.

## 5. MR 7215 of 1938. *Kate*

Aside from the 20hp and 40hp tractors built for the First World War, the 20/28hp type was to become the most ubiquitous of all the locomotives that Motor Rail produced. Some 190 locomotives of this type were built for either the War Office or the Admiralty between 1943 and 1945. It is sobering to consider that A. Gloster bought well over 200 of the same type for South Africa over a similar time period in the early 1950s!

No. 7215 was an early one having been built in 1938 for the Ham River Grit Co. Ltd in Surrey. This company were major users of Simplex locomotives but eventually moved to other means of transport. Around 1965 the loco moved on to Joseph Arnold & Sons Ltd at Leighton Buzzard where it was unusual in being a 3½ ton machine whereas most of their quarry locos were only of 2½ tons. It had a stint at their outlying quarry at Stone, near

Aylesbury, from 1965 to 1973 where it was numbered 8 but became 21 when returned to the centre of operations. In due course the cannibalised frame went to the Teifi Valley Railway in West Wales in 1982.

It then came into Alan Keef Ltd's hands and, following re-engining with a new Deutz F3L912 engine, plus acquiring the name 'Kate', commenced on a peripatetic career that would have been typical of locomotives in the Diesel Loco Hirers fleet. At various times it was with Taylor Woodrow at their Isle of Grain segment plant for the Channel Tunnel, with Pirelli in the Woodhead Tunnel, involved in the restoration of the Rochdale Canal, once again with Taylor Woodrow at their Southall segment plant and then sold in 1995 to the peat operation of Joseph Metcalf Ltd on Chat Moss, near Manchester, for which the weights were removed to reduce it to 2½ tons. Although that system has closed it remains in store; perhaps for future use?

202. (*Left*) As No. 21 in the fleet of Joseph Arnold Ltd, MR 7215 climbs out of New Trees Quarry in 1973 with a train of sand for the lorry loading tip. It is being banked from behind by MR 5859 of 1934 which also started life with Ham River Grit. With both being 3½ tonners, unusual at Leighton Buzzard, it gives a measure of the steepness of the gradient. The 24 RB excavator in the background will have been used to load the train. *Courtesy S.A. Leleux*

203. (*Below*) *Kate* emerges into the daylight with a train of concrete tunnel segments whilst with Taylor Woodrow at their Southall, Middlesex, plant. It was on hire here whilst a new Alan Keef K40 locomotive was in build. Note the underslung weights at each end that increase the weight from the more common 2½ tons to 3½ tons. In practice, with the much lighter Deutz engine and the removal of the Simplex radiator it is probably not much over 3 tons in this guise.

204. *Kate* in use on the restoration of the Rochdale Canal. A remarkably good track was laid along the towpath for the movement of materials for this job.

## 6.  32/42. MR 10409 of 1954. No. 43. *Trotter*

Along with the 20/28, the 32/42 was a staple of Motor Rail production for many years until superseded by what became the 60S. Fitted with the Dorman 2DL engine of, as the classification suggests, around 40hp and fitted with a 3-speed gearbox it could be supplied in weights up to 6 tons. It could be fitted with cabs of various types and on occasion with full Westinghouse air braking. It was a popular locomotive and large numbers were sold to both East and South Africa.

This particular locomotive is perhaps unusual in that whilst it has had a number of different owners it has worked on the same railway all its life and is still doing so today. It was sold to the Leighton Buzzard Light Railway Co. Ltd and despatched on 14th January 1954, where it was numbered No. 11. This railway served the two principal sand companies in the Leighton Buzzard area, Joseph Arnold & Sons Ltd and George Garside Ltd. The railway's purpose was to transport sand some 4½ miles from the pits to the main line railway. The railway company only owned the track and the locomotives, upon which and with which it hauled the sand companies' wagon loads of sand. The railway company was always independent of the sand companies even if their destinies were inextricably intertwined.

By 1958 the LBLR became simply the owner of the track; the locomotive stock was divided up and sold to Arnold and Garside, with No. 11 going to the former, who renumbered it 43 in their stock. It continued to carry out its function of two or three trains a day of twenty-four wagons each, to be delivered to the washeries or the main line. In 1968 the railway moved into the preservation era, with No. 43 being purchased by one of the society members. It continued to work the same length of track but now as a passenger operation. Not being fitted with air brakes it may have been used on passenger duties in the early days but latterly was a workhorse of the line for maintenance and similar purposes. More recently it has been fitted with air brake controls which allow it to operate either with another compressor-fitted locomotive or with a brake van containing an independent compressor. It remains in very much as-built condition and can be seen working on its original railway today.

205. Probably taken shortly after the transfer of the Leighton Buzzard Light Railway locomotives to the sand quarry owners at the end of 1958, this is now Arnold's No. 43 in more or less the same position as the protected 40hp tractor shown in Plate 54. The overall white cab denotes an Arnold locomotive, those transferred to Garside having a white triangle on the back of the cab. Also, Arnold did not name their locomotives whereas Garside did, usually after racehorses.

206. On the double track of the LBLR between Stonehenge tile works and Double Arches quarry, No. 43 rattles along with the standard load of twenty-four sand wagons heading for the exchange sidings at Billington Road. It is obviously a warm midsummer day, with the second man riding outside in his shirt sleeves. *Courtesy Frank Jux*

207. (*Below*) *Trotter* looks as though it has just arrived at Pages Park Station on the Leighton Buzzard Railway. It is standing more or less where the right hand track is in Plate 1. It is working double headed with Arnold's No. 44, MR 7933 of 1941 The difference between the 6 ton and 5 ton locomotive is striking. The first vehicle of the train is a brake van converted from MR 5608 of 1931 and contains a compressor for the train's air brake system. *Courtesy Mervyn Leah*

## 7.  G Series. SMH 104G063 of 1976

This was one of a pair of G series locomotives supplied in 1976 by Simplex Mechanical Handling Ltd, to Severn Trent Water Authority for use in their Newstead sewerage treatment works near Stoke-on-Trent. It was fitted with a Kirloskar RA2 engine amidst a fanfare of trumpets as this was intended to be an introduction of this Indian copy of a Deutz engine to the UK market. These engines proved to be dirty and unreliable but got over the problem of what appeared at the time to be a worldwide shortage of small diesel engines.

In the programme of closure of their sewerage works railways this locomotive was sold at auction into preservation at the Old Kiln Light Railway in Surrey in 1986. Surprisingly, in 1988 it was then sold back into industrial service with ERS Mining Ltd at Whittle colliery, County Durham, via Alan Keef Ltd. Apparently they were desperate for a small locomotive to work the surface stockyard. This did not last long as the engine finally expired.

It then passed through Alan Keef Ltd's hands again in 1991, back into preservation with Tim Shelton who operated a replica mineshaft in his garden. He re-engined it with a Petter engine with which many of the G series were fitted and continued to use it. It then passed through several enthusiasts' hands before finally arriving at the Apedale Valley Light Railway at Newcastle-under-Lyme, near Stoke-on-Trent, and in the process acquired the Deutz equivalent of the Kirloskar engine. Coincidentally, it thus ended up not so very far from where it first started work.

208. Seen it its working days at the Severn Trent Water sewerage works in Stoke-on-Trent, it is hauling clinker for the filtration beds. These locomotives could cope with lightly laid track, were small, compact and powerful, if slow with it. This view was taken sometime after delivery, probably around 1978.

209. Looking suitably well used, this is it back in industrial use as a stock yard loco with ERS Mining at Whittle Colliery, near Morpeth in County Durham. This followed its short spell in preservation at the Old Kiln Light Railway in Surrey.          *Courtesy Jim Hay*

210. (*Right*) In preservation again, SMH 104G063 was used on a replica mine railway built into a very congested site. As a consequence pictures of it tend to be cluttered with other things.

## 8. 40SD. SMH 40SD530 of 1987

Technically this was the last locomotive of any type built by Motor Rail/Simplex Mechanical Handling and was completed in 1987 for Butterly Building Materials Ltd to be used at their Star Lane Works, Rochford Essex. In fact the frame was made in Bedford with the remainder by Alan Keef Ltd, who had the year before moved to Ross-on-Wye. This was part of the sub-contract arrangement between the two companies. It was in the middle of the manufacture of this 3½ ton locomotive that Alan Keef Ltd took over the locomotive business of Simplex Mechanical Handling Ltd (see Chapter 9).

The machine was slightly modified at Star Lane by having the cab roof raised a few inches to make egress marginally easier. (Later locomotives supplied to this works and built by AKL in their own right had much more commodious cabs.) In 1997 the railway at this works was cut for the installation of a new gas main for a period of some months. When that job was completed Butterley decided that railways were too old fashioned for their smart works and the line closed for good, this despite the representations of local management.

Along with the other locomotives in use at this and their Cherry Orchard works, it was bought back by Alan Keef Ltd and subsequently re-gauged to 2ft 8½ins for use on Volk's Electric Railway at Brighton where it can still be seen. Here it is used on the world's oldest electric railway for maintenance and car transfer purposes in the winter when power is switched off. In the process it was raised slightly to give clearance over the third (live) rail.

211. The frame of 40SD530 was made in Bedford but the remainder was built by Alan Keef Ltd during the period of the takeover. It was for the Star Lane Works of Butterley Brick Co. Ltd at Southend-on-Sea and is seen leaving the tipping shed with a train of empties. The locomotive is so new that this could be its first load of clay. Only a few years later the railway was closed for somewhat petty reasons.

212. After the line was closed the locomotives were simply abandoned. The Simplex cab on the 40s and 40SD locomotive was always very awkward and it is obvious here that at some stage the roof has been raised in an effort to alleviate the problem.

213. All the locomotives were bought by Alan Keef Ltd and this one was re-gauged to 2ft 8½ins for maintenance purposes on Volk's Electric Railway at Brighton. The loco has been visibly raised to clear the electric pick-up rail and had the cab removed to make the driving position easier for frequent access.

## 9.   60S. MR 11004 of 1956.
## Later AK 29R of 1989

At the time of its manufacture this locomotive was classed as being of 50hp and only later did the type become the 60S. It was fitted with a Dorman 3LA engine, later to become the 3LB and eventually the 3LD, rated at 72hp, driving a 'beefed up' version of the 3-speed gearbox fitted into the 32/42. Initially these machines were weighted to 6 tons but later, with the more powerful engine, 7 tons became the norm.

Possibly few locomotives have had such a chequered career as this one which started before it was even built! The records state that it was ordered in 1956 as a 5 ton locomotive by Wigglesworth for Tanga in Tanzania and even suggest that it was despatched. Then it was returned to Motor Rail stock and became part of the Diesel Loco Hirers fleet. In 1960 it was sold to Mitchell Plant Ltd of Peterborough as a secondhand 7 ton loco. It presumably had had the ballast weights changed and possibly the engine as well although that is not recorded. It was probably used on the Morar Dam in the north of Scotland.

About 1971 Alan Keef bought it from Anglo Scottish Plant Ltd of Peterborough, who may or may not have been successors to Mitchell Plant, and sold it on to Reed & Mallik Ltd for use on the aqueduct they were driving through the mountain at Foyers on Loch Ness. It was bought back at the end of this contract and

prepared for use on the Channel Tunnel Project that was getting under way at that time. When this was cancelled it went on hire to Balfour Beatty Ltd for use on the contract for the second Dartford Tunnel. There it was thrashed unmercifully on the 1:30 grade up out of the tunnel but survived to be used another day. This time it was converted to 4ft gauge by welding on channels to the sides of the frame to carry the axleboxes and making longer axles to suit the gauge. In this form it was used by Taylor Woodrow Ltd for the rebuilding of the Glasgow Underground, known officially as the Subway and colloquially as 'The Clockwork Orange' after the colour of its new rolling stock. In the process of this contract it also acquired fail-safe air brakes.

At the end of the contract the locomotive languished in Taylor Woodrow's yard and later in Alan Keef Ltd's. It was then completely rebuilt to the point that it carried a new AKL works number 29R. This included a new Perkins engine, alteration to 3ft 6ins gauge, full height and width headstocks, pockets for main line couplers, side steps and a canopy over the driver. In this form it was exported to Kaduna in northern Nigeria to shunt main line wagons for its new owners Fertilizers & Chemicals (Nigeria) Ltd. From the fact that spare parts are still occasionally supplied one can only presume that it is still there and still in use. For the record, a second locomotive of the same type was supplied to the same customer a year later for use at Kano, albeit that this time it was new throughout.

214. As the works number suggests, MR 11004 of 1955 was a very early 50hp locomotive that after various vicissitudes ended up in 7 ton form in use with Balfour Beatty on the construction of the Dartford road tunnel. Here it is on the 1:30 ramp up from the air lock at the tunnel entrance. From the name on the side it will be noted that this is before the days of Alan Keef Ltd which was formed in 1972.

215. Here is MR 11004 in 4ft gauge form ready for the journey north to Glasgow to assist in the rebuilding of the Glasgow Subway (Underground). It has acquired a cab, outriggers for the lengthened axles and been repainted in Taylor Woodrow colours. The black box is the water bath exhaust conditioner with which it would have been built for Mitchell Construction and beside it can be seen the air reservoir for the braking system.

216. As AK 29R of 1989, it has been rebuilt yet again and is ready for shipment to Karduna in Nigeria for Fertilizers & Chemical (Nigeria) Ltd. It has now been re-engined, converted to 3ft 6ins gauge and will be used for shunting main line wagons in the company's sidings. Couplings are due to be fitted upon arrival.

## 10.  60hp Standard Gauge. MR 9932 of 1972

This was the penultimate standard gauge locomotive supplied by Motor Rail Ltd. As an 8 ton shunter it went to Fort Dunlop in Birmingham which was the major storage and distribution point for tyres made by the Dunlop Rubber Co. Ltd. Underneath it was basically a 60S with standard 3LB Dorman engine and 3-speed gearbox mounted in a slightly modified 60S frame. This allowed for an extended wheelbase of 4ft 7ins and the frames were cut away to

go over the wheels. The controls were arranged for the locomotive to be driven with the driver in a standing position from the comfort of a modest cab. Over this was arranged a frame to carry the heavy duty headstocks with standard gauge buffing and coupling gear. All this is obvious in the pictures.

When this facility closed in 1988 the locomotive was purchased by Alan Keef Ltd and converted back into the basic 60S locomotive that was beneath all the cladding. This was a slightly unusual machine, not only because of the extended wheelbase and the

217. In very workaday condition in 1978 the locomotive stands in front of the bulk of Fort Dunlop, Birmingham. Note the step for the shunter and his pole lying along it.
*A.J. Booth. Collection Industrial Railway Society*

218. These latter-day shunters were basically a 60S chassis with the standard gauge accoutrements hung round it. This is the completed chassis in the works. Note how the frame has been cut away to take the longer axles and wheels.

cutouts in the side frames, but made more so because it was intended for a long hire to contractors Balfour Beatty working in the Woodhead Tunnel. Space was tight on one side of the track so it was set with the wheels 3ins off centre in order to give adequate clearance!

On return from that contract, the wheels were corrected and it was sold to the Dean and Chapter of Salisbury Cathedral who were repairing the cathedral spire with stone from the original

stone mine – which at that time happened to be within an MoD site that only had rail access. The negotiations were carried on in a Portakabin on the cathedral roof! On completion of the spire repairs the stone operation was taken over by the Rare Stone Company who in various guises worked the system, which included a stretch of roadside tramway, after the MoD left, until 2013 when yet again it passed through Alan Keef Ltd's hands before going on to private preservation in Mid Wales.

219. When brand new to the job MR 9932 is bringing a short train of containers from the main line to the storage facility of Fort Dunlop. One of the two people in the cab is a Motor Rail employee there to commission the machine. Note the viaduct on the M6 in the background.

220. How are the mighty fallen! In 1988, 9932 was bought by Alan Keef Ltd and re-gauged to 2ft gauge. After a six month hire to Balfour Beatty working in the Woodhead Tunnel for National Grid it was sold on to what became the Rare Stone mine at Chilmark in Wiltshire. It is here seen with two large blocks of stone being transferred by roadside tramway from mine to cutting shed.
*Courtesy John Stevenson*

## 11. U Series. SMH 122U136 of 1973

This is also a locomotive that has not changed much over the years, and does not wholly meet the criteria of this section, but has the distinction of being one of very few U series still in commercial use anywhere in the world. It was bought through the agents Parbury Henty & Co. Ltd on behalf of the Colonial Sugar Refining Co. Ltd for use at their Lautoka Works in Fiji. Weighing in at 10 tons, the limit for the U series, it was fitted with a Dorman 6DA air cooled engine rated at 94hp driving through a Twin Disc transmission unit. Thus it was what Motor Rail described as having a Hydrokinetic drive. It was one of five, all bought separately over a period of a few years and all fitted with couplings and wheel profiles peculiar to Fiji.

At some stage it was re-engined with a GM water cooled engine of the same power. This has raised the height of the bonnets by a few inches, otherwise the locomotive looks very much as it did when built. The wings to the cab roof give some slight protection from driving tropical rain. It was still doing the job it was bought for in 2013 and that is hauling wagons of sugarcane over the weighbridge until they reach a point when the chain haulage into the tippler can pick them up. In passing, it is worth mentioning that CSR were extensive users of other types of Simplex locomotive in particular the 10 ton mechanical drive units and a few very dilapidated and much rebuilt ones still exist.

221. This is certainly a locomotive for Fiji although it may not actually be 122U136. It stands on the multi-gauge track outside the erecting shop at Bedford and awaits its full complement of ballast weights to bring it up to 10 tons weight. For obvious reasons Motor Rail packed the window glass separately to be fitted upon arrival. In hot climates it often was not!

222. In 2013 the locomotive was doing what it was built for, hauling wagons of sugar cane over the weighbridge situated just beyond the footbridge until the creeper in the foreground can pick them up. It has been re-engined with a General Motors engine but the appearance has changed very little.

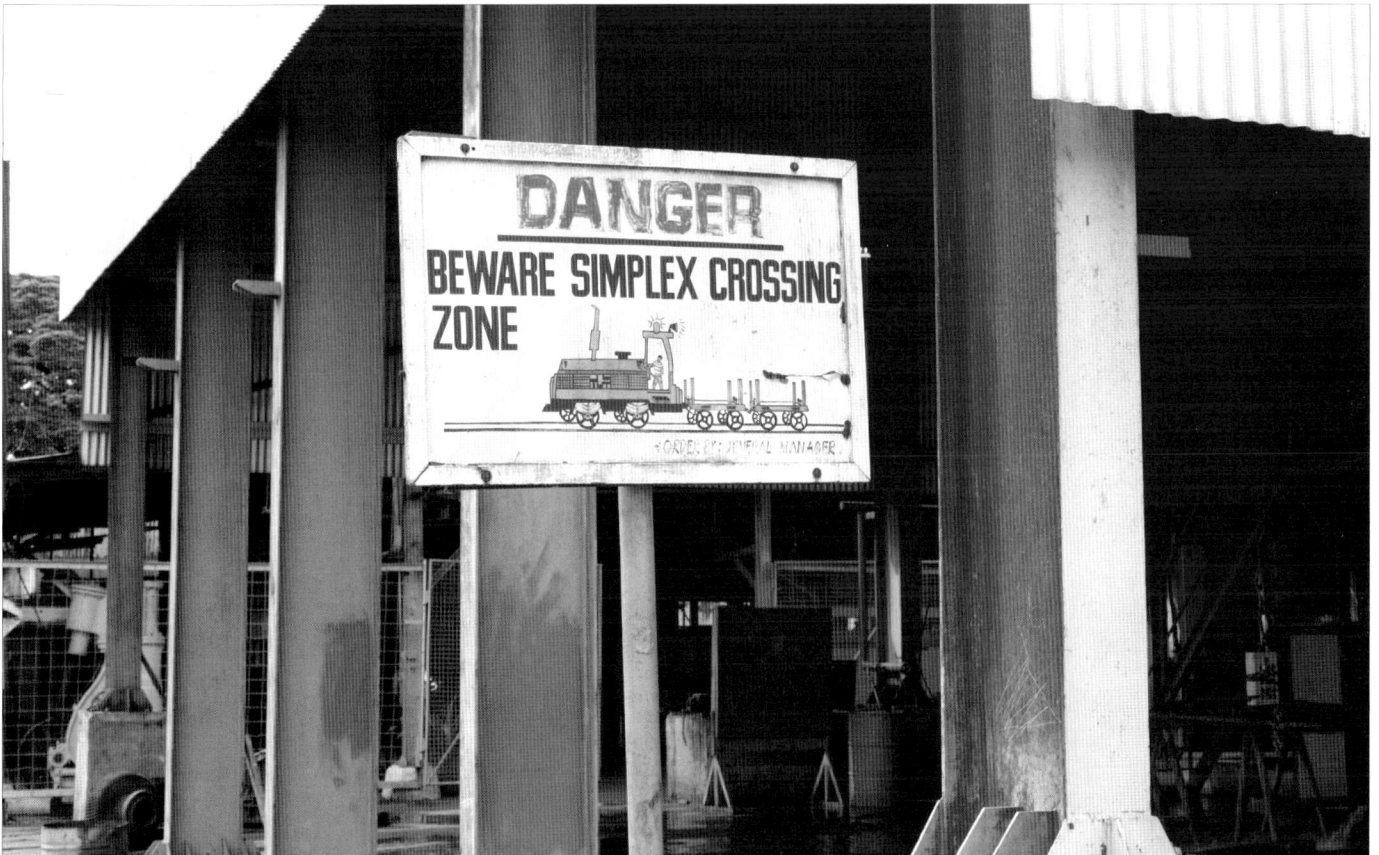

223. The warning sign is very specific and does not preclude one being run down by another make of locomotive!

## 12.  T Series. SMH 102T007 of 1974.
## 3ft gauge. Later AK 78R of 2007

This locomotive was supplied to Associated Portland Cement Manufacturers Ltd for their gypsum quarry at Kilvington, Nottinghamshire in 1974. It was the standard design of T series locomotive fitted with a Deutz F6L912 air-cooled engine set at 104hp and weighed 14 tons. It was used to haul rock gypsum from the quarry a distance of about 1½ miles to a tipping dock beside the main line for onward transmission to various APCM works where it was used to give plasticity to newly made cement.

When the operation closed in 1984 it was bought by The Lord O'Neill for use on his railway in the grounds of Shanes Castle in Northern Ireland, which was then open to the public. In due course O'Neill abandoned this operation and, whilst the majority of the equipment went to the revived Giants Causeway and Bushmills

Railway, this locomotive moved to the Fin Valley Railway. This is a revival of a few miles of the Glenties Branch of the erstwhile County Donegal Railways. It remained in its original condition through these vicissitudes, was painted black and affectionately known as 'The Black Pig'!

In 2007 it received more than just a makeover but sufficient for it acquire a new works number. Alan Keef Ltd carried out a modification that they had already done for a similar locomotive on the Leighton Buzzard Railway. This involved extending the buffer beams outwards and building new bodywork to suit the loading gauge of the railway. Part of this was a full stand-up, independently mounted, cab with dual controls from each side. The existing bonnets were used, as was the engine and transmission. Visually it is hard to believe that it is the same locomotive but of course this is what Simplex should have done years ago.

224. Seven years old but still looking remarkably smart, SMH102T007 of 1974 pushes a loaded train of rock gypsum into the tipping dock at Kilvington. Despite the company by then being Simplex Mechanical Handling, note the Motor Rail roundel on the rear headstock and the shunter on the main line. This locomotive was fitted with INCO style ballast weights and couplings left over from when Canadian orders ceased.

*A.J. Booth. Collection Industrial Railway Society*

225. By 1998 it had moved on from Shanes Castle to Fintown. Here it stands in the old County Donegal Railway station on the Glenties Branch and is about to depart with a train of tramcars that originated in Belgium. At this stage it was known affectionately as 'The Black Pig'!

226. In 2007 it turned itself into a 'proper' locomotive and became Alan Keef Ltd's No. 78R in the process. Just delivered, it is about to start trial running on a push pull basis with CDR railcar No. 18. Incompatibility of coupling heights was always a problem between Irish 3ft gauge railways so note the additional jaw coupling above the normal buffer block.

## 13.  MR 8389 of 1947 Dumper

This is almost certainly the last remaining Motor Rail dumper and is currently preserved, along with the G series above, at the Apedale Valley Light Railway. It seems appropriate that it should be included in this chapter. The Dorman 2DWD engine as fitted in the 20/28 locomotives was the norm at the time, driving through a modified 3-speed gearbox as, being rear control, it didn't need equal speeds in both directions. This was very much the machine with which Motor Rail made their name in the world of dumpers. Later models were largely variations and improvements on the theme.

Dumpers do not have their careers recorded in the way that locomotives do! Thus its history is a bit obscure as it was built for the contractors W.G. Turriff Ltd of Leamington Spa but with no delivery address recorded. Just where it worked for Turriff is not known but it is later reputed to have worked in a 'white stone quarry' at Blakeney on the edge of the Forest of Dean, Gloucestershire. Turriff are on record as having had a quarry at Tintern on the opposite side of the Forest so maybe this is where it worked for them. Along with other plant from the quarry, perhaps when it closed it went to a vehicle dealers at Whitchurch, near Monmouth, from whence it was ultimately bought for preservation.

227. It is good to see that this preserved dumper has been left in 'scruff' order so as to give an idea as what these machines might have looked like in their working environment. The starting handle typical of the 20/28 locomotive is tucked under the driver's right leg, and the raised mudguards to take account of seriously rough ground are prominent. Although speeds were not very high the driver could well have found himself well covered in mud on a bad day and wet if it rained. Cabs were not de rigeur in those days!                    *Courtesy Moseley Railway Trust*

# Appendix I: Light Railways of the First World War

The light railway systems used by all the combatants during the First World War gave a huge boost to the development of the internal combustion engined locomotive and it is upon this conflict that the business of the Motor Rail & Tramcar Co. Ltd and its successors was instigated. The transport situation and the *raison d'etre* for the use of light railways has been touched upon in Chapter 4, but more details of the sheer scale of the operation will give some indication of what Motor Rail achieved in what was, by any standards, a very short time frame indeed.

In 1914 the War Office had appointed an officer of the Royal Engineers, Sir Percy Girouard, to review transport arrangements in general. He had extensive railway experience in South Africa and elsewhere but they did not think it necessary to appoint him, or anyone else, to be in charge of war transport in France. There had been problems in providing an adequate supply of arms and ammunition in the early days of war and David Lloyd George had been made Minister of Munitions in March 1915. His success at the very considerable task of increasing output led to his being appointed Secretary of State for War fifteen months later. With typical ruthlessness and energy he proceeded to trample on Army traditions and appointed Sir Eric Geddes to study the transport situation on the Western Front. Deputy General Manager of the North Eastern Railway, Geddes immediately initiated a statistical review to ascertain what would be required to handle the anticipated traffic and how matters could be better organised and co-ordinated. The War Office had little experience of such organisational work, particularly in handling such huge quantities of material, since previous wars had been wars of movement on a lesser scale and against a lesser adversary.

The perceived thinking was that there were three stages to the delivery of supplies to the front line. First, the main line railway to a point some ten to twenty miles behind the front line. Second, from there to a point of safety that was out of sight of the enemy's front line. Third and finally, by man or horse powered trench tramways where they existed to the point on or near the front line where the material was needed. It was for the second stage that the powers-that-be decided that light railways could be utilised with steam traction for the main haul. Trials were also made with light petrol driven units for operating over the lightly laid trench tramways as well as on the French lines that had been taken over. Generally speaking these tracks were far too light for satisfactory locomotive operation. However, Canadian troops had laid their lines using 20lbs/yd rail, as opposed to the 9–16lbs/yd rail used by the trench tramways, and these tracks were much more suited to the task. Trial orders were placed for a small number of locomotives, which included the initial seven to be built by Motor Rail. They obviously made their mark as increasingly large orders were placed along with later orders for the 40hp version of the same basic design, the latter fitted with varying types of armour plate protection.

Whilst initially the light railways were laid from the main line railheads to serve specific points on the front line, these soon developed into more elaborate systems to serve each Army unit. In turn this was followed by interconnecting lines between systems in order to allow movements along the front line. Finally, lateral lines

228. Despite the numbers that were in use, Simplex locomotives tend to be nearly invisible in accounts of the Great War. This is taken from one account and shows a train of wounded soldiers. This is equipment in use by Canadian troops and they emblazoned the engine covers with large painted running numbers that bore no relation to either works or WDLR numbers.

229. A German official photograph of a train at Zandvoorde in Belgium. The whole railway seems to be very much more substantial than most British light railways and one wonders if this is in fact a section of the extensive sugar beet railways common in the area and often taken over for military use. However, the German lines often did have quite elaborate stations, but whether these were official or a local means of producing normality in an abnormal world is unknown.                                                                                          © IWM

between the existing systems were provided parallel to the front to allow even greater flexibility and to cope with any advance or withdrawal at any particular point. In all there was laid in 1917/18 something like 1,800 miles of light railway track by the British alone, which in itself has to have been no mean achievement. The German advances in March 1918 were particularly successful and many locomotives and much equipment was evacuated. Even so, some 300 steam and diesel locomotives were left behind in immobilised condition together with large stocks of track materials and wagons, much of which was burnt. A good deal of this material was later reclaimed for re-use.

One reason for the use of 600mm rail gauge was that German track, locomotives and equipment could be, and was, used when captured by the Allies. The reverse, of course, was also true! The proposition has also been put forward that when what became known as the Western Front stabilised it spanned, particularly on the German side, a series of 600mm gauge railways largely provided by Decauville for the haulage of sugar beet from field to mill. Whilst these railways continued to haul sugar beet even while hostilities lasted, the Germans also used them for the haulage of munitions and extended them as required. This may account for the apparently substantial nature seen in some pictures of German military railways. Maybe it was pre-planned or maybe it was purely coincidental.

Prior to the start of the War, less than a hundred internal combustion locomotives are known to have been built in Britain, to which may be added a handful of German imports. One of the reasons put forward for this situation was that German locomotives were built at a price that could not be matched by UK manufacturers but there seems also to have been a difference in culture. Many of the earliest motor cars in this country were also of European design and manufacture while in Britain coal remained the mainstay of the economy. In contrast, by 1914 Germany had built between 1,500

and 2,000 petrol locomotives of which Deutz contributed around 1,500 with Montania, Ruhrthaler and Oberursel being among the other builders. During the war years Deutz alone were to build some 4,000 locomotives of all types.

German military railways were used in most areas of the conflict including on the Russian borders and in East Africa. Deutz produced about 1,000 locomotives for the Heeresfeldbahnen – the organisation that managed the light railways – the bulk of which were of the standard 10hp design, but with examples of both 40hp and 50hp. Oberursel and Montania also built locomotives for the HFB and of course there were large numbers of steam locomotives including the well known 'Feldbahn' 0-8-0T type, many of which still survive. (As was the case with the British, many locomotives were under construction at the time of the Armistice and never saw war service.) A large batch of German locomotives was used in Turkey to assist with the attempted completion of the Baghdad Railway. To assist with the spring offensive of 1918, and having made peace with Russia, the Germans were able to transfer to the Western Front no less than 300 steam locomotives, 3,500 wagons and, no doubt, an unrecorded number of i/c locomotives!

Of the Allies, the French had perhaps the most interesting mix of locomotives – including the iconic Pechot-Bourdon articulated design (similar to the Ffestiniog Railway's double Fairlie), 280 built by Baldwin in America, 15 by North British Locomotive Co. in Glasgow and a quantity of the 0-6-0 Joffre design built by Kerr Stuart. Also available to them were the normal Decauville steam locomotives, with petrol powered locomotives including a 6-coupled 60hp design by Schneider (some of which were built by Baguley in England) and 200 of a petrol-electric double bogie design by Crochat. They also bought a batch of 600 petrol locomotives of 45hp from Baldwin. When the Americans entered the war in April 1917 they also adopted the same design and a further 126 units of both 35hp and 45hp were brought to France. Indeed Baldwin came by a very considerable amount of business due to the war and built in the order of 5,000 locomotives in all gauges for the conflict. These include 300 750mm gauge locomotives for Russia, but as a result of the Russian revolution few are thought to have been used.

By contrast, British steam locomotive production was restricted as many builders were fully occupied with other types of war work, primarily munitions and later on manufacturing tanks. None was geared for mass production on the American scale and the largest single class was the Hunslet 4-6-0 of which 155 were built. Again Baldwin came to the rescue by building 495 of their ubiquitous 4-6-0 design in seven months, reputedly without affecting the rest of their scheduled production! A batch of 100 2-6-2 locomotives of very similar type were built by the American Locomotive Co. for the American forces. So far as petrol locomotives were concerned, a small number were built by Avonside and Baguley but aside from Simplex the largest quantity was 200 petrol-electric locomotives built by Westinghouse and Dick Kerr. These were very successful, not least because they could be used as generators to drive mobile workshops,

but had the disadvantage of being heavy at 8 tons and also slow when on the move. There was also a fairly large number of tractors converted from cars, of which the Crewe tractor is perhaps the best known. These were converted from Model T Ford cars and a good number were also converted by the railway workshops in Nairobi, Kenya, but these were no substitute for 'proper' locomotives, either then or after the war. These latter seem to have caught the popular imagination as they appear in many photographs, whilst the more common Simplex workhorse is nearly invisible!

By contrast, the 2½ ton Simplex was a speedy machine that could be used over virtually any track that had been laid. However, they had no cab and no armour and accordingly the 40hp version was developed. This weighed in at some 6 tons and could not only haul heavier loads but also came with three levels of armour plating. The driver thus had some protection from flying debris, rifle fire or, in its fully armoured state, something much more serious! The record shows that 749 of the 20hp version and 327 of the 40hp design were built for the War Department light railways although not all

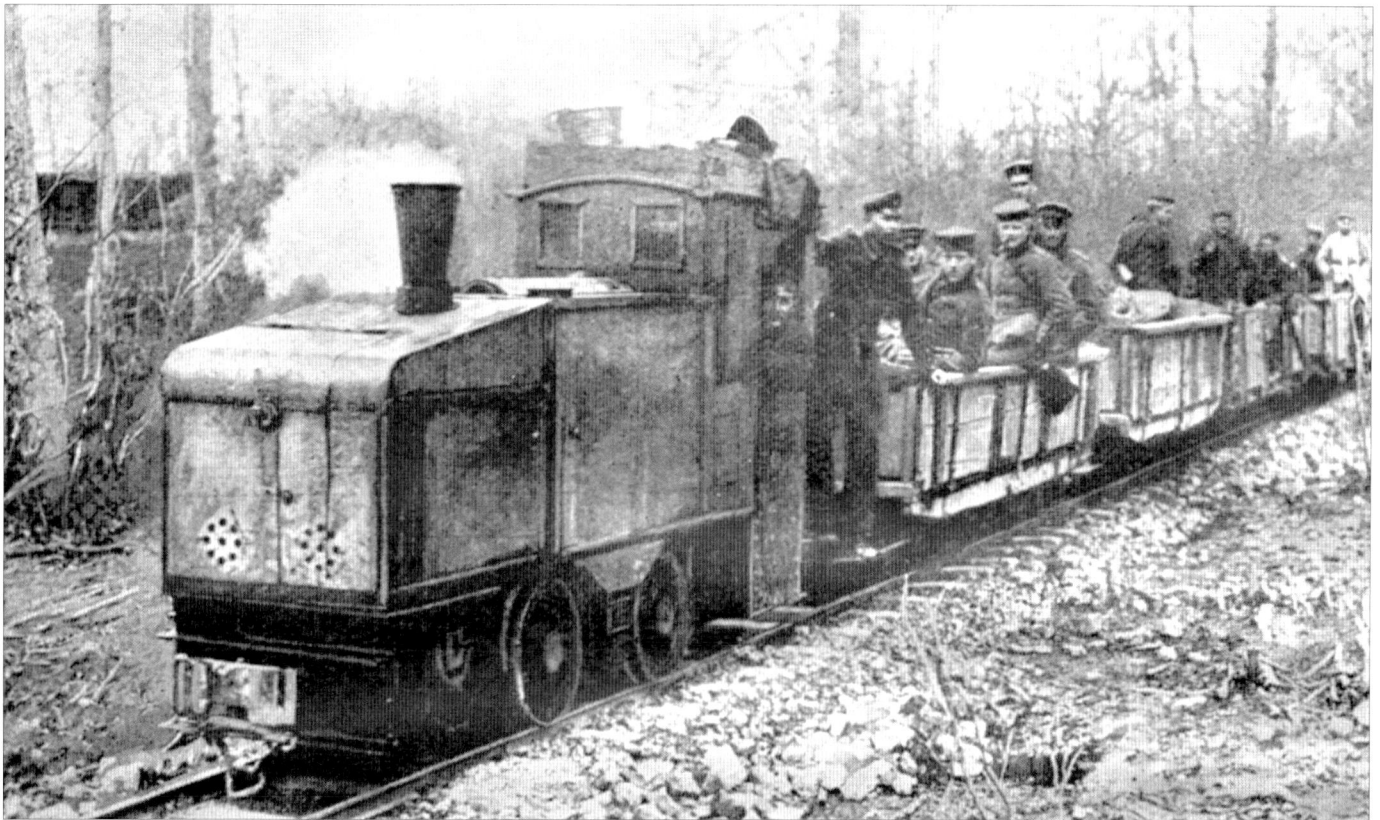

230. (*Above*) The original caption to this picture suggests that it is of retreating German troops behind the Hindenberg Line. If true they don't look particularly perturbed! The locomotive is of Deutz manufacture and was the workhorse of the German military railways. The steam from the 'chimney' is part of the cooling system and the cage on the cab roof, which was invariably added to these locos, contains some buckets perhaps for its replenishment.

231. (*Right*) Another Deutz locomotive but this time in French hands. It is subtly different from the two above (smaller wheels, different cab, different couplings, etc) so was it of pre-war supply to the French or simply captured and put to good use transporting water to the front line?

went overseas and some never saw any kind of war service. These were by far the largest class of any type of internal combustion engined locomotive used by the Allies and for them to have been built at all was no mean achievement. It seems that the design was drawn up from scratch and had no initial teething troubles making it an immediate 'best seller'. Prior experience with the gearbox in the Karachi trams together with the use of the Dorman engine (also used in the Dick Kerr and Westinghouse petrol-electrics) no doubt helped, but the sheer organising ability to achieve these numbers in the time available is astounding. In numerical terms it represented around twenty-five locomotives per week! It was also profitable and set up the firm's reputation for the future.

Although perceived thinking equates the First World War to France, Belgium and the Western Front, the war involved other areas in German and Turkish colonies. Simplex locomotives operated in North Russia (after the Bolshevik Revolution), East Africa, Salonika, Palestine, Italy, Mesopotamia and even found their way to such unlikely places as Jerusalem. (In passing it is worth noting that for those who fought in both, East Africa was considered worse than the Western Front!) However, in these places their duties were different to France, being used around Army bases and ports for the internal transport of supplies.

Among the Allied troops there were contingents from the British Colonies and Dominions, and these included railway operating companies from Australia, New Zealand, Canada and the USA who thus gained valuable experience in the use of Simplex locomotives. The Canadians in particular seem to have had a penchant for making good use of their railways. Simplexes were used on construction duties as well as serving the front line, not only taking ammunition and supplies where required but also, for example, roadstone to

dumps for road repairs. Trains of ammunition would often consist of one or two bogies wagons travelling in convoy after dark with each train branching off to its own separate destination. Initially these could well be sidings from where the material was collected as required and moved forward by hand-worked trench tramway or horses. However, as the light railways became more established, artillery batteries were sited with their own siding from a more permanent line so that ammunition could be delivered almost directly into the guns. The down side of this was that enemy shelling could and did cause much damage to light railway installations and no doubt a good many locomotives were destroyed, although damage to the track and subsequent derailment was likely to have been a bigger and more annoying problem. There are no statistics as to how many locomotives survived the conflict, but a best guess is about half of them including those that never left the UK.

With the German advance of early 1918 the main repair depot at Berguette had to be abandoned and for a time locomotives were returned to England until a new workshop and facilities was set up at Beaurainville. The repair depot in England was conveniently situated at Richborough in Kent from whence a ferry service operated to France. About 100 petrol locomotives were there at the cessation of hostilities. Spares for light railway locomotives – both steam and diesel – were accumulated at Purfleet in Essex, where the Royal Engineers had a riverside depot, for onward distribution as required. Once again there were large stocks of spares available after the war, most of which went for scrap. This depot became a concentration point for locomotives and material being returned from France and at one stage there were line upon line of locomotives awaiting potential buyers, but the market was flooded and again much of it was sold for scrap.

232. Spoils of war. The troops, including their officer, are looking extremely pleased with themselves for having captured this Deutz locomotive. The officer, in shiny leggings, is sitting on a 20hp tractor, which may have brought it in, and there are at least three Baldwin steam locos on the track behind. There is just a glimpse of the flywheel, several feet in diameter which was a prominent part of the horizontal engine with which these machines were fitted.
*Courtesy Frank Jux*

# Appendix II: Railway Materials Department

I am indebted to Chris West for this document. It appears to show the total quantities of railway materials ordered, delivered, cancelled or still awaited by the Ministry of Munitions of War as at 5th December 1918, less than a month after the Armistice.

Of interest to this history is the record of 5ft gauge railcars for Murmansk that seems to have been given to the Motor Rail & Tram Car Co. Ltd in compensation for the cancellation of orders for 20hp tractors. Both 20hp and 40hp tractors are listed along with the track

and rolling stock to go with them. However, the products of other companies such the Westinghouse petrol-electric locos or the tiny McEwan Pratt machines are not mentioned. The same applies to steam locomotives from both Hunslet and Baldwin.

For all that, one can only but be astounded at the sheer quantity of material listed, ranging through over 23,000 60cm gauge wagons to 3,500 miles of 20lbs/yd rail (1,750 miles of track). It is always remarkable what gets achieved in wartime!

---

## MINISTRY OF MUNITIONS OF WAR

### RAILWAY MATERIALS DEPARTMENT.

### REPORT NO. 106.

### Week ending December 5th. 1918.

**REQUISITION.**

Total received to date 2,280 or 6 for the week.

The requisitions are covered to date by 5,975 contracts.

The principal items requisitioned during the week are:-

```
    54 Sets of Taps for Loco. Shops, Mesopotamia.
 1,500 Brass Tubes for Loco. Boilers,       "
 5,500 Steel    "      "    "     "         "
20,000 Ferrules for above,                  "
    20 Simplex Rail Trollies, 20 H.P., 5 ft. gauge, Murmansk.
     1 Welding Equipment, low pressure, portable, acetylene, with
         oxygen cylinders, sufficient for 72 days, Archangel.
   200 feet Bright Steel Shafting, 2½" dia. with couplings,
         Plummer Blocks and Brackets, Mesopotamia.
    14 Sets Tools and Spares for 20 H.P. Drewry Rail Cars,
         Archangel and Murmansk.
```

The following requisitions have been cancelled:-

Req. 1541. Items 13 & 14. Spare Engine and Tender Tires, 50 each, for 0-6-0 Locos, Mesopotamia.

" 1901. 6,000 Gedge Screw Couplings, France.

" 1929. 1,000 Corrugated Skylights, France.

" 2017. Fittings, steel, screwed and socketted for 5" Water Piping, France.

" 2071. 120 Miles 75 lb. Rails, with Fishplates, Fishbolts and Dogspikes for same, France.

" 2072. 555 Sets Points and Crossings for 75 lb. Rail, France.

" 2079. (Part). 100 40-Ton Bogie Flat Wagons.

" 2095. 100 Hand Power Track Drilling Machines, 5/8" to 1¼" Chuck, France.

" 2096. Extra Spares and Equipment for Repair of Baldwin 4-6-0, 60 c.m. Locos returned from France.

" 2145. Items 5-9. 73,000 feet Steel Wire Rope for Hawsers, Towlines, Cranes, Winding Gear etc., France.

" 2169. 300 Toolboxes with Tools for Hamilton Ropeway, France.

Req. 2197. 15 W.I. Turntables for 20 lb. 60 c.m. Track, D.I.W.D.

" 2200. (179 Items) Spares for 14 H.P. Coventry Simplex Engines, France.

" 2210. Experimental Equipment for 400 yards length of existing Ropeway, France.

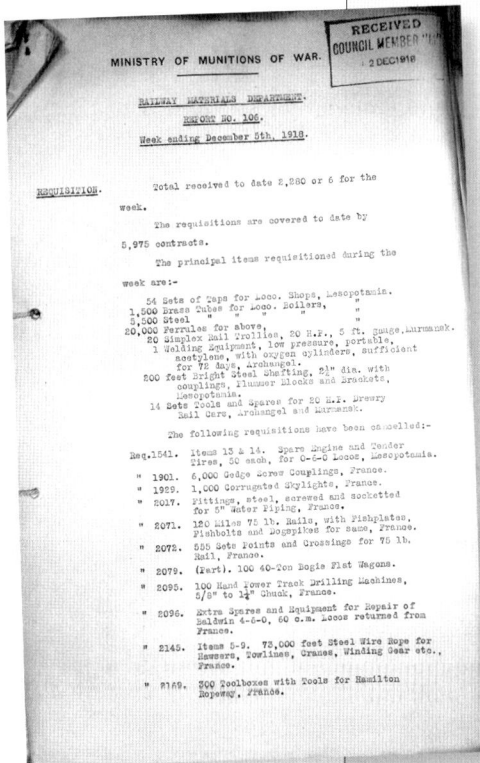

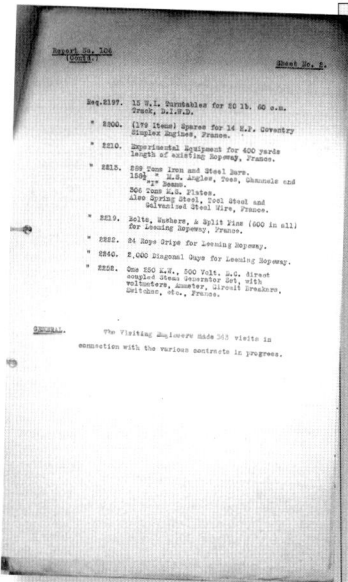

" 2213.  289 Tons Iron and Steel Bars.
        158½ " M.S. Angles, Tees, Channels and "I" Beams.
        306 Tons M.S. Plates.
        Also Spring Steel, Tool. Steel and Galvanized Steel
            Wire, France.

" 2219.  Bolts, Washers, & Split Pins (600 in all) for Leeming
        Ropeway, France.

" 2222.  24 Rope Grips for Leeming Ropeway.

" 2240.  2,000 Diagonal Guys for Leeming Ropeway.

" 2252.  One 250 K.W., 500 Volt. D.C. direct coupled Steam
        Generator Set, with voltmeters, Ammeter, Circuit
        Breakers, Switches, etc., France.

GENERAL.          The Visiting Engineers made 383 visits in connection with
            the various contracts in progress.

WAGONS.           The following statement shows the output of Standard Gauge
            and 60 c.m. Gauge Wagons:-

| Description | No. Requisi-tioned. | To Nov. 28th | Manufactured | | | | To Date | Balance to complete |
|---|---|---|---|---|---|---|---|---|
| | | | December | | | | | |
| | | | 5 | 12 | 19 | 26 | | |
| **4'8½" GAUGE.** | | | | | | | | |
| 20 Tons Covered | 10,750 | 7,853 | 54 | | | | 7,907 | 2,843 |
| "   "   Open | 4,750 | 4.750 | - | | | | 4,750 | 0 |
| 12  "   " | 8,679 | 6,789 | 33 | | | | 6,822 | 1,857 |
| 10/12 " Covered | 2.950 | 1.719 | 14 | | | | 1,733 | 1,217 |
| Brake Vans | 790 | 790 | - | | | | 790 | 0 |
| 25 Tons Bogie | 76 | 76 | - | | | | 76 | 0 |
| 30  "   " | 480 | 100 | 10 | | | | 110 | 370 |
| 40  "   " | 1,043 | 702 | 12 | | | | 714 | 329 |
| Secondhand and) miscellaneous) | 697 | 485 | - | | | | 485 | 212 |
| Total for Overseas: | 30,215 | 23,264 | 123 | | | | 23,387 | 6.828 |
| Iron Ore Wagons for Home Traffic: | 4,206 | 2,779 | 54 | | | | 2,833 | 1,373 |
| | 34,421 | 26,043 | 177 | | | | 26,220 | 8,201 |
| **60 C.M. GAUGE.** | | | | | | | | |
| Low Side, Bogie | 4,360 | 3,726 | 30 | | | | 3,756 | 604 |
| Open Well, Bogie | 2,138 | 2,038 | - | | | | 2,038 | 100 |
| Ambulance     " | 250 | 250 | - | | | | 250 | 0 |
| Tank, &c. | 223 | 223 | - | | | | 223 | 0 |
| Total Bogie Wagons: | 6,971 | 6,237 | 30 | | | | 6,267 | 704 |
| Ration, 4 wheel | 3,850 | 3,466 | 42 | | | | 3,508 | 342 |
| Tip, Box, &c. | 12,299 | 10,542 | 93 | | | | 10,635 | 1,664 |
| Total 4-wheel: | 16,149 | 14,008 | 135 | | | | 14,143 | 2,006 |
| Monorail Trucks: | 2,000 | 2,000 | | | | | 2,000 | 0 |

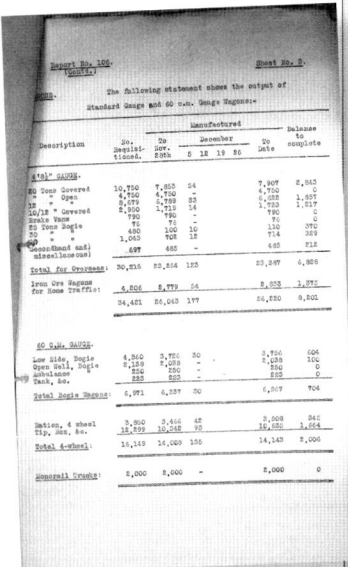

LOCOMOTIVES.      The position of Consolidation Locomotives on order in the
            United Kingdom is as follows:-

| Contractor | No. Ordered | To Nov. 28th | Manufactured | | | | To Date | Balance to complete |
|---|---|---|---|---|---|---|---|---|
| | | | December | | | | | |
| | | | 5 | 12 | 19 | 26 | | |
| North British Loco Co. | 249 | 178 | 3 | | | | 181 | 68 |
| Kitson & Co. | 32 | 32 | - | | | | 32 | 0 |
| Stephenson & Co. | 82 | 42 | - | | | | 42 | 40 |
| Nasmyth Wilson. | 32 | 24 | - | | | | 24 | 8 |
| Great Central Rly. | 6 | 0 | - | | | | 0 | 6 |
| TOTAL: | 401 | 276 | 3 | | | | 279 | 122 |

The position of locomotives ordered in U.S.A. is as under:-

| Description. | Ordered. | Completed. | Shipped. | Balance available for shipment. |
|---|---|---|---|---|
| 0-4-0 | 50 | 50 | 50 | - |
| 2-8-0 | 50 | 50 | 50 | - |
| 0-6-0 | 50 | 50 | 50 | - |
| 2-8-0 | 100 | 100 | 100 | - |
| 4-6-0 | 70 | 70 | 70 | - |
| "Mallet" | 40 | 40 | 35 | 5 |
| 4-6-1 | 50 | 25 | - | 25 |
| 4-6-0 | 485 | 460 | 430 | 30 |

## PETROL TRACTORS.

| Contractor | No. Ordered | Manufactured | | | | | To Date | Balance to complete |
|---|---|---|---|---|---|---|---|---|
| | | To Nov. 28th | December | | | | | |
| | | | 5 | 12 | 19 | 26 | | |
| Motor Rail & Tram Car Co. | | | | | | | | |
| 40 H.P. | 334 | 309 | 9 | | | | 318 | 16 |
| 20 H.P. | 724 | 686 | 10 | | | | 696 | 28 |
| TOTAL: | 1,058 | 995 | 19 | | | | 1,014 | 44 |

## TRACK.

| Description | Mileage requisitioned | Manufactured | | | | | Mileage to date | Balance to complete |
|---|---|---|---|---|---|---|---|---|
| | | To Nov. 28th | December | | | | | |
| | | | 5 | 12 | 19 | 26 | | |
| **4'8½" GAUGE.** | | | | | | | | |
| 1st Programme. | | | | | | | | |
| 75 lb. ex U.K., New | 693 | 693 | Completed | | | | 693 | 0 |
| 80 lb. ex Canada, 2nd hand. | 300 | 300 | " | | | | 300 | 0 |
| 90 lb. ex R.E.C., 2nd hand. | 207 | 207 | " | | | | 207 | 0 |
| 2nd Programme. | | | | | | | | |
| 80 lb. ex Canada, 2nd hand. | 141 | 141 | " | | | | 141 | 0 |
| 75 lb. ex U.K., New | 1,485 | 919 | 22 | | | | 941 | 544 |
| TOTAL: | 2,826 | 2,260 | 22 | | | | 2,282 | 544 |
| **POINTS AND CROSSINGS. 75 LB.** | | | | | | | | |
| 1st Programme. | | | | | | | | |
| Points & Crossings | 6,345 | 6,345 | Completed | | | | 6,345 | 0 |
| Double Slips | 66 | 66 | " | | | | 66 | 0 |
| Three Throw Switches | 36 | 36 | " | | | | 36 | 0 |
| 2nd Programme. | | | | | | | | |
| Points &Crossings | 5,985 | 1,645 | 136 | | | | 1,781 | 4,204 |
| Double Slips | 250 | 75 | 20 | | | | 95 | 155 |
| Single " | 25 | 25 | - | | | | 25 | 0 |
| Three Throw Switches | 50 | 25 | - | | | | 25 | 25 |
| TOTAL: | 12,757 | 8,217 | 166 | | | | 8,373 | 4,384 |
| **60 C.M. GAUGE, 20 LB.** | | | | | | | | |
| 1st programme | 1,072 | 1,072 | Completed | | | | 1,072 | 0 |
| 2nd Programme | 1,191 | 1,191 | " | | | | 1,191 | 0 |
| 1918 Programme | 1,299 | 1,078 | 35 | | | | 1,113 | 186 |
| Total to 31,12.18. | 3,562 | 3,341 | 35 | | | | 3,376 | 186 |
| **60 C.M.GAUGE, 9 LB.** | | | | | | | | |
| 1917 Programme | 377 | 377 | Completed | | | | 377 | 0 |
| 1918 Programme | 666 | 508 | 8 | | | | 516 | 150 |
| Total to 31.12.18 | 1,043 | 885 | 8 | | | | 893 | 150 |
| **METRE GAUGE, 45 LB.** | 83 | 83 | Completed | | | | 83 | 0 |

NOTE: Contractors have been advised of the cancellation of the outstanding balance of 20 lb. and 9 lb. Rail oontracts

# Appendix III: Locomotive Prices

The prices given below are taken from actual sales from around 1968 to the end of Simplex Mechanical Handling Ltd and beyond. They are generally for the same type and size of each class of locomotive. All are of 2ft nominal gauge unless otherwise indicated. The weight of a locomotive makes an obvious difference to price – there is that much more steel to be supplied. Whilst the rail gauge could be changed within certain parameters, those over 2ft 6ins gauge required a different arrangement of wheels and axleboxes with associated cost increases. The chronological gaps represent years when locomotives of this series were not built (or the files are missing). There also seemed to be quite wide variations in selling price for apparently the same thing, except perhaps for sales through RMP who worked from an agreed price list.

## G Series Locomotives

These were generally sold as a standard machine with little variation although Enfield, Kirloskar and Petter engines were used. Mostly they were 2¼ tons in weight but occasionally are specified as being 2½ tons or even 3 tons.

| Year | Agent/Customer | Country | Price (£) | Comment |
|------|----------------|---------|-----------|---------|
| 1986 | | | | |
| 1985 | | | | |
| 1984 | RMP | Egypt | 9,700 | |
| 1983 | | | | |
| 1982 | | | | |
| 1981 | | | | |
| 1980 | ENU | Portugal | 6,680 | ? per RMP |
| 1979 | | | | |
| 1978 | RMP | Singapore | 4,892 | |
| 1977 | RMP | Iran | 4,659 | |
| 1976 | Severn Trent | UK | 4,610 | |
| 1975 | RMP | Turkey | 2,600 | |
| 1974 | RMP | Singapore | 1,815 | Batch of 15 |
| 1973 | RMP | Colombia | 1,650 | |
| 1972 | RMP | Ghana | 1,720 | 18ins gauge |
| 1971 | | | | |
| 1970 | RMP | Pakistan | 1,353 | |
| 1969 | ICI | UK | 1,300 | |
| 1968 | | | | |

233. An Enfield engined G series with Vulcan Street in the background.

## 40S Locomotives

As the successor of the renowned 20/28 it might be expected that the 40S would have had the most sales over the period, but this does not seem to have been the case. Generally these are of 2½ tons weight but for work in oil palm plantations they were often sold at 4½ tons. The gap in 1977/78 seems to have been caused by the cancellation of an order for eleven locomotives, all with Perkins engines. It appears that RMP took these into their own stock and subsequently sold them independently of Motor Rail; indeed they had RMP plates affixed to them. There may be a gap in the records here, or eleven locomotives built were sufficient to cover orders in hand.

| Year | Agent/ Customer | Country | Price (£) | Comment |
|------|-----------------|---------|-----------|---------|
| 1989 | Butterley | UK | 22,900 | Built & sold by AKL |
| 1988 | Butterley | UK | 20,300 | Built & sold by AKL |
| 1987 | | | | |
| 1986 | Butterley | UK | 19,710 | Built by AKL |
| 1985 | | | | |
| 1984 | Severn Trent | UK | 14,475 | |
| 1983 | RMP | Indonesia | 12,810 | |
| 1982 | | | | |
| 1981 | RMP | Peru | 9,625 | |
| 1980 | RMP | Bolivia | 8,750 | |
| 1979 | Severn Trent | UK | 8,760 | |
| 1978 | RMP | Singapore | 7,915 | |
| 1977 | | | | See text |
| 1976 | | | | See text |
| 1975 | Geest | St Lucia | 6,083 | |
| 1974 | RMP | Malaysia | 3,717 | 4½ ton |
| 1973 | RMP | Singapore | 3,388 | |
| 1972 | RMP | Chile | 2,645 | |
| 1971 | Mixconcrete | UK | 2,453 | |
| 1970 | RMP | Malaya | 2,397 | |
| 1969 | | | | |
| 1968 | | | | |

234. A 3½ ton 40S in the works and on skids awaiting side covers and buffers before despatch.

## 60S Locomotives

The 60S was a popular locomotive during this period and it happens that the Loxroy machine listed below was the very last locomotive to be assembled at Elstow Road. For the purpose of this list they are generally taken as the 7 ton version, although when the Deutz engined 60SD nomenclature became standard the weight was limited to 6 tons. For reasons of vibration the Perkins engine was not a success in this locomotive. Those for Bord na Móna are included for interest' sake. They were a very different style of 60S but were a batch of fifteen and there was an enquiry for a further thirty-five of the same type. It is as certain as anything ever is that the locomotive for Guyana Sugar Corporation will be the last traditional Simplex to have been built.

| Year | Agent/Customer | Country | Price (£) | Comment |
|---|---|---|---|---|
| 1992 | Fletcher Smith | Guyana | 31,200 | Built & sold by AKL |
| 1991 | | | | |
| 1990 | | | | |
| 1989 | | | | |
| 1988 | | | | |
| 1987 | | | | |
| 1986 | Ghana Bauxite | Ghana | 20,819 | 3ft 6ins gauge Built AKL |
| 1986 | Loxroy | Tanzania | 18,830 | |
| 1985 | | | | |
| 1984 | | | | |
| 1983 | | | | |
| 1982 | NCB | UK | 19,110 | NCB Spec |
| 1981 | RMP | Sabah | 11,717 | |
| 1980 | Bord na Móna | Ireland | 14,250 | 3ft gauge BnM Spec |
| 1980 | NCB | UK | 15,920 | NCB Spec |
| 1979 | RMP | Indonesia | 10,770 | |
| 1978 | RMP | Sabah | 8,700 | |
| 1977 | RMP | Singapore | 8,374 | |
| 1976 | RMP | Somalia | 7,250 | SD, 6 tons |
| 1975 | RMP | Malaysia | 5,967 | |
| 1974 | RMP | Malaysia | 4,883 | |
| 1973 | RMP | Malaysia | 3,881 | |
| 1972 | RMP | Bangladesh | 3,352 | |
| 1971 | RMP | Fiji | 3,352 | |
| 1970 | Wigglesworth | Tanzania | 2,675 | 5 tons |
| 1969 | RMP | Pakistan | 2,730 | |
| 1968 | Pilkington | UK | 2,710 | 5 tons |
| 1967 | RMP | | 2,147 | 5 tons |

235. Metre gauge 11152, 7 ton 60S sold per RMP to Iraq. Looked at closely it seems that the multi-gauge track did not include metre gauge as the nearer wheels are in the mud! Note the unusual coupling arrangements.

## U Series

The U series of hydrostatic and hydrokinetic locomotives were subject to a host of problems as described elsewhere, but for this purpose a locomotive of 8–10 tons weight with around 100hp has been settled upon as being the most common. A very large number were sent to Canada under the aegis of Jarvis Clarke for the nickel mines there, some of which may still be at work.

| Year | Agent/ Customer | Country | Price (£) | Comments |
|---|---|---|---|---|
| 1988 | Patterson Simons | Korea | 39,500 | Built & sold by AKL |
| 1987 | | | | |
| 1986 | | | | |
| 1985 | | | | |
| 1984 | | | | |
| 1983 | | | | |
| 1982 | | | | |
| 1981 | | | | |
| 1980 | Selection Trust | Zambia | 22,450 | 3ft 6ins gauge |
| 1979 | | | | |
| 1978 | Selection Trust | Zambia | 17,139 | 3ft 6ins gauge |
| 1977 | Paterson Simons | Korea | 13,060 | |
| 1976 | Paterson Simons | Korea | 10,960 | 5½ tons |
| 1975 | RMP | Indonesia | 11,966 | |
| 1975 | RMP | Turkey | 6,769 | |
| 1974 | Selection Trust | Zambia | 6,885 | 3ft 6ins gauge |
| 1973 | Parbury Henty | Fiji | 6,891 | |
| 1972 | Selection Trust | Zambia | 6,100 | |
| 1971 | RMP | Iraq | 4,900 | |
| 1970 | Mogul of Ireland | Ireland | 3,950 | |
| 1969 | Selection Trust | Zambia | 3,822 | |
| 1968 | Carl Strom | Sweden | 3,700 | Prototype |

236. A 2ft gauge U series hydrokinetic. The lack of any ballast weights on what is obviously a new locomotive suggests this might be one of the ones for either Somalia or Cameroon.

## T Series

The T series came out of a requirement for a locomotive heavier and more powerful than could be achieved with the U Series, albeit that they often had the same engine fitted. They were also intended as a mining locomotive although none was ever built for underground use. This is the more surprising considering that the first eleven units were for use on a sugar plantation. The vast difference in price for those supplied to the National Coal Board is accounted for by the fact that these machines were fitted with full Westinghouse air brakes and Willison auto couplers, or possibly SMH thought they could get more out of nationalised customer!

| Year | Customer | Country | Price (£) | Comments |
|---|---|---|---|---|
| 1985 | NCB | UK | 45,910 | See text |
| 1984 | | | | |
| 1983 | | | | |
| 1981 | NCB | UK | 42,735 | See text |
| 1979 | NCB | UK | 32,000 | See text |
| 1979 | RMP | Indonesia | 19,961 | |
| 1978 | | | | |
| 1977 | | | | |
| 1976 | APCM | UK | 17,825 | 3ft gauge |
| 1975 | TPC | Tanzania | 12,185 | |
| 1974 | APCM | UK | 9,497 | |
| 1973 | Krinsen/TPC | Tanzania | 6,852 | |
| 1972 | Krinsen/TPC | Tanzania | 6,547 | |

237. 101T001, the first of the T series, ready for despatch to Tanganyika Planting in Tanzania.

# Appendix IV: The M & R Story

I am grateful to John Middleton for providing the information for, and indeed writing, most of this appendix. Inevitably there is some duplication with Chapter 6.

The business of gold mining in South Africa was operating on a vast scale and had become of world-wide importance by the turn of the twentieth century. The use of railway equipment within that industry had blossomed on a similar scale with innovation being the name of the game. Electric trolley locomotives were in use on the surface as early as 1894 and underground by 1900. Internal combustion locomotives had been tried in the mines before the First World War but the petrol engines of the time were, unsurprisingly, not suitable for underground usage. The first diesel locomotive was tried in 1928, by which time there were recorded 183 locomotives in use underground in South African mines with all of them being battery or trolley electric.

During the 1930s, large new reserves were proven in the Orange Free State, but development, and therefore production from these areas, was interrupted by the Second World War. Pre-war levels of production were not regained until 1950. However, this period showed a change in operations, with a shift from the old mines around Johannesburg to new areas of production in the Orange Free State. This in turn led to new methods of mining and a vast increase in the use of railway equipment. Despite earlier innovations many of the older mines relied heavily on rope haulage systems. This was the era in which the diesel locomotive came into its own even if it in turn was to be superseded by its predecessor, the battery electric locomotive.

It is difficult to find a superlative to describe the numbers of locomotives involved in South African gold mining. Statistics from the Chamber of Mines show a dramatic increase during the period

238. This is the locomotive that all the fuss was about. This is pure Simplex, even down to the box-like exhaust quencher, and is working on the construction of new groynes on the foreshore at Durban in 1984. The M & R on the side refers to the contractors, Murray & Roberts, not the locomotive! Built in 1962, Lenning's numbering system classed this as L35213, Locomotive, 3.5 tonnes, number 213. In fact their numbers started at 101 for this type and a total of 270 were built including variations on the theme.

*Courtesy John Middleton*

1950-70, although the peak year was not reached until 1982. In that year there were 2,706 diesel, 2,660 battery and 416 trolley electric locomotives recorded in use, giving a grand total of 5,782! Where Motor Rail was concerned, the peak period was from the 1950s and the highest concentration of diesel locomotives was reached in 1975 with 3,225 recorded. To put these figures in context, the Vaal Reefs mine had over 700 locomotives on their books. The oil crisis of the 1970s affected South Africa badly and prompted a rethink on the use of diesel fuel resulting in a wholesale change to battery electric operation. Health and safety considerations also played a part with the elimination of fumes underground. Thus, in 1980 alone, no less than 500 new battery electric locomotives were introduced.

In fact Motor Rail came onto this scene relatively late. In the early years the supply of locomotives, largely electric, to the gold mining industry had been dominated by American companies such as General Electric, Westinghouse and Goodman. The latter opened a local manufacturing facility as early as 1923 and by 1963 all Goodman locomotives had 100% local content. Charles Funkey, an American engineer, set up a local manufacturing business prior to the Second World War and built his first diesel locomotive in 1939. Funkey went on to become one of Motor Rail's most serious competitors with, ultimately, nearly 3,000 of its locomotives in the country. Hunslet Engine Co. Ltd from Leeds combined with the local firm of C.C. Taylor (Pty) Ltd to form Hunslet Taylor (Pty) Ltd and went on to build some 2,700 locomotives up to 1984 that included large main line shunters and the iconic 2ft gauge Beyer Garrett's for South African Railways. Hubert Davies was originally Goodman's local agent who had installed that first electric mine tramway in 1894. His company obtained the rights to market locomotives built by Ruston & Hornsby of Lincoln and in due course some 500 of their products came to South Africa. They were in fact the largest competitor to Motor Rail for locomotives exported from the UK; thus mirroring their relative positions in the home market.

It remains hard to understand Motor Rail's attitude in this maelstrom of activity, although the situation in a family firm is rather different to that in conventional business. Going for the biggest market, the highest turnover and the best profits is not always the object of the exercise. An enjoyable lifestyle may have a higher priority. To make the most of the South African opportunity one of the Abbotts would have had to move to the country on a near permanent basis and, understandably they may not have wanted to do so (or more likely their respective wives did not!). One must also remember that at that time it was a fortnight at sea to get there, not a few hours in an aeroplane. In addition, the company was perennially short of money and it is more than likely that they did not have the financial resources to take on South Africa in this way whilst to take in other partners would have meant the loss of family control. In addition, Motor Rail had been well served over the years by their network of agents and Gloster was doing a splendid job for them in South Africa. Why lose control of your business for an additional profit when you do not actually need to do so? Why indeed?

The exact origins of M & R Engineering (Pty) Ltd are unclear, but certainly they were one of many firms pirating Simplex spare parts. The principals were Messrs Margolis and Ralph and it seems an unlikely coincidence that their initials were so similar to Motor Rail. There is some circumstantial evidence that the company was an arms-length creation of Lenning which they could disown if their intentions did not work out (not dissimilar to Motor Rail's later experience with Lenze). It is believed that T.D. Abbott visited their works on the occasion of his 1958 visit when M & R were experimenting with torque convertors in Simplex locomotives. At that stage the experiments were unsuccessful due to attempts to use the existing gearbox, but later use of a Brockhouse convertor and a direct drive proved wholly satisfactory. By 1959 Lenning could afford to officially take over M & R and allow their relationship with Motor Rail to deteriorate. They were happy to admit that the wheels, axles and brakegear of the locomotive exhibited at the Rand Show of that year were all Motor Rail and it seems likely that the frame was a Bedford product too as the Simplex logo on the buffer heads had been chiselled off! M & R locos used both Perkins and Dorman engines and the latter may have been a sop to Simplex as Motor Rail had helped Lenning obtain the Dorman agency for South Africa. Understandably the Bedford firm considered all this in breach of their agreement with Lenning and gave notice to terminate that agreement on 14th May 1959.

In December 1959 legal action ensued between Motor Rail and Lenning but the laws on so-called 'piracy' in South Africa did not favour Motor Rail and Lenning won the day. To illustrate just what Motor Rail lost: M & R/Lenning went on to build some 780 locomotives of which 270 were a direct copy of the 3½ ton Simplex with the last being supplied in 1977. Even with the benefit of hindsight this would in itself hardly have been enough to warrant a full scale factory in the country. Perhaps the Abbotts were right after all!

The M & R name continued to be used until about 1966. However, what is presumably an internal sales list in the Motor Rail records contains a full list with specifications, drawings,

photographs and prices of the entire M & R range from 3 to 28 tons. This carries E.C. Lenning's name and address throughout and where dated is of 1960/61 vintage. Initially they are thought to have rebuilt Motor Rail locomotives imported by Lenning by the process of fitting a torque convertor drive and discarding the Motor Rail gearbox. When that supply dried up with the cancellation of Lenning's agency agreement they started to build their own machines completely from scratch. Of whatever parentage, all these locomotives were badged and plated with M & R (and later Lenning) works plates.

Whilst M & R generally concentrated on small locomotives up to about 10 tons, they did build a few larger shunters up to 28 tons for use in South African Railways' workshops. Their 5 ton design also seems to have been pirated back to the UK by Bagnall's of Stafford, courtesy of W.H. Dorman Ltd! When Motor Rail abandoned South Africa in 1962 Dowson & Dobson did build a few locomotives but these did not follow Simplex practice.

For interest's sake it is necessary to complete the Lenning story although it is in no way germane to that of Motor Rail. With the oil crisis of the 1970s and the decline of the diesel locomotive in underground use, Lenning set up CKK Engineering (Pty) Ltd to build battery locomotives taken from the designs of Goodman of Chicago, many of which were made in South Africa anyway. In this they ploughed a very similar furrow to that with Motor Rail with the ultimate effect that Goodman's became isolated from their markets and the only way back in was through Lenning. In 1985 Lenning took over the Goodman manufacturing license, renamed CKK as Goodman-Lenning and went on to build around 1,500 further battery and trolley locomotives until Lenning decided to leave the locomotive market in 1994. Despite the supposed new venture they even carried on the CKK numbering system!

As a postscript to that, some of Lenning's staff joined Trident Engineering who, in conjunction with Bateman Industrial Holdings, concluded an agreement with Goodman to manufacture and sell their entire range in South Africa. In 2003 Goodman ceased operations in the USA and all new Goodman equipment is now supplied by Trident. In this guise Trident have built over 2,000 locomotives since 2003.

239. In its many variants this was Lenning's most popular locomotive with something over 300 having been built including two by Bagnalls of Stafford in 1961 after Dorman's took over that company. Dorman was the standard engine for this type but a few were built with Perkins engines and this is one of those. Two of the standard design were modified for surface use by fitting cabs and were used at the Craddock ballast quarry of South African Railways. When road transport took over, L5054132 of 1974 was plinthed and was still there in 1990.                                    *Courtesy John Middleton*

240. Lenning tried a range of different types, weights and powers of locomotive and this is perhaps one of their less successful. Only thirteen were built of which this is the first, and the only one not to go underground. L6037-101 was built in 1967 to 3ft 6ins gauge for President Stein Gold Mines in Welkom. It seems that it was intended as a general works shunter but was little used and spent most of its timed stored at the end of this siding, being still there in 2011! The handbrake looks very much an afterthought but the hoop, the screw, the wheel and the brake block are recognisable Motor Rail parts.
                                                  *Courtesy John Middleton*

# Appendix V: Hire Fleet

A list of the numbers in the hire fleet is interesting, as is the fact that Petrol Loco Hirers also bought in secondhand locomotives from other sources from time to time. These tables show the position of the hire fleet as reported to the meetings of the partners or directors, and were no doubt intended to provide the information necessary to manage the business by giving levels of utilisation and whether additions to the fleet were required.

The first column gives the cumulative total of locomotives that had passed through the hire fleet's hands since inception, with the second column being a similar total for those sold. The third column gives the number out on hire at the end of the month shown, with the final column showing the total in hand and available. It will be seen that at times of heavy demand the reserve of locomotives available for hire was virtually nil.

The locomotive records that survive have been annotated with notes of subsequent users or owners from information in spares orders, but it is known that some of these were already hiring the locomotives concerned.

## PETROL LOCOMOTIVE HIRERS

| DATE | OWNED | SOLD | ON HIRE | IN HAND |
|---|---|---|---|---|
| June 1924 | 22 | 6 | 13 | 3 |
| Dec 1924 | 24 | 8 | 11 | 5 |
| June 1925 | 25 | 8 | 15 | 2 |
| Dec 1925 | 25 | 11 | 13 | 1 |
| June 1926 | 31 | 11 | 18 | 2 |
| Dec 1926 | 35 | 18 | 13 | 4 |
| June 1927 | 52 | 19 | 28 | 5 |
| Dec 1927 | 54 | 20 | 27 | 7 |
| June 1928 | 62 | 31 | 23 | 8 |
| Dec 1928 | 71 | 36 | 34 | 1 |
| June 1929 | 94 | 46 | 42 | 6 |
| Dec 1929 | 99 | 57 | 24 | 18 |
| May 1930 | 103 | 64 | 33 | 6 |

NOTES ON ADDITIONS:

| | |
|---|---|
| October 1924 | Two new locos added. |
| May 1925 | One 6 ton loco added. |
| February 1926 | Three new and two secondhand locos added. |
| April 1927 | Six 20hp 2½ ton locos bought from Manchester Corporation. |
| June 1928 | Five locos bought at auction in Leicester. |
| October 1928 | Seven secondhand locos bought. |
| February 1929 | One secondhand loco bought. |
| August 1929 | One secondhand loco bought from Walls & Alexander. |
| October 1929 | Four secondhand locos bought. |
| February 1930 | Three secondhand locos bought. |

## MOTOR RAIL & TRAMCAR CO. LTD (MOTOR RAIL LTD FROM 1931)

| DATE | OWNED | SOLD | ON HIRE | IN HAND | ON HIRE | DUMPERS IN STOCK | SOLD |
|---|---|---|---|---|---|---|---|
| June 1930 | | | 38 | 1 | | | |
| Dec 1930 | | | 51 | 2 | | | |
| June 1931 | 173 | 94 | 77 | 2 | | | |
| Dec 1931 | 182 | 118 | 57 | 7 | | | |
| June 1932 | 185 | 131 | 38 | 15 | | | |
| Dec 1932 | 188 | 137 | 14 | 37 | | | |
| June 1933 | 192 | 148 | 17 | 27 | | | |
| Dec 1933 | 192 | 156 | 10 | 26 | | | |
| June 1934 | 199 | 168 | 21 | 10 | | | |
| Dec 1934 | 206 | 176 | 21 | 8 | | | |
| June 1935 | 223 | 185 | 24 | 14 | | | |
| Dec 1935 | 224 | 196 | 18 | 10 | | | |
| June 1936 | 248 | 209 | 31 | 7 | | | |
| Dec 1936 | 272 | 229 | 37 | 6 | | | |
| June 1937 | 287 | 246 | 35 | 6 | | | |
| Dec 1937 | 295 | 264 | 22 | 9 | | | |
| June 1938 | 303 | 274 | 13 | 16 | | | |
| Dec 1938 | 340 | 279 | 56 | 5 | 1 | 7 | |
| June 1939 | 353 | 282 | 70 | 1 | 10 | | |
| Dec 1939 | 361 | 304 | 56 | 1 | 13 | | |
| June 1940 | 367 | 312 | 53 | 2 | 7 | 1 | 5 |
| Dec 1940 | 375 | 321 | 52 | 2 | 8 | | 5 |
| June 1941 | 379 | 322 | 51 | 6 | 5 | 1 | 7 |
| Dec 1941 | 393 | 324 | 69 | 0 | 6 | 1 | 7 |

# Appendix VI: A. Gloster

Sent by Olivia Hall Craggs. I knew that she had been a secretary to A. Gloster and wondered if she knew what the 'A' stood for and got this!

*I need time to give you a thumb nail sketch of AG as it is pretty extraordinary. He was probably Anthony and in those days I called myself a bilingual secretary, but he never used my French!*

*I shared the secretarial job with another girl called Julia. We did 24h on 24h off. On duty you slept in his house in the maids' bedroom at 25 Porchester Terrace, rose quite early and had to take the Armstrong Sapphire over to the Savoy where he swam and had breakfast. We hung around with the other chauffeurs who were pretty glad to have a girl to chat up. We then proceeded to his office in the City. I vividly remember him insisting that I take shorthand whilst going round Hyde Park corner. Once arrived at the office you had to arrange the flowers brought from home for*

*his office. You left quite early in the afternoon and would often stop for a cafe frappee at Fortnum & Mason. Mrs G was nicer than AG, a comely lady, they were both keen pyscho-analysts and I would get quizzed in the traffic. Disaster struck when Julia got into difficulties with the automatic garage door in the mews, panicked and left her leg behind so that it was crushed. Then I was expected to be on duty ALL the time. AG summoned a taxi to take me away and I was crying so much the taxi man asked if he should call the Police. The most nightmarish job I had was to take some Nigerian potentate's daughter to a private school outside London and I got on to the M1 and couldn't get off!! He never made advances to either of us, I think he just liked our youth. He gave me a book called* Olivia *by 'Olivia' which wasn't my style, being a lesbian's tale. Suspect he was trying more analysis but I didn't even understand.*

*Alan, I hope you get my drift and I hope it makes you laugh!*

241. The ultimate indignity. A 5½ ton 50hp on Pangani beach, Tanzania.

# Index

# Other Books by Alan M. Keef

## Industrial History

### *A Tale of Many Railways: An Autobiography & History of Alan Keef Ltd*
Black Dwarf Lightmoor (2008) ISBN 978-1-899889-30-3

## Fiction

### *The Finding*
Iponymous Publishing Ltd (2015) ISBN 978-1-908773-97-5

### *Slave to Ariconium*
Iponymous Publishing Ltd (forthcoming) ISBN 978-1-908773-86-9